THE DIGITAL ACCESSIBILITY
HANDBOOK FOR LIBRARIES

ALA Editions purchases fund advocacy, awareness, and accreditation programs for library professionals worldwide.

THE DIGITAL ACCESSIBILITY HANDBOOK FOR LIBRARIES

Carli Spina and
Rebecca Albrecht Oling

CHICAGO **2025**

IN COLLABORATION WITH CORE

© 2025 by Carli Spina and Rebecca Albrecht Oling

Extensive effort has gone into ensuring the reliability of the information in this book; however, the publisher makes no warranty, express or implied, with respect to the material contained herein.

Isbns
979-8-89255-286-8 (paper)
979-8-89255-314-8 (PDF)
979-8-89255-315-5 (ePub)

Library of Congress Cataloging-in-Publication Data
Names: Spina, Carli, author. | Oling, Rebecca Albrecht, 1968– author.
Title: The digital accessibility handbook for libraries / Carli Spina and Rebecca Albrecht Oling.
Description: Chicago : ALA Editions in collaboration with Core, 2025. | Includes bibliographical references and index.
Identifiers: LCCN 2025000288 (print) | LCCN 2025000289 (ebook) | ISBN 9798892552868 (paperback) | ISBN 9798892553148 (pdf) | ISBN 9798892553155 (epub)
Subjects: LCSH: Libraries and people with disabilities—United States. | Electronic information resources—United States. | Library resources—United States. | Computers and people with disabilities—United States. | Accessible Web sites for people with disabilities. | Assistive computer technology. | Universal design.
Classification: LCC Z711.92.H3 S65 2025 (print) | LCC Z711.92.H3 (ebook) | DDC 027.6/63—dc23/eng/20250331
LC record available at https://lccn.loc.gov/2025000288
LC ebook record available at https://lccn.loc.gov/2025000289

Cover design by Kim Hudgins. Text design and typesetting by Karen Sheets Design in the Arno and New Frank typefaces.

♾ This paper meets the requirements of ANSI/NISO Z39.48-1992 (Permanence of Paper).

Printed in the United States of America
29 28 27 26 25   5 4 3 2 1

Contents

Preface: Libraries as Community Equalizers vii

Acknowledgments xi

CHAPTER 1
The What and Why of Accessibility
1

CHAPTER 2
The Wares: Spaces, Hardware, and Software
23

CHAPTER 3
Principles of Web Accessibility
47

CHAPTER 4
The Accessible Library Website
73

CHAPTER 5
Digital Media and File Accessibility
95

CHAPTER 6
Accessible Communications and Events
115

CHAPTER 7
Automated and Manual Testing
133

CHAPTER 8
Accessibility of Emerging Technologies
147

CHAPTER 9
Accessibility of eXtended Reality
161

CHAPTER 10
Artificial Intelligence, Libraries, and Accessibility
179

CHAPTER 11
Best Practices for Working with Vendors
199

CHAPTER 12
Preparing the Profession
215

CHAPTER 13
Digital Accessibility on a Budget
229

CHAPTER 14
A More Inclusive Tomorrow
253

Appendix: Recommended Resources 257

Glossary of Acronyms 259

About the Authors and Contributors 263

Index 269

PREFACE

Libraries as Community Equalizers

Whether as a community partner or a protector of our freedoms, the modern library sets out to serve all equally. That mission includes everyone, regardless of ability. It is critical when we think about the scope of our work as librarians that we ground that work in an understanding that disability is intersectional and is perhaps the only at-risk population any one of us can fall into at any moment. When we think of users in risk groups, a slice of those users will experience one or more disabilities as well. Those users experience an ever-heightened risk of marginalization due to information scarcity caused by lack of accessibility. Libraries have long held a role as community centers and equalizers ensuring access to resources and support for all—for members of their local communities and beyond. They support job seekers, those needing to build a skill set, older adults needing engagement and recreation, students doing homework or research, those seeking Wi-Fi access or who might be unhoused, and even act as cooling centers or charging stations during weather emergencies or natural disasters. Libraries are also trusted spaces, making them "an opportune space for the coordination and delivery of health-promoting services."[1] In "Lunch at the Library: Examination of a Community-Based Approach to Addressing Summer Food Insecurity," Bruce et al. note that libraries "across the country began serving lunches to low-income children throughout the summer, with one of the earliest documented programs starting at an Oakland (California) public library in 2011."[2] Libraries can do this because they have long been "flexible to community needs, responding to changing social issues and demands," and even sustaining their constituents by meeting basic needs as a "natural extension" of their mission.[3] Feeding the community is just one of many examples of the library's role as a community partner rooted in equity.

For all these uses, library resources and services—from websites, e-books, and databases to registrations and events themselves—must be made available to those with disabilities. Leaving those with disabilities, permanent or temporary, behind without equal access to information is not merely an unfortunate by-product of the fast pace at which technologies change or the perennial budget deficits that keep many libraries short-staffed. It is contrary to our core values, which embrace full inclusion and equity, in theory. Too often, librarians lack the training and practical guidance needed to move this from theory to practice.

It may seem obvious that libraries can leverage their websites to list all available assistive technology and include options for reporting barriers or accessing content in an alternative format. However, many libraries haven't done this yet. Moreover, when libraries do add this information to their website, they don't always confirm that this information is presented in a clear and accessible format. Prioritizing these types of changes can have a major impact on our communities at a very low cost and sends a clear signal of the importance the library places on inclusion.

Part of our inherent ableism is thinking that disability is a fixed state. Often we forget, for example, that our patrons might be losing their sight and are still dealing with that transition. Or, as mentioned earlier, they may face multiple risk factors. We need to keep in mind that disability is a spectrum, not a monolith (one can be blind and still see shadows or colors, for example). The mythology of disability is strong. We forget that not all d/Deaf patrons know or use American Sign Language (ASL), any more than all our blind patrons embrace braille. These are very personal choices among a host of languages and options, and they are often tied to the educational resources and support that the individual has had access to throughout their life. Needing assistance or an assistive technology, along with other aspects of having a disability (such as reduced financial capacity, reduced leisure time, and reduced opportunities in a society full of barriers), form an equation only users can calculate how to manage for themselves.

Large organizations will have a slate of options available, in addition to the built-in capabilities of each operating system or technology offered. Users with evolving needs may seek the guidance we provide via our website recommendations or transparent conformance information without their ever needing to stop and ask us. This preserves their independence and ensures they need not disclose personal information they are uncomfortable sharing. We have little idea how great the impact of those web pages can be, or how ignorant we might be of the diversity of disabilities we need to serve in our ever-growing and changing disabled populations.

Our communities are morphing with more young people having disabilities, an aging population, and the long-term effects of COVID-19. This suggests that we will see an increase in disability all around us—in the workforce, among our colleagues and friends, and with those we serve. It means that more of us will encounter barriers, even amidst greater opportunities for workplace accommodations, and we will all increasingly depend on our culture's (and our profession's) ability to meet this challenge, expand our skill set, and cement truly equitable access to information. The rise in the number of disabled people in the workforce changes both who we serve and the demographics of who we are. Librarians are well-positioned to lead in improving equity and creating a more universally inclusive landscape. Vendor and publisher relationships, procurement, consortial networking, and the like provide natural intersections within our axis of influence.

In this book, we will delve into digital accessibility to ensure your library's online presence is welcoming and inclusive for all and your other digital offerings avoid barriers that can exclude users with disabilities. We will start with background information on understanding what is meant by disability and the obligations libraries have to support disabled users. We then consider the software and hardware libraries can use to create inclusive spaces and services. From there, we will dive into the overarching principles of online accessibility before applying them specifically to library websites, digital media and files, digital communications, and emerging technologies, including augmented reality, virtual reality, and artificial intelligence. Along the way, we will explain how libraries can verify the accessibility of the tools they develop or subscribe to, and we'll discuss best practices for working with vendors to optimize the accessibility of their library products. We will conclude with some considerations for the future, particularly around education and hiring to ensure accessibility remains central to the work done at all libraries. We hope you will come away from this book with a concrete plan to improve accessibility, and also a greater understanding of the accessibility needs of those with a wide range of disabilities.

Notes

1. Morgan M. Philbin et al., "Public Libraries: A Community-Level Resource to Advance Population Health," *Journal of Community Health* 44, no. 1 (February 2019): 192–99, https://doi.org/10.1007/s10900-018-0547-4.
2. Janine S. Bruce et al., "Lunch at the Library: Examination of a Community-Based Approach to Addressing Summer Food Insecurity," *Public Health Nutrition* 20, no. 9 (June 2017): 1641, https://doi.org/10.1017/S1368980017000258.
3. Bruce et al., "Lunch at the Library," 1641.

Acknowledgments

A work of this scope is made possible because of the community of library accessibility professionals within which we work and, particularly, the professional generosity of contributors with whom we collaborated to ensure we had the most up-to-date perspective from practitioners and experts in the field. Additionally, we want to thank our families and Susan Suffes, Doris Patrao, and Michael Pardo for their support throughout this project.

• • •

CHAPTER 1

The What and Why of Accessibility

A patron with declining vision stops by the library to ask for help obtaining an accessible version of their book club's latest reading selection, so they can continue to participate in this important aspect of their social life.

A college student who uses a screen reader needs to find peer-reviewed journal articles about French history using the library's databases.

A library employee who is deafblind is watching required training videos.

In all these scenarios, digital accessibility is the difference between the individual being able to participate equitably in what the library has to offer and their facing barriers to access. These and countless other scenarios influence the direction of digital accessibility in libraries. This book will guide libraries working to improve the digital accessibility of all their offerings and provide a barrier-free experience for all patrons and employees.

Before diving into digital accessibility, it is vital to understand the fundamental concepts surrounding disability and accessibility. This foundational knowledge informs the types of accessibility features offered and the ways in which accessibility and disability topics are integrated into ongoing workflows. You will benefit from a clear understanding of who you serve with this work and why it is central to every library's mission.

1

2 ••• CHAPTER 1

This chapter sets the stage for topics covered in subsequent chapters and offers a context for understanding disability inclusion and accessibility at your institution and beyond.

▶ Defining Disability

There is no one, universal definition of disability. The Americans with Disabilities Act (ADA) defines a disability as "(A) a physical or mental impairment that substantially limits one or more major life activities of [an] individual; (B) a record of such an impairment; or (C) being regarded as having such an impairment."[1] By contrast, the UN Convention on the Rights of Persons with Disabilities states that "persons with disabilities include those who have long-term physical, mental, intellectual or sensory impairments which in interaction with various barriers may hinder their full and effective participation in society on an equal basis with others."[2] While the definition found in the ADA, and therefore often central to legal discussions in the United States, focuses exclusively on an individual having an impairment, the UN definition incorporates both the idea of impairment and the way that external barriers impact the individual and interact with that impairment.

These definitions relate to different models of understanding disability, as discussed in the next section of this chapter. Under either definition, disability impacts a significant portion of the population. As of 2022, U.S. Census Bureau data found that 13.9 percent of Americans have some form of disability.[3] Data based on whether survey respondents self-identified as disabled set that number even higher at 25.7 percent of non-institutionalized adults, or a total of approximately 61.4 million individuals.[4] Worldwide, the World Health Organization sets this number at 16 percent of the population, or 1.3 billion people total.[5] With these percentages, it is clear that disabled individuals make up a significant portion of the population no matter where they are in the world. Moreover, this makes it clear that all libraries serve communities that include disabled individuals as not only patrons but also as current or potential library employees.

In the United States, census data from 2006 suggests that "as the Baby Boomer population ages, the largest population in the USA to date,

THE WHAT AND WHY OF ACCESSIBILITY ● ● ● 3

the demand for services to the elderly will increase over the next several decades."[6] According to the Congressional Budget Office (CBO), "by 2050, one-fifth of the U.S. population will be age 65 or older, up from 12 percent in 2000 and 8 percent in 1950. As a result, expenditures on long-term services and support for the elderly will rise substantially in the coming decades."[7] The CBO concludes that "if those rates of prevalence continue, the number of elderly people with functional or cognitive limitations, and thus the need for assistance, will increase sharply in coming decades." However, the aging population is only one part of the disability picture in the coming years.

At the same time the population is aging, a surge in the rates of disability among students ages 3–21 is occurring, as reflected in the number of students who received special education or related services under the Individuals with Disabilities Education Act (IDEA). According to the National Center for Education Statistics,

> In 2022–23, the number of students served under IDEA reached an all-time high of 7.5 million, which was 3 percent higher than it was in 2019–20. As a result, the percentage of public school students served under IDEA continued its upward trend each year during the pandemic and was higher in 2022–23 (15 percent) than in 2019–20 (14 percent).[8]

For librarians in K–12 institutions, communities, and higher education, it is clear that we must pay attention to this ever-growing and diverse disabled population.

COVID was a mass-disabling event, a fact supported by data from the Bureau of Labor Statistics that shows that the number of adults over sixteen in the civilian population with disabilities spiked after the first wave of cases and then continued to increase with each subsequent wave.[9] This information helps librarians understand the scale of the community being served by accessibility services and can be useful in allocating resources to and advocating for the importance of prioritizing accessibility improvements. This ever-growing disabled population is reflected in the workforce. So, while we consider who our patrons are and how we can serve them best, we must also consider our own colleagues in our efforts to create a more accessible culture.

4 ●●● CHAPTER 1

❱ Models of Disability

There are many ways to conceptualize disability beyond just a simple definition. Every individual, whether or not they have consciously considered it, has a concept of disability that comes to mind for them. This may be in the form of a specific individual or the archetype, or perhaps even the stereotype, they think of when calling to mind a "disabled person." It may also be a broader notion of what disability means as a concept or category. For some, this understanding may have developed from a young age based on the dominant conception in their society. For others, it is a source of serious study and even advocacy. But when it comes to formally defining these conceptions or models of disability, three models are particularly important to understand: the moral, the medical, and the social models.

The Moral Model

The moral model of disability was the earliest of these three models to develop and was arguably the original model of disability in many societies.[10] This model conceived of disability as a result of moral failures and was often, though not always, tied to the religious morality of the society.[11] Today, with the advent of greater medical understanding, the moral model has receded in importance, but ripples of its influence can still be felt in the way that disability is viewed by many in modern society. As Julie Smart notes, "much of the shame and stigma surrounding disabilities, especially psychiatric disabilities, is due to the enduring effects of the Moral/Religious Model."[12] This continuing stigma is particularly pronounced when the person with the disability is perceived as being "at fault" for their condition.[13] For this reason, it is important to understand this model to understand the stigma and discrimination still faced by many disabled individuals in a wide variety of contexts.

The Medical Model

As the medical field and the scientific understanding of many disabilities and medical conditions expanded, the way of conceiving of disability also continued to develop and evolve. With the advent of this new understanding of disability as a result of advances in medical and scientific knowledge, a new mode emerged: the medical model. As its name suggests, this model focuses on the medical aspects of disability, including diagnosis and treatment. As Rhoda Olkin describes it, this model "posits the problem as residing in the individual, and the solutions are medical intervention, aid in 'adjustment' to disability, modifications of the disabled person's lifestyle."[14] While this model does not have the same focus on personal fault present in the moral model, it does place the responsibility for "correcting" the problem of the disability on the disabled individual, through compliance with medical interventions such as medications, treatments, or devices. As Tobin Siebers phrases it, this model sees disability as "a defect that must be cured or eliminated if the person is to achieve full capacity as a human being."[15] As such, its approach to disability is a negative one, seeing only a flaw or a weakness in need of improvement, whether through personal effort, medication, or technology. This focus on seeing disability as an issue, or even a "defect," to be remedied is all too present. Look no further than the legalistic focus on accommodation recognized in many approaches to disability around the world. Over time, this focus not only on diagnosis and interaction with the medical establishment but also on "fixing" the "problem" of disability came to be challenged, particularly by disability activists and scholars who questioned this negative approach to the topic.

The Social Model

More recently, the social model has emerged as a way of thinking about disability and the barriers disabled people face from a societal perspective. The social model shifts the focus from the individual to the barriers society creates for those with disabilities. A good example of this is the recent trend of colleges not requiring an official (and often costly) medical diagnosis before they will accommodate a disabled student's needs. Colin Barnes summarizes the social model as "a deliberate attempt to shift attention away from the functional limitations of individuals with impairments onto the problems caused by disabling environments, barriers and cultures."[16] Often, the social model is presented as it relates to the medical model. For example, Anita Silvers describes the two models' relationship this way: "while the medical model takes disability to be a problem requiring medical intervention—and as both the prerogative and the responsibility of medical professionals to fix—the social model understands disability as a political problem calling for corrective action by citizen activists who alter other people's attitudes and reform the practices of the state."[17] A consequence of thinking about disability in this way is to move away from the idea of the accommodation or remediation of inaccessible spaces or services that is initiated only when a disabled individual requests to use that space or service. Rather, a social model would suggest we take the forethought to include a disabled perspective in the design phase for new spaces and services. This understanding informs much of the advocacy for disability inclusion that has occurred over the last several decades.

The social model is not without its detractors, however. Recent critiques of this approach have pointed out the ways that the social model may exclude some disabled individuals or discount their own experiences. Anita Silvers describes this critique, saying:

> The social model stands accused in some quarters of misrepresenting disabled people by abridging who they are, or of even more malignant distortions such as promoting values that exclude people with certain kinds of physical or cognitive limitations. These complaints are connected, in that the former criticizes the social model for suppressing rather than showcasing disabled people's differences, especially dysfunctional ones, while the latter objects to advancing an ideal of independence that some disabled people's dysfunctions make unrealizable for them.[18]

This perspective has shaped the evolution of this model and overall approaches "to better account for pain, nonphysical disabilities, and attitudinal and behavioral (rather than just physical and sensory) access barriers."[19] Ongoing critiques and reconsiderations of the social model point to the complicated nature of understanding the diverse range of disability experiences, however transient some of those might be, which make up the disability community.

For the purposes of those working on digital accessibility in libraries, the most important aspect of these varied models is to understand the implications that all three of them continue to have for societal attitudes toward disability, legal approaches to accessibility, and institutional responses to inclusion. With these models in mind, it's much easier to understand, reconsider, and challenge how disability inclusion and accessibility are integrated into workflows and approached throughout our institutional decision-making processes. Understanding these models can lead to a deeper understanding of how to evaluate the existing frameworks around accessibility, both at the library and within our community. More significantly, it reshapes our inclusive approaches and helps remove barriers at all libraries, whether through legal means or through local policy framework shifts.

▶ Types of Disabilities

While it may initially seem as though it would be easy to categorize disabilities into different types, the reality is this is often a very complicated proposition, and the categories depend on context. In addition, each disabled person is unique in their own experience of their disability (or disabilities) and their own personal needs and preferences. This limits the value of categorizing disabilities as a way to understand an individual's specific accessibility needs. However, it can be helpful for overall planning and evaluation purposes to understand some of the ways that disabilities can be categorized.

Legal frameworks often require a formal diagnosis to qualify for protection under the law, which can force a more diagnostically focused definition of disability. For example, the Individuals with Disabilities Education Act (IDEA) defines individuals with disabilities as those "having an intellectual disability, a hearing impairment (including deafness), a speech or language impairment, a visual impairment (including blindness), a serious emotional disturbance (referred to in this part as 'emotional disturbance'), an orthopedic impairment, autism, traumatic brain injury, an other health impairment, a specific learning disability, deaf-blindness, or multiple disabilities."[20] These categories can be useful in understanding and evaluating different aspects of accessibility. But like any labels, categories obscure the full range of experiences individuals may have and can limit responses to the needs of individuals who have multiple different conditions simultaneously.

By contrast, as mentioned earlier, the ADA only divides disabilities into two categories by saying "a physical or mental impairment that

8 ••• CHAPTER 1

substantially limits one or more major life activities of such individual."[21] However, the subsequent definition of "major life activity" in the ADA connects these two categories to particular types of disabilities by saying "major life activities include, but are not limited to, caring for oneself, performing manual tasks, seeing, hearing, eating, sleeping, walking, standing, lifting, bending, speaking, breathing, learning, reading, concentrating, thinking, communicating, and working."[22] This is significantly different from the more diagnostically focused approach of the IDEA, but it can be instructive when designing for inclusion.

Another way to categorize disabilities is by visibility. Disabilities within each of the categories listed earlier might be evident or could potentially be *invisible disabilities*, a term that refers to disabilities that are not immediately apparent when interacting with an individual. Some disabilities can be invisible in certain contexts but not in others. As an example, an individual with an artificial leg may have a visible disability when walking while wearing shorts, but their disability may be invisible when seated and fully clothed. Many individuals with invisible disabilities, particularly those that are fully invisible, such as chronic illness and conditions causing chronic pain, experience situations where others question whether they are eligible or deserving of the accommodations or other assistance they need due to their disability. For this reason, they may be reluctant or unwilling to request necessary accommodations or assistance and may even be hesitant to use accessible spaces and services if the latter are designated as solely available to those with disabilities.

Accommodations and Identity

For those with disabilities (visible or not), there can be a reluctance to request accommodations for a multitude of reasons. The process for requesting accommodations generally requires medical documentation. This in turn requires access to medical professionals, an expensive and time-consuming process, particularly in areas where medical care is scarce. The process can take a considerable amount of time and effort. Finally, many individuals with disabilities may be uncomfortable with disclosing their disability due to concerns about discrimination, fears that they will not be believed, or other privacy reasons.

While considering types of disabilities, it is worth noting that individuals may classify themselves differently than an outsider would, based on these categories of disabilities. These cases can exist at multiple points on the spectrum of disability. Some people may not consider themselves disabled even if they meet the legal or institutional definitions for it. As an example of this, an individual who has declining vision may not consider themselves disabled even if they would qualify for the resources and support offered to individuals with vision disabilities. At the same time, individuals with conditions that fit within a specific definition of disability may not consider their condition a disability at all. For one example of this phenomenon, many Deaf individuals do not see themselves as disabled and instead see themselves as part of Deaf culture, one that has not only a language but also social practices and a shared history.[23] Other individuals may consider themselves disabled without a formal medical diagnosis, which can make it impossible for them to pursue formal accommodations in many institutions. There can be many reasons for this, from a lack of affordable access to the medical care necessary to pursue a diagnosis, to a preference to avoid interactions with the medical system. These individuals may have the same need for accommodations as those with formal diagnoses, but lack the ability to pursue accommodations in many cases.

Comprehensively classifying disability and the complex situations explained earlier demonstrate why it is preferable to approach accessibility with a universal lens that opens access to all users. Requiring accessibility accommodations presents a range of barriers to access for many individuals who would benefit from these features. While this may not always be possible, offering options that are open to those who do not have a formal accommodation is a good place to focus on as a starting point when aiming to shape inclusive offerings at libraries. This is why it is helpful to ensure that information regarding accessibility features and assistance is available throughout the library's online and physical presence at the points of need. Having guidance at the "point of need" means that information is available, even to those who may not think to refer to a discrete section labeled as "disability services."

▶ The Language of Disability

The language used to discuss disability has changed significantly over the last several decades. It is important to keep up with current best practices and terminology when referring to topics related to disability and accessibility. Terms such as *handicapped, differently abled,* and *special needs* are considered outdated and may be offensive to some individuals. Using the appropriate terminology is important for inclusion, as it will help individuals with disabilities to feel welcome at your institution, and it will also help users who are searching by keyword to find your information about services for patrons with disabilities.

There is no consensus on whether *person-first language,* such as "a person who is blind," or *identity-first language,* such as "a blind person," is preferable. Each approach serves its own purpose. As Kodi Laskin notes, "person-first language is meant to show that even though the person might have a difference from the norm, they are a person first. Identity-first language, in contrast, is used as a way to show that the disability is nothing to be ashamed of and can instead be an empowering fact."[24] In this way, the choice of language can be something that reflects people's relationship to their disability and also their relationship to their larger community. For example, many people with disabilities see the shift toward person-first language as part of society's bias toward people with disabilities, which Erica Mones describes by pointing out that "much of this confusion [around language choice] comes from the unconscious but prevalent understanding of disability as inherently negative. Disabled people rail against this narrative, insisting that disability is just another part of the human condition."[25] A 2022 global survey of over 500 disabled people from across 23 countries found "that 49% of disabled people preferred identity-first language, 33% favored person-first language, and 18% did not have a preference." At the same time, the study found "that language preferences varied within and across gender identities, age groups, and countries. For example, women 36 years or older had a dominant preference for person-first language (53% vs. 29%; 18% had no preference)."[26] The same study identified differences between its results and those found in past studies, which they argued pointed "to the evolution of preferences over time . . . presenting a necessity for up-to-date data on the language preferences of disabled people."[27] Both the evolution of preferences over time and the differing preferences across demographics point to the importance of understanding the preferences of specific individuals, for example in the case of disabled presenters at events, as well as the preferences in specific library communities.

However, for some communities, there is a clear preference for one approach over the other. For example, members of the Deaf community and the autism community generally prefer identity-first language.[28] Even within each community there may be no consensus on the preferred language and terminology. For some individuals, these preferences can be deeply personal, so when discussing a specific individual, it is best to ask for their preferred language, particularly if you will be referring to them publicly, for example when introducing a speaker at a library program. Language preferences and appropriate terminology continue to develop and evolve over time, so this is an area where it is important to remain up-to-date and willing to adapt as the appropriate terminology and individual preferences change. In this book, person-first and identity-first language will be used interchangeably except when referring to a specific individual, in which case that individual's preference will be respected if known.

❯ What Does Accessibility Mean?

When we use the word *accessibility*, we can mean many different things. Librarians often use accessibility to refer to access to a space or material, such as the off-campus accessibility of subscription databases. The word might also be used to refer to more general ease of access to a space, such as a statement that "the library is accessible by bus and car." However, a major use of the term *accessibility* is, of course, to refer to the ability of disabled people to access, participate in, and use a specific space, service, product, or experience. Needless to say, these multiple uses can cause confusion at times, as in the example of referring to a library database as accessible. In one context, this might mean that it is available no matter the user's location. In another, it might refer to its usability for individuals with disabilities or those who use assistive devices.

In addition, different organizations may use the word in more subtly different ways. The United Nations has defined accessibility as "the provision of flexibility to accommodate each user's needs and preferences,"[29] without a specific mention of disability, though access for disabled individuals is incorporated into the definition. By contrast, when legal entities in the United States use the term accessibility, they often define it more narrowly with respect to disabled individuals. For example, Digital.gov defines accessibility by noting that "in the federal government, accessibility means that agencies must give disabled employees and members of the public access to information comparable to the access available to others."[30] Thus, even when being used to refer to offering inclusive access to all, the term accessibility can have different meanings in different contexts, such as in a U.S. context versus an international context or when used by different institutions.

Adding to the confusion around the word *accessibility*, even when it is being used to refer to access for disabled individuals, an item may frequently be accessible for individuals with one type of disability or one specific need, while being inaccessible to other users. For example, a video that has closed captions available at the bottom of the screen may be accessible to a deaf person, but inaccessible to a deafblind person. If the captions are not able to be turned off, they might even make the video less accessible for a person with a learning disability, who may find them distracting. In libraries, it is best to provide multiple alternatives or offer access to different accessibility features to ensure that a resource or service is accessible for a range of individuals and in a wide variety of use cases. We must be thoughtful using the term *accessibility* if we are to ensure that the final outcome maximizes inclusion.

In this book, we will focus on using the word *accessibility* to mean usability for disabled individuals, with specific reference to whom an item will be accessible or inaccessible as relevant. When using this word, it is important to always remember to clarify the sense in which it is being used and also specify for whom an item is being made accessible. It should never be assumed that just because an item is called "accessible," it is equally usable by all individuals no matter their specific needs. This is why it is always important to be prepared to support requests for accommodation even when accessibility has been a focus of the design. Accommodations may be requested to enable use for even the most accessibly designed service or product.

▶ Legal Requirements for Accessibility

This book is not intended to serve as an introduction to the legal rules around accessibility for a number of reasons, including the evolving nature of these rules and the fact that they vary across legal jurisdictions, both within individual countries and across countries. However, it is worthwhile to understand the influence the law has had on accessibility and the basics of the current state of accessibility, with a focus on the legal framework in the United States. It is also helpful to understand what recent trends and changes may mean for the future of this work in the United States and around the world.

In the United States, there are several federal laws that impact the accessibility requirements placed on libraries. In particular, three of note are the Rehabilitation Act of 1973, IDEA, and the Americans with Disabilities Act (ADA). These laws, along with other federal, state, and local laws and regulations, set the legal minimum for accessibility at different types of facilities and prohibit disability discrimination across various types of institutions and interactions, from employment to physical building access. Though the exact rules that apply to libraries vary based on their type, all three of these laws can help in understanding how accessibility is approached.

The Rehabilitation Act of 1973

The Rehabilitation Act of 1973 seeks to prevent disability discrimination in individuals' access to any programs funded by the U.S. federal government and in federal government employment. This scope covers many libraries, including federal libraries and also those that receive various types of federal funding. Section 508 of this Act is particularly important for those working on digital accessibility because it sets forth the specific "requirements for electronic and information technology developed, maintained, procured, or used by the Federal government. . . . [and] requires Federal electronic and information technology to be accessible to people with disabilities, including employees and members of the public."[31] This section of the Act is one of the most important laws to consider when discussing digital accessibility requirements in the United States. Because it extends to any technology purchased or used by the federal government, many vendors will design their products and services with these requirements in mind, especially if they work with the U.S. government or hope to in the future. It is also one of the specific sections of law that is frequently mentioned in institutional accessibility policies. A good example of this is the appearance of Section 508 in many of the information-technology accessibility policies enacted by both public and private institutions of higher education in recent years.[32] As of January 2018, the Access Board, responsible for rules and standards related to Section 508, revised the Information and Communication Technology Standards and Guidelines that apply to entities covered by Section 508 so as to incorporate the Web Content Accessibility Guidelines (WCAG) 2.0,[33] which will be discussed in greater detail later in this book (particularly in chapter 3, "Principles of Web Accessibility").

IDEA

The IDEA is a federal "law that makes available a free appropriate public education to eligible children with disabilities throughout the nation and ensures special education and related services to those children."[34] Because it focuses on public education, this law primarily applies to school libraries in public K–12 institutions. The law covers a range of aspects of education and has implications for the types of hardware, software, and assistive technology that schools are required to provide for their students. For those working on digital accessibility for K–12 institutions in the United States, this is a law that will be very important, particularly for public schools.

ADA

The ADA is a broader anti-discrimination law than the Rehabilitation Act of 1973 or the IDEA. It applies in a wide range of settings, including state and federal governmental entities, as well as "public accommodations," the definition of which specifically includes libraries, museums, private educational institutions, and other social service centers.[35] This means that the ADA applies to the majority of libraries in the United States and has implications for a wide range of activities done within libraries, from patrons using virtual reference services at their local public library to the setup of employee workstations in a university library. While the original provisions of the ADA do not deal as directly with digital accessibility as do those of the Rehabilitation Act, the fact that the ADA has always required all services and employment processes of covered entities to be accessible means that it often requires accessible software, hardware, and workstations. As with other laws, the related rules, regulations, and technical standards are at least as important to the application of the ADA in libraries as the text of the law itself. In this case, the Department of Justice has recently formally adopted WCAG 2.1 as the technical standard for state and local governments under the ADA, with some limited exceptions.[36] This rule clarification sets a new minimum standard for web accessibility for libraries that are affiliated with state or local governments, and will likely prove influential on the practices of other libraries as well. This rule has near-term implications for many libraries, thus demonstrating the importance of keeping up with the changing requirements under all federal laws to ensure ongoing compliance with accessibility requirements.

Other Legal Considerations

In addition to these federal laws, in the United States there are some individual states and even cities that have more stringent accessibility and anti-discrimination requirements. For this reason, it is always important to consider local requirements as well as federal law when making decisions and setting policies for a library in the United States.

Internationally, legal rules in individual countries vary widely, though many of the principles underlying the civil rights laws in the United States relating to disability are also reflected in the laws of other countries. In addition, WCAG has been influential not only on U.S. legal requirements but on laws around the world. The World Wide Web Consortium's (W3C) Web Accessibility Initiative (WAI) remains an online resource that tracks international laws related to accessibility and whether they incorporate any version of WCAG.[37] In addition to the laws of individual countries, there have also been international efforts to improve access and inclusion. The United Nations has been active in working toward greater inclusion for disabled people worldwide. Adopted in 2006, the Convention on the

16 ●●● CHAPTER 1

Rights of Persons with Disabilities is at the core of these efforts and outlines the rights of disabled people. It has many provisions around access to justice, equality, and education that relate to digital accessibility[38] and has also influenced the accessibility of the United Nations' own work globally. The World Intellectual Property Organization–administered Marrakesh Treaty has also had a significant impact on international approaches to accessibility. It establishes internationally recognized exceptions and limitations on copyright to make the creation and sharing of accessible books easier across borders.[39]

❱ Aiming for Inclusion

While the legal requirements in a library's location will necessarily influence that library's accessibility efforts, it is important not to focus entirely on meeting the legal requirements to the exclusion of all other factors. In all cases, the law should serve as a minimum requirement rather than the end point for accessibility efforts. It is true that institutions must meet the legal requirements of their jurisdiction, but they can and should strive to then continue to work with disabled individuals to make their spaces, collections, services, and communities inclusive, usable, and user-friendly for those with a wide range of disabilities, needs, and preferences. In many cases, meaningful inclusion will require an approach that goes beyond the minimum standards of your jurisdiction to consider how spaces, services, and policies can be designed to be equitable and inclusive for those with a wide range of needs and preferences, including users with a variety of different disabilities. This work can be challenging and will require a willingness to continually adapt and evolve, particularly as technology changes and new tools emerge. However, it is the only way to offer equitable access to all the resources libraries can offer their communities.

The focus of the advice in this book is on ensuring the most comprehensive version of accessibility and inclusion possible. While this book will touch on legal minimums and international standards for accessibility along the way, this is not its exclusive or even primary focus. Instead, the advice in this book aims to offer support in complying with legal requirements while also demonstrating how exceeding the minimal levels of accessibility will lead to greater inclusion for all members of the community. During institutional discussions of accessibility, legal requirements are often a major focus and are sometimes even treated like a checklist for compliance. With this book, we aim to offer the tools needed to advocate for an approach that focuses on inclusion beyond legal compliance, so as to ensure libraries are welcoming and usable to all members of their communities.

Digital Accessibility Skills in Libraries

Interview with **Clayton A. Copeland**, *Director of the Laboratory for Leadership in Equity of Access and Diversity (LLEAD), University of South Carolina's School of Information Science*

What do you see as the current state of library education around digital accessibility skills and broader skills related to serving patrons with disabilities?

We have an unprecedented opportunity and responsibility to integrate digital—and other—accessibility skills in library education. Such opportunities must be integrated throughout the curricula. This process must begin in foundational or core courses and then continue throughout high-division electives. We must design the curriculum such that students have this critical and essential knowledge regardless of their individualized programs of study or areas of emphasis. These skills must also be integral to internship and service learning opportunities, such that students have opportunities for preservice training. It is possible for programs to also consider offering students opportunities to earn specialized certificates as a part of their undergraduate or graduate studies. Continuing education and professional development opportunities and perhaps even certificates of advanced study/credentials may be offered.

What, if anything, are you hearing from other library leaders about necessary skills and competencies?

Something that is at the forefront of everyone's minds right now is the Department of Justice's (DOJ's) final rule on Title II of the Americans with Disabilities Act (ADA), which became effective on June 24, 2024. Public universities are required to follow this new final rule by making digital content accessible at the Web Content Accessibility Guidelines 2.1 Level AA standard by April 24, 2026. Additionally, library leaders share concerns about ensuring accessible digital content, including articles and materials retrieved from databases. Sadly, many platforms are continuing to release content that does not meet accessibility requirements or needs and then necessitates that libraries remediate the documents for accessibility. Research indicates that students are often hesitant to request this service from the library or simply do not have the time to wait for the remediation process, and this results in inequitable access to information for students with accessibility needs. Accessibility and remediation skills should not be limited to a specific or limited number of library staff members. Cross-training is paramount, as every single staff member working with a library should (1) Advocate for accessibility; (2) Be equipped with the skills and tools necessary to advocate for accessibility; and (3) Be equipped with the skills and tools they need to immediately respond to accessibility needs, including negotiating with vendors to ensure purchases will not be made when platforms and the materials within them are not accessible. Moreover, all library staff should have the skills necessary to remediate documents on the spot, such that they are not delayed in bureaucratic processes that often cost students or other patrons timely, equitable access to information.

How do you think this will change in the future? How do you hope it will change (short-term and long-term)?

Personally, I choose to believe in the innate goodness in the human spirit. I believe that people want to be a part of creating and ensuring an accessible, inclusive world. This requires that people have opportunities to develop awareness of accessibility needs and barriers, as well as solutions, such that they can then make critical contributions to effecting change. I am also very hopeful that factors such as the DOJ's final rule and the Marrakesh Treaty will bring increased attention to accessibility needs and also equip librarians with the necessary knowledge and skills. Perhaps the most significant opportunity and responsibility we have is to work with patrons who have personally lived experiences with accommodation needs to learn from them and work with them to ensure their needs are met.

What are the key digital accessibility skills all librarians should aim to develop?
Website accessibility, document remediation, seeking training provided by people who have accessibility needs, as they have so much invaluable information, knowledge, and strategies to share.

Notes

1. Americans with Disabilities Act of 1990, 42 U.S.C. § 12102 (1990), www.ada.gov/pubs/adastatute08.htm.
2. United Nations, "Convention on the Rights of Persons with Disabilities," *Treaty Series* 2515 (2006): 3.
3. Institute on Disability, "Percentage of People in the U.S. Who Had a Disability from 2008 to 2022," Statista chart, March 1, 2024.
4. C. A. Okoro, N. D. Hollis, A. C. Cyrus, and S. Griffin-Blake, "Prevalence of Disabilities and Health Care Access by Disability Status and Type among Adults—United States, 2016," *Morbidity and Mortality Weekly Report* 67, no. 32 (2018): 882–87, http://dx.doi.org/10.15585/mmwr.mm6732a3.
5. World Health Organization, "Disability," March 7, 2023, www.who.int/news-room/fact-sheets/detail/disability-and-health.
6. Laurie J. Bonnici, Stephanie L. Maatta, and Muriel K. Wells, "US National Accessibility Survey: Librarians Serving Patrons with Disabilities," *New Library World* 110, no. 11/12 (2009): 512–28, https.//doi.org/10.1108/0307 18009 11007532.
7. Congressional Budget Office, "Rising Demand for Long-Term Services and Supports for Elderly People," June 26, 2013, www.cbo.gov/publication/44363.
8. National Center for Education Statistics, "COE – Students with Disabilities," https://nces.ed.gov/programs/coe/indicator/cgg/students-with-disabilities.
9. Bureau of Labor Statistics, "Bureau of Labor Statistics Data," https://data.bls.gov/timeseries/LNU00074597.

20 •• CHAPTER 1

10. Julie Smart, "Models of Disability: Another Way to Describe Disability," in *Disability Definitions, Diagnoses, and Practice Implications: An Introduction for Counselors* (Routledge, 2018), 79.

11. Jackie Leach Scully, *Disability Bioethics: Moral Bodies, Moral Difference: Conceptualizing Disability* (Rowman & Littlefield, 2008), 22, https://search.alex anderstreet.com/view/work/bibliographic_entity%7Cdocument%7C3237185.

12. Smart, "Models of Disability," 79.

13. Nancy J. Evans, Ellen M. Broido, Kirsten R. Brown, and Autumn K. Wilke, *Disability in Higher Education: A Social Justice Approach* (John Wiley & Sons, 2017), 56.

14. Rhoda Olkin, *What Psychotherapists Should Know about Disability* (Guilford, 2001), 27.

15. Tobin Siebers, *Disability Theory* (University of Michigan Press, 2008), 3.

16. Colin Barnes, "Understanding the Social Model of Disability: Past, Present and Future," in *Routledge Handbook of Disability Studies* (Routledge, 2019), 20.

17. Anita Silvers, "An Essay on Modeling: The Social Model of Disability," in *Philosophical Reflections on Disability* (Springer, 2010), 19–36.

18. Silvers, "An Essay on Modeling."

19. Sami Schalk, *Black Disability Politics* (Duke University Press, 2022), 34.

20. Individuals with Disabilities Education Act of 2004, Pub. L. No. 108-446, 118 Stat. 2647 §300.8(a)(1) (2004).

21. Americans With Disabilities Act of 1990, 42 U.S.C. § §12102(1)(A) (1990).

22. Americans With Disabilities Act of 1990, 42 U.S.C. § §12102(2)(A) (1990).

23. Jackie Leach Scully, "Deaf Identities in Disability Studies: With Us or Without Us?" In *Routledge Handbook of Disability Studies*, ed. Nick Watson, Alan Roulstone, and Carol Thomas (Routledge, 2012), 111.

24. Kodi Laskin, "Introduction: Disability Is Not a Bad Word," in *Serving Patrons with Disabilities: Perspectives and Insights from People with Disabilities* (American Library Association, 2023), viii.

25. Erica Mones, "I Refer to Myself as Disabled, Because My Disability Is Central to Who I Am," Popsugar, March 9, 2021, www.popsugar.com/fitness/why-i-use -identity-first-language-as-disabled-person-48170684.

26. Ather Sharif, Aedan Liam McCall, and Kianna Roces Bolante, "Should I Say 'Disabled People' or 'People with Disabilities'? Language Preferences of Disabled People between Identity- and Person-First Language," in *Proceedings of the 24th International ACM SIGACCESS Conference on Computers and Accessibility* (2022), 12, https://doi.org/10.1145/3517428.3544813.

27. Sharif, McCall, and Bolante, "Should I Say," 12.

28. Shannon Woolridge, "Writing Respectfully: Person-First and Identity-First Language," National Institutes of Health, April 12, 2023, www.nih.gov/about-nih/ what-we-do/science-health-public-trust/perspectives/writing-respectfully-person -first-identity-first-language.

29. See United Nations, Department of Economic and Social Affairs, "Accessibility and Development: Mainstreaming Disability in the Post-2015 Development Agenda," December 2023, www.un.org/disabilities/documents/accessibility_and _development.pdf; Leo Valdes, "Accessibility on the Internet," report to the United

Nations (June 16, 1998, updated March 31, 2004), www.un.org/esa/socdev/enable/disacc00.htm.

30. U.S. General Services Administration, "An Introduction to Accessibility," Digital.gov, 2024, https://digital.gov/resources/an-introduction-to-accessibility/.

31. U.S. Department of Justice, Civil Rights Division, "Guide to Disability Rights Laws," ADA.gov, February 28, 2020, www.ada.gov/resources/disability-rights-guide/.

32. See, for example, Harvard University, "Harvard University Digital Accessibility Policy," June 1, 2023, https://accessibility.huit.harvard.edu/digital-accessibility-policy; University of Cincinnati, "Electronic and Information Technology (EIT) Accessibility Policy," April 5, 2018, www.uc.edu/about/policies/electronic-information-technology-accessibility.html; Colorado State University, "Accessibility of Electronic Information and Technologies," Colorado State University Library Policy, November 11, 2022, https://policylibrary.colostate.edu/policy.aspx?id=739; State University of New York, "Electronic and Information Technology (EIT) Accessibility Policy," June 20, 2019, www.suny.edu/sunypp/documents.cfm?doc_id=883.

33. Federal Register, "Information and Communication Technology (ICT) Standards and Guidelines," January 18, 2017. www.federalregister.gov/d/2017-00395.

34. IDEA, "About IDEA," https://sites.ed.gov/idea/about-idea/.

35. Americans with Disabilities Act of 1990, 42 U.S.C. §12181(7) (1990).

36. U.S. Department of Justice, Civil Rights Division, "Fact Sheet: New Rule on the Accessibility of Web Content and Mobile Apps Provided by State and Local Governments," April 8, 2024, ADA.gov, www.ada.gov/resources/2024-03-08-web-rule/.

37. W3C Web Accessibility Initiative, "Web Accessibility Laws & Policies," December 4, 2023, www.w3.org/WAI/policies/.

38. United Nations, "Convention on the Rights of Persons," 3.

39. WIPO, "Marrakesh Treaty," www.wipo.int/en/web/marrakesh-treaty.

● ● ●

CHAPTER 2

The Wares

Spaces, Hardware, and Software

A theater student working a crew position sprains both wrists but needs to complete a paper.

A blind music production student is unable to read the sheet music in a library database.

A professor comes into the library preparing for cataract surgery and hoping to learn how they can read and grade their students' papers in the meantime.

I n these real situations, librarians were caught off guard, felt helpless, and struggled to assist the patrons. They didn't know where to begin and were unsure what they could and could not ask. What disclosures, if any, would be necessary? What was possible? What barriers had we unintentionally created? What asks were reasonable? What solutions would be most inclusive? While this book is focused on digital accessibility in libraries, we need to appreciate that digital accessibility includes spaces, hardware, and assistive technology devices as well as access to materials and resources discussed throughout.

While offering a wide array of assistive devices is not a legal mandate, doing so ensures that all users can access your collections. Of course, you will not be able to meet every need and preference of every user. Input devices for some motor impairments might, for example, require costly sensory switches like the one used by the famed theoretical physicist Stephen Hawking. Hawking's sensor attached to his cheek enabled him to activate the switch using small movements. A "sip and puff" switch allows

24 ••• CHAPTER 2

the user to control the cursor using breath control or, like the FLipMouse, via light pressure from one's lips, finger, or toe. Such devices are helpful for those without confident use of their hands, but they are not easily shareable and are extremely expensive (the base price is currently about $200). So your job becomes a kind of alchemy, balancing an inclusive approach and making educated guesses on what would be most advantageous to fulfill your goals.

❯ Assistive Technology Considerations

There are many devices libraries might provide patrons depending on local demographics, budget allowance, grant opportunities, and the library's vision to have a fully inclusive set of options. While it is difficult to predict the needs your users might have in a year or two, planning should move forward with a sense of the library's priorities and an understanding of your community and the diversity of disabled individuals served. Planning needs to be iterative, constantly adapting to new technologies and needs. We know that both younger and older members of the workforce are declaring one or more disabilities and that overall numbers are on the rise. How can libraries see to it that all users have the tools they need to equitably engage with library resources? Acquiring hardware that can assist a variety of users and reviewing those acquisitions over time should be an objective of any digital accessibility program. Accessibility contacts or teams at each library should work closely with IT (information technology) personnel to ensure that equipment is regularly tested, updated, and maintained in working order.

Keyboards get unplugged or lose keys, mice go missing, system upgrades can cause programs to disappear, furniture can block computing spaces, and other barriers to access can pop up before patrons ever enter the library. Promoting your assistive technology and accessibility features to your users is certainly important. But it means little if users arrive on site to find equipment lacking, computers out of date, or programs missing. A healthy library is one that shifts, as a kind of living organism. Attending to your library's assistive technology must be a regular part of the workflow. Ensuring proper maintenance of equipment and spaces is critical in making sure that those with disabilities feel welcome. Your goals should always be to build that upkeep into the planning from the start.

❯ Welcoming All Users

Though we don't always define this as "digital accessibility," a patron with disabilities cannot access your resources without flexibility and the dignity that autonomy brings. Signage must be in appropriate font, size, and contrast such that low-vision users can navigate your spaces without personal assistance. This is the welcome mat of your space. Keep it clean and clear.

Generous network ports, Wi-Fi hot spots, and outlets in all your spaces (for the public or your staff) can make or break accessibility efforts. Wiring for audio systems should take disability into account before construction begins or a renovation commences. Ideally, equipment for those with disabilities should be easy to access, with clear emergency egress instructions readily available and accessible. Any rooms dedicated to assistive technology should also be accessibly designed, centrally located, regularly maintained, and updated.

❯ Operating Systems

Though the personal computing era began in the late 1970s, it was not until the mid- to late 1980s that we saw computers appearing in every home. In 1995, five years after the ADA passed, accessibility features were folded into operating systems using the leverage of the law. The ADA's passing was a touchstone for advocacy groups looking to push for a more equitable and inclusive environment. According to the American Federation for the Blind, the rollout of Windows 95 became a seminal moment, when advocates, and states like Massachusetts and Missouri "openly pushed Microsoft to commit to much greater accessibility for Windows 95 or face possible refusals by those states to purchase the program when it was released."[1] This kind of advocacy, using the law to push the landscape further and faster, has yielded positive developments.

In April 2024, the Department of Justice released a final rule revising Title II of the ADA so as to specify compliance with WCAG 2.1 digital accessibility standards by 2026 for public entities with populations of over 50,000 people and 2027 for public entities with populations under 50,000 people. We would expect advocates and users to employ this newly clarified rule to their advantage in pushing efforts forward to create a more universally accessible environment. It is possible that more and more states, consortia, and entities will put pressure where needed to ensure that their adoptions meet the current regulations or that there is a road map for getting there fast. In the following sections, we outline some of the most common, existing, and anticipated accessibility features that are folded into operating systems (OS).

Common OS Accessibility Features: Vision Support

Built-in Screen Readers

Most operating systems include some type of base-level screen reader. The screen readers can read content in the operating system itself, allowing users with little or no vision to navigate through the system and options. Linux "Orca," Windows' "Narrator," and Apple's "Voiceover" are examples of this assistive technology. Screen readers are discussed at length later in this chapter.

Screen Magnification and Zoom/Zoom Apps

A screen magnifier is a software feature that can enlarge the text and graphics shown on a computer screen. It can enlarge the content of an entire screen or zoom in on just parts of it. Sometimes, these magnifiers have a hover feature that will enlarge anything over which the user lingers with their mouse. This is also a built-in feature for web browsers.

Dark Mode, Contrast, and Night Light

All operating systems allow visual customization appropriate for those with low vision, migraines, and fatigue. These features control the sharpness of contrast, the tint of the screen, and other visual elements.

Common OS Accessibility Features: Fine Motor Support

Sticky Keys and Slow Keys
Sticky keys ensure that those with tremors or fine motor issues can activate key combinations like Command-S using only one hand. Slow keys deliberately ignore multiple fast-repeat keystrokes from users who have trouble quickly lifting their fingers off the keys. The program indicates to the OS that it can wait before accepting more movements.

Switch Control
A switch control allows users to activate commands without the traditional mouse. Users can engage with a joystick, or plate switch (controlled with one's hand or foot like a pedal).

Dictation/Speech Recognition
Both of these features discern spoken words and convert them to text or commands. Users can control their devices and input text without the fine motor skills involved in typing on a keyboard. This technology can present barriers for those with speech impediments or slurred speech. Moreover, it normally requires significant time to "train" the technology in dictation applications. A speech recognition app might be an individual program (e.g., Dragon by Nuance), or it may be incidental or built into another application (e.g., Texthelp's Read&Write literacy program). Dedicated applications tend to have higher accuracy and allow the customization of commands and vocabulary. Sometimes they are paired with other technologies and platforms to allow for more professional speech recognition. Dedicated programs also tend to have fewer issues with the nuances of a user's speech because they require the user to train the application. Like other applications that accept a user's input, libraries should consider privacy issues, including the security of user profiles on shared computers. Staff who are trained to assist patrons with such programs need basic training.

Common OS Accessibility Features: Hearing Support

Visual Alerts

Some operating systems have visual indicators when an OS alert is sounded, enabling hard-of-hearing or deaf users to have a visual cue of an event that is normally dependent on sound. In most cases, a system notice, pop-up, or dialog box opens, or else it might be buried in multiple windows or tabs. This feature will flash the screen or taskbar when an alert goes off.

Mono Audio

Some people with hearing issues have stronger hearing on one side or another. Mono Audio allows users to focus on one side without getting distracted or confused trying to distinguish sounds on the weaker side where sounds may be muffled or distorted.

Customization of Captions

This feature allows users to determine the foreground and background colors, specify the placement of captions on the screen, and choose the size and type of font desired for video content and live captions.

Common OS Accessibility Features: Cognitive Support

Focus Mode

Most operating systems have some option to minimize distractions by silencing all or most notifications, thereby enabling the user to focus better on what they're doing. Like the driving mode on a cell phone, a user can selectively silence unwanted or unnecessary notifications and shut down access to certain sites or apps.

Predictive Text

Predictive text is a software feature that suggests words or phrases the user might wish to insert as they type. It helps to make composing messages easier. This feature may allow for prediction in several languages. Predictive text can assist in engaging and focusing the user who needs cognitive support, but it is also helpful for those with mild mobility issues as it often takes a single stroke to accept predictive suggestions.

Immersive Reader
An *immersive reader* is a tool that assists reading comprehension and focus by enabling users to customize a text's appearance; for example, by altering the font, style, line spacing, and background.[2] Immersive readers will high-light words as they are read aloud, often include a focus mode (described earlier), and may integrate translation support for non-native speakers.

▶ The Future Is Customizable

As shown with the common features described in the previous sections, several operating systems include granular customizations for each indi-vidual's accessibility needs. As tech companies race to ensure that they integrate keyboard shortcuts, customizable display settings, and content or screen magnification as a baseline, the disabled community will likely push for total inclusion. Hopefully, these companies will see the value of including accessibility in everything they do—using a universal design approach. Simple things like setting the display to night mode to soften the contrast might be helpful for some users, but for others, such as those with migraines, for example, it is essential. Changes that are often targeted to an audience with disabilities can potentially benefit every user. As oper-ating systems mature, we will see more voice control, guided access, eye tracking, haptics, and so on. As a result of the ADA rule update,[3] we will likely see American consumers (individuals and larger institutions alike) clamor for more accessibility features sooner rather than later.

▶ Anticipated and Future OS Enhancements

Enhanced Speech Recognition
Current speech recognition technology fails in several ways. It yields high inaccuracy rates for non-native speakers, speakers with irregular speech

patterns, or those suffering from cerebral palsy, stroke, or degenerative diseases like Parkinson's. With advances in natural language processing, new AI integrations promise more precise outcomes.

Haptic Integration

Haptics is a technology that transmits information through the sense of touch and vibrations. As haptics evolve, we expect to see more of that growth, integrating music more seamlessly so that users with hearing impairments can better enjoy the experience. We will also see more haptic integration into screen reading technology and images.

Cognitive, Mood, and Mental Health Support

Look for more mood-tracking and stress-reduction tools integrated into operating systems that trigger reminders for mindfulness and breathing.

▶ Essential Technology

Screen Readers

A screen reader is an application that allows visual information and navigation to be read aloud so that a blind or low-vision user can navigate and interact with content using the keyboard. This can be essential for those with severe mobility impairments as well. It is important, however, to remember that a screen reader can only do so much. For a screen reader to be useful, it must be asked to read something that is accessible by nature. The text needs to have proper optical character recognition, tagging, and heading; these improve the reading experience, create a navigational structure throughout the document, and ensure that the content can be consumed. Screen readers can output text to either audio or braille.

While most operating systems have screen readers integrated, some users will use a combination of screen reading technologies. In fact, of over 1,500 users surveyed by Web Accessibility in Mind (WebAIM), "almost 72% of survey respondents said they use more than one screen reader, 43% use three or more, and 17% use four or more."[4] The fact that users combine adjuvant technologies is not unusual and is something libraries should consider, as well as what percentage of workstations and loaner laptops will have this technology installed and ready for use.

THE WARES: SPACES, HARDWARE, AND SOFTWARE ● 31

From workstation to workstation, if a user does not bring their own laptop, they need a screen reader with which they are familiar. For years, JAWS (Job Access with Speech) has been the most popular screen reader and was considered the industry standard in screen-reading technology. JAWS is a proprietary software with a minimum cost to individuals of around $100 per year and a price tag for institutions of over $1,500 (usually allowing for three seats). It has the most granularity when customizing settings like the pitch, speed, and expression of the synthesized voices. JAWS is beginning to lose market share to NVDA (Non-Visual Desktop Access), however. Since the inception of the WebAIM survey, users' habits have shifted. In 2009, 48 percent of respondents insisted that cost was a factor in their choice of a screen reader, but this percentage has risen dramatically with almost 80 percent of respondents citing this as a factor. As more users become comfortable with the more economical NVDA as an option, JAWS may continue to lose ground.

What Are the Best Screen Readers for Library Computers?

What does this shift mean for libraries? It is important to keep an eye on such trends so we know where to place our planning energies. Many libraries invest in Apple computers, which benefit from the VoiceOver screen reader. This application is highly regarded, but because the Apple ecosystem is so expensive, it has a much smaller adoption rate among those with disabilities, coming in at under 10 percent in the WebAIM survey.[5] Of course, it is always useful to survey your local population so as to understand which technologies they embrace and why. For now, however, many libraries offer both NVDA and JAWS at a minimum.

❱ Essential Hardware

Keyboards and Other Assistive Input Devices

Large print and high-contrast keyboards are small investments, well-suited for those with declining or low vision. Other devices like an ergonomic keyboard, trackpad, foot mouse, switch device, or joystick can allow users with fine motor issues to have alternate means of inputting queries. Given the aging population and the rise of disability overall, such investments are

AAC Augmentative and Alternative Communication Devices

Augmentative and alternative communication (AAC) devices are designed to facilitate communication with nonverbal individuals. A patron may be verbally limited (such as having aphasia) or experience slowed speech (such as in the aftermath of a stroke). Some users may benefit from a simple picture board or an alphabet board.

AAC devices can also be higher tech such as a speech synthesizer board that speaks a word when a button or icon is activated. The higher the tech product you acquire, the higher the cost generally. Beyond cost alone, however, libraries should consider the needs of their local communities and their inclusivity goals. For a fuller and up-to-date discussion of augmentative and alternative communication options, refer to the American Speech-Language-Hearing Association.[6]

CCTV and Magnification

A closed-circuit television (CCTV) system can be used as a tool for magnification. It features a monitor on a stand above a flat surface with vertical and horizontal guides to align the book or similar item. The book or item is placed on the surface and a camera inside the bottom of the monitor then displays that image on the monitor above. The guides ensure that the reader stays on the line or column, thus increasing the reader's ability to focus. These units can allow for a magnification of up to 170x, though 75–80x is more common.[7] According to the American Foundation for the Blind, a "camera mounted on a fixed stand and x-y table is in the $1,800 to $4,000 price range."[8] A traditional CCTV is generally not portable, though some new technologies increase manageability by combining a handheld device with a portable stand (or none at all), allowing the device to be stronger than a handheld magnifier. Today, CCTVs come in a wide range, with some that are lighter and more portable and some that are tablet-based, with external cameras or Wi-Fi enabled to project on a television. The smallest handheld device is a 5-inch portable CCTV that allows output to a TV using HDMI cables and can achieve 22x magnification.

Such a tool may be useful individually but can cause a host of issues for a library (circulation, maintenance, etc.), making the larger, more traditional CCTVs preferable, even with the higher price tag. Many new high-tech CCTV devices now come with an integrated OCR (optical character recognition) component, document export, and read-aloud options. The Perkins School for the Blind maintains a list of options.[9]

The visual assistance that a traditional CCTV provides is stronger than any that a handheld device could achieve. While this kind of assistive technology does many of the same things as app-based screen magnifiers, a basic CCTV can do this without a computer. It allows users, especially technology-averse users, to enjoy everyday activities like reading the newspaper or a magazine.

Magnification Software

Desktop computers and mobile devices may include programs that mimic the magnification of a CCTV using less bulky technology, such as software programs like ZoomText or MAGic. By contrast, these programs enlarge digital content. The capacity of these programs to magnify is not as strong as a traditional CCTV, and many apps can only enlarge up to 30x. Some of these programs may shift the user's field of vision without recentering to establish the user's visual context, making it confusing to get oriented properly. This disorientation can cost the user time and cause frustration. Other programs might have great magnification within a user's context, but they may not be easy to toggle, or they may require finer hand-motor coordination to change font colors or contrast.

When it comes to magnification software, there is no one-size-fits-all solution. Not every tool fits every user, and librarians need to consider many factors in the equation to adopt the best technologies for their populations. Considerations might include looking at some of the WCAG criteria for success (for example: criterion 1.4.10, which enables a user to enlarge text while staying inside the viewport), combined with real-time usability studies for your population where you test to see if the target sizes make sense once someone engages the magnifier. A user may be forced to roam the screen to find the target link on a website that does not have resizable text. It is important for anyone procuring software to recognize that users have preferences, and not every tool is appropriate for each user.

There are a host of options for desktop computers and mobile devices, including tablets and smartphones.

Portable Scanners

A document scanner is a device that converts the text and images of physical documents into a digital format. The resulting digital images are stored on a computer and can be viewed and edited. One simple thing every library can do is acquire portable document scanners with high-quality OCR for use by all patrons. The units should be plug-and-play, easy to use, able to scan up to 600 dpi (dots per inch; a measure of image resolution), and should have clear buttons and controls. When items that were not "born digital" need to be made accessible, high-quality scanners should be readily available for those creating content (following a set of reasonable best practices).

It isn't the user's responsibility to make items in the library's collection accessible by scanning them. While not the user's responsibility, these same scanners could be used by patrons who themselves may want to make their own content accessible. For example, a user who wishes to scan a personal document from a doctor or employer, or a professor who needs to make a document accessible before adding it to their course site. In these cases, patrons may seek access to appropriate scanners and OCR software to make their own materials usable. However, we must be clear that it is the library's responsibility to curate a usable collection for our patrons and, failing that, ensure that we have a clear path to helping them get what they need. Users should not be expected to remediate library materials themselves. If a user comes in with an item and needs assistance, we should have a process that is useful and guided by clear policies. Libraries should do what they can to ensure that users can achieve their goals even if the materials are not our responsibility to remediate.

THE WARES: SPACES, HARDWARE, AND SOFTWARE   ••• 35

Best Practices for Document Scanning

- Scan from a clean original (no skewing, no markings or stains, highlighting, shaded text, black gutters, etc.).
- Set higher quality dpi, such as 300 dpi or above (with 600 dpi for scientific images, graphs, etc.).
- Scan only one page at a time—don't attempt to save time by pressing the spine down to do two pages at the same time. It is difficult to do both without creating a skew or a larger black column, which will be interpreted by the OCR application as an image.
- Take a moment to crop out shadows, etc., so that the page is as clean as possible.
- If there is bleed-through because of thin pages (you see dots from the text on the verso page), try placing a piece of black paper behind the page being scanned and scanning the page as grayscale or color.
- Try to avoid color scans because they are heavier files, but in some cases, like yellowing or foxed pages, using color makes a lot of sense.
- Be sure the reading order of the document is clear (that paragraphs aren't located unusually).

Adapted from "Scanning & Linking," Purchase College, 2024, www.purchase.edu/library/services/course-reserves/scanning/.

Braille Embosser and Refreshable Braille Displays

Louis Braille invented the braille system in the early nineteenth century, and it slowly took hold as the "national reading standard in the United States" for those with low or no vision.[10] The braille alphabet is a series of tactile dots, normally raised or embossed, on paper that allow the visually impaired to read by touch. It is its own system and is not comprehensible to the untrained user. Braille is not universally embraced by blind patrons. Adoption of the braille writing system may depend on one's cultural background, age, or acumen with the technology. More often than not, we encounter users who take advantage of our collections using digital accessibility best practices, but they do not consume braille content. While the number of braille users has shrunk, perhaps due to "the lack of access to skilled Braille instructors," it is equally possible that the assimilation of students with disabilities into the modern classroom, along with advances in technology, have had some effect.[11] As technology becomes more advanced and more blind users mainstream, we may see a further decline. Notwithstanding this, libraries serving large, diverse, or aging populations may want to invest in braille technology. This is especially important for educational institutions to ensure they are protecting the access rights of patrons. Adoption is always community- and user-dependent, with an eye toward flexibility in choice.

A braille embosser is an impact printer that collects text or other data from a computer and prints it out in braille on paper, which a user can then read by touch. Some considerations for the adoption of braille embossers include their speed, noise, size, cost, and maintenance. Braille embossing can be a slow and noisy process, so the space in which the technology resides should be chosen with this understanding. While there are sound abatement products, this equipment is better suited to a separate room. It should go without saying that the room should be centrally located and easy to find. While this may be difficult to arrange, it is important that users feel the value of their inclusion and not feel marginalized by the library's desire to put the embosser out of the way so as not to disturb other users. All users should feel equally cared for and included.

The cost of the embossers is generally high and is higher in the long term than, say, using a screen reader for digital accessibility. The equipment most libraries will have to invest in is costly and requires heavyweight embossing paper that can handle the printing process. This paper looks a bit like the old dot matrix paper that needs to be loaded using a tractor feed, looping the guide holes on either side evenly to pull the paper forward. The paper itself can be costly, as can the maintenance and support needed to ensure the whole process can go forward.

The embosser and paper are only part of the braille equation. The embosser cannot work without braille output provided by programs

THE WARES: SPACES, HARDWARE, AND SOFTWARE　●●● 37

like JAWS. This tells the embosser what strikes to make onto the paper. Embossers are not the only way to read braille. Refreshable braille displays are also available. These are similar to pin art toys, where a screen of many pins can be pushed to make a three-dimensional image, except that the refreshable braille display connects to a computer or mobile device and has a series of pins that correspond to braille dots. This enables a user to read and then refresh the display to read the next set of characters. While the price for such units is extremely high ($5,000 to 11,000), according to the American Federation for the Blind, the "improved efficiency justifies the additional cost"[12] and provides an uninterrupted reading experience.

Considerations for the adoption of a refreshable braille display include many of the same concerns as for a braille printer. Is there tech and training support available? What is the compatibility with your chosen screen readers? How important is the size? (This may affect the number of pins and how frequently the display needs to be refreshed.) What kind of power is needed to run the display? Is it rechargeable or does it require a USB, and do you have available ports sufficient for a user's needs? With a price tag as high as that of a refreshable braille display, it is particularly important to consider all these factors, as well as what extra features might be available and how well your library can grow with the unit. As with any of these costly purchases, libraries in dense and diverse populations or in the academic sector will be more likely to consider adoption.

Audio Assistance

In your physical space, there are several ways to ensure that your hearing-impaired patrons can hear clearly and feel included in your events and other programming. A hearing loop or induction loop is one of the best ways to broadcast speakers, events, and meetings. The hearing loop system transmits audio directly to audience members' hearing aids and cochlear implants by using a broadcast signal. The hearing loop technology can send sound to a wide range of hearing devices. Moreover, the system transmits signals while strippling out background noises, thus resulting in excellent sound quality for the listeners (often better than its predecessor, the FM system).

A frequency modulation or FM system consists of a speaker who uses a microphone, and the sound is delivered directly into audience members' headphones or hearing aids by means of an FM radio signal. This type of system has been around for some time and was for years the gold standard for inclusive programming and services. However, the need for testing, lending, and checking-in of equipment, as well as the maintenance of headphones to ensure hygienic practices, can be a deterrent. Another potential downside of FM systems is that they can sometimes experience interference with others who are using FM technology, including security personnel who cross your frequency. While not the most popular choice nowadays, FM systems are much more affordable and can serve your hard-of-hearing population, many of whom do not yet have hearing aids.

Both induction loop and FM transmission systems have pros and cons. It is important that each library weighs the potential use of each type for various types of events. This kind of technology may be very helpful to hearing-impaired users during an event, especially in older buildings or structures with open floor plans and poor soundproofing.

Closed Captioning and Transcription Services

Closed captioning is a kind of subtitling in which the audio portion of a program is transcribed and appears (at the bottom of the TV or video screen) as text that the user can read while watching the video portion of the program. This technology is a standard tool enabling hearing-impaired viewers to comprehend all sorts of audiovisual programs. Unlike subtitles, however, captions may include additional details relevant to the content. For example, closed captioning may detail the horn blast of enemy troops in the distance if it is essential information for a town's historical reenactment. This is especially useful for the hearing-impaired to comprehend speeches, lectures, meetings, and other live events remotely. A variant called "live captioning" is used for captioning live audio in real time on a screen. The technology typically uses speech-recognition software to automatically generate the captions.

Despite the obvious tragedies, challenges, and dangers of the COVID-19 pandemic, the crisis held some hidden gifts for some in the disabled community. The shift during the lockdown to virtual meetings and videoconferences arguably sped up the development of more accurate live captioning in programs like Zoom, Teams, and apps like Otter.ai. For those with hearing impairments and focus or processing issues, the move to more ubiquitous captioning meant support in ways they traditionally lacked. The use of AI to improve speech recognition and typical speech patterns has informed large language models and has increased the overall efficiency of live captioning. However, there is still a long way to go in interpreting what's captured when the speaker has a speech impediment or is a non-native English speaker, for example.

Live captioning for events is crucial to the success and inclusivity of your events both in person and online. WCAG success criterion 1.2.4 calls for captions that "not only include dialogue, but also identify who is speaking and notate sound effects and other significant audio."[13] What is important for librarians to remember is that not all captioning is equal. In some systems, speech-recognition software is used to automatically generate the captions, while in other systems, human input is used to generate them. The latter type, known as "steno captioning" or "human captioning," still far outperforms even AI-enhanced automated captioning as far as quality is concerned. Steno captioning is as it sounds; a highly trained stenographer represents phonetic sounds on their keyboard to build the words we see in the captions. This is also referred to as CART (communication access real-time translation). Once the stenographer inputs the phonetic sounds, a computer converts them to English.

Human captioning does not necessarily mean that someone types every word. It could be that the captioner respeaks what they hear to clarify it for the AI, as they are trained to pronounce the way they know the AI needs to hear it. The AI then processes it and outputs what we see as live captions on a large screen or personal devices for in-person events or to television or device displays. Both CART services/steno captioning and human captioning are resource-intensive prospects, but they are essential for large-scale live programming. The policy driving the decisions for necessary live captioning can allow for flexibility of choice for each event, or it can create a flat rule that at every event a specific style of captioning will be provided.

Besides dialogue (its main use), closed captioning may also convey non-dialogue-related content like sound effects or background noises like laughter or cheering. Transcription services typically process the spoken words into text and create a written record of the content. Closed

40 ••• CHAPTER 2

captioning can also be useful for meetings, events, and lectures. The captions are timed to the speaker's words, but transcription will, more often than not, ignore timing. Transcripts are often considered separate, though some applications like Teams will allow a pop-out, time-stamped transcript of a meeting and will identify speakers based on their user profiles. Whether you engage captioning or transcription, both have a basis in speech recognition, and for both, artificial intelligence is shifting the costs.

Automated AI-enhanced captioning, using speech-recognition software, is by far the most ubiquitous and the least expensive kind of captioning, but it lags in accuracy and fails to account for speech impediments and non-native names and speech patterns. The least expensive solution is not always the most reliable or useful one. It is important, then, to understand the audience's needs and the importance of the event. When libraries are trying to ensure that such content is fully accessible, prioritizing events like press conferences, emergency management, and election information sessions is important, where the stakes are higher and we risk misinforming or excluding a vulnerable population. (There is a fuller discussion of AI enhancement of speech-recognition captioning in chapter 10, "Artificial Intelligence, Libraries, and Accessibility.")

Literacy Software

Literacy software programs can help students improve their reading and writing skills and are particularly useful for those with learning disabilities. A grouping of accessibility features, often bundled, become the ingredients in these multilayered literacy software programs. These applications might include speech recognition but also add options for word prediction, increasing or maintaining focus, and annotating content. They may have a built-in dictionary and thesaurus. Such literacy programs aim to improve reading and writing skills overall. Some even use graphics of lips to help users properly pronounce words. This kind of literacy package has universal appeal and can be essential for those with learning disabilities or for non-native speakers. Read&Write (Texthelp) and Kurzweil 3000 (Nuance) are two such programs, providing support for those with literacy and learning disabilities, dyslexia, and ADHD, or who have English as a second language. Once licensed, these programs also offer browser extensions so that the support is integrated into the web browsing experience. Some applications, such as Read&Write, offer support for all rather than specifically focusing on disabled users, so they can be popular throughout the community and attract a wide audience.

Optical Character Recognition and Text-to-Speech Technology

A sighted individual sees a PDF file, reads it, and assumes that because they can read it, anyone can. The truth is that PDF files can be extremely complex when it comes to their accessibility, especially if they have been hand-scanned. For a file to be truly accessible to all users, the characters in a PDF file need to be recognizable by screen reading and text-to-speech programs. Most word processing and design programs allow for "Save as PDF" and will secure accessibility features of born digital documents, as discussed in greater detail in chapter 5, "Digital Media and File Accessibility."

Because programs, more and more, allow for the file processing to save accessibility settings, text-to-speech (TTS) programs can be used without the need for OCR technology. The characters will already be recognizable, and no conversion is necessary. Thus, people can use TTS to have born-digital documents read aloud independently, so they can listen to the content of an e-book, article, website, text file, and so on. This is what you will often see embedded in databases as a "read aloud" or "play" option.

For many uses, however, as with scanned documents, the processing of materials using OCR is a necessity. While OCR technology may be integrated into multiple programs, such as HP's scanning software, sometimes these bundled elements will create a searchable PDF but not a fully editable one and they can lock editing on the OCR portion of a file, making it more difficult to fine-tune and correct. A dedicated OCR program like ABBYY FineReader allows for higher accuracy and more flexibility in supporting languages other than English. Furthermore, dedicated OCR programs will allow the user or library to set a document for multiple languages more easily. For example, let's assume that a love poem is written in both Spanish and English versions, side by side. To isolate the English version would be to miss part of the poet's intention and fail to align it with the Romance language text to highlight their commonalities. The instructor's lesson is focused on this pattern in the poem, and so separating the parts would degrade that purpose. Having a program that allows you to specify both English and Spanish, where relevant, is critical to supporting the lesson. An experienced user of Adobe Acrobat Pro DC can do this.

Dedicated OCR programs, like ABBYY FineReader or programs like Kurzweil 1000 for low vision and blind users who use ABBYY Fine-Reader as a basis for OCR, will also handle other complex issues with more aplomb than a bundled program. Discrete parts of the document, like decorative fonts, tables, multiple columns (as in the side-by-side poem in English and Spanish), and even handwritten text, may be more easily distinguished with the more advanced algorithms in a separate program created for the unique issues that OCR'd documents may present. Dedicated TTS programs may offer more customizations for voice options, noise reduction from stray markings on the pages, etc., than out-of-the-box or free solutions.

OCR programs include options with various levels of functionality. Free programs or sites may cost time and effort in the end. They tend to offer one thing or another, but librarians would need to string together several of these free programs and learn them all to do what a suite can. Some programs do basic OCR, others do tagging of parts, and so on. By contrast, suites can do most of what is needed to ensure that PDF files are accessible (examples include Adobe Acrobat Pro and OmniPage), but these programs can be costly and may have a learning curve. So, the considerations remain cost, training, and personnel.

Once a library has the technology and trained staff to properly create OCR'd documents, it should consider where these workflows come into play. Many electronic information technology accessibility plans and policies, commonly called EIT plans, attempt to re-situate older workflows and establish more updated guidance and expectations for library employees. Awareness among ILL (interlibrary loan) librarians of accessibility needs and historically inaccessible practices is growing and is changing the way ILL departments provide materials. "By providing scans that are searchable, ILL units can feel more confident that they are providing patrons with the information they need in an accessible format."[14] OCLC, a member-run nonprofit organization for technology and services, hosted an executive subgroup on accessibility that produced a set of guidelines in 2022. With these guidelines they outlined workflows, best practices, and cited other resources to guide scanning quality, including OCR, for as many articles as possible for all library types. They laid out a variety of tech options available for scanners and OCR software, and suggested that the group adopt Tesseract, an open-source OCR engine that can detect words embedded in images and which supports over 100 languages.[15]

In June 2023, the Reference & User Services Association amended the American Library Association's U.S. ILL Code to include guidance on accessibility, with explanatory text for those unaware of best practices.[16] Best practices that were once limited to organizations like the American Federation for the Blind or the National Federation of the Blind are becoming more commonplace. These best practices are being woven into a myriad of projects and efforts, including those that oversee some of the trickiest materials to remediate, such as the materials in archives, local history collections, and institutional repositories.

Designing Accessible and Inclusive Library Computer Labs and Workstations

Brady Cross, *Associate Librarian for Collections, Resource Sharing, and Technical Services, Tri-County Technical College*

- Integrate all assistive technology/adaptive technology (AT) into the existing spaces rather than creating a single "special" workstation. This will reduce the need for those with disabilities to self-identify and thus reduce barriers to access.
- Some AT may be more appropriately checked out at the circulation desk. Some patrons may not understand the role of the AT and could inadvertently misuse or abuse the equipment.

CHAPTER 2

- Consult with the IT department to discover if there are any existing licenses for expensive AT software such as JAWS. Unused or underutilized licenses may be available for immediate implementation.
- Negotiate institutional site licenses (a license that may be used for all college/university computers) for AT software such as Kurzweil. This will reduce possible barriers, such as the need for self-identification.
- Consider universal design when making furniture purchase and design decisions.

  - Are the furniture unit and space appropriately designed to be accessible by all users? Will patrons with a wheeled conveyance be able to collaborate with peers in the space?
  - Ensure that furniture is modular so it may be rearranged to suit future needs.

- Ensure that all workstation seating has casters so it may be moved with low effort, thereby ensuring that patrons with walkers and wheelchairs can easily utilize the workstations.
- Install dimmer switches (especially in labs and study rooms), solar shades, and blackout shades, and offer earplugs to accommodate users with sensory overload needs.

Notes

1. American Foundation for the Blind, "A Brief History of Microsoft and Accessibility," www.afb.org/aw/1/4/16165.
2. LEEDS Beckett University, LibAnswers, "What Is 'Immersive Reader' and How Do I Use It?" https://libanswers.leedsbeckett.ac.uk/faq/243635.
3. "Nondiscrimination on the Basis of Disability; Accessibility of Web Information and Services of State and Local Government Entities," Federal Register, April 24, 2024, www.federalregister.gov/documents/2024/04/24/2024-07758/nondiscrimination-on-the-basis-of-disability-accessibility-of-web-information-and-services-of-state.
4. Colleen Gratzer, "Key Findings from the WebAIM 2024 Screen Reader User Survey," Medium (blog), March 20, 2024, https://medium.com/@colleengratzer/key-findings-from-the-webaim-2024-screen-reader-user-survey-bb15864d3bc8.
5. Gratzer, "Key Findings."

THE WARES: SPACES, HARDWARE, AND SOFTWARE ● ● ● 45

6. American Speech-Language-Hearing Association, "Augmentative and Alternative Communication (AAC)," www.asha.org/njc/aac/.
7. American Foundation for the Blind, "CCTVs/Video Magnifiers," www.afb.org/blindness-and-low-vision/using-technology/assistive-technology-products/video-magnifiers.
8. American Foundation for the Blind, "CCTVs/Video Magnifiers."
9. Perkins School for the Blind, "Choosing the Appropriate Video Magnifier," www.perkins.org/resource/choosing-appropriate-video-magnifier/.
10. "Disability in American Life: An Encyclopedia of Concepts, Policies, and Controversies," 2 vols., Ebscohost.
11. National Industries for the Blind, "Impact of Technology on Braille Literacy," January 4, 2024, https://nib.org/connecting-the-dots-how-technology-is-impacting-braille-literacy/.
12. American Foundation for the Blind, "Screen Reading Technology," https://afb.org/blindness-and-low-vision/using-technology/assistive-technology-videos/screen-reading-technology.
13. Web Accessibility Initiative, "Understanding Success Criterion 1.2.4: Captions (Live)," www.w3.org/WAI/WCAG21/Understanding/captions-live.html.
14. Michelle Courtney Lee, "Improving Accessibility in Interlibrary Loan Using OCR," *Journal of Interlibrary Loan, Document Delivery & Electronic Reserve* 29, no. 1/2 (January 2020): 76, https://doi.org/10.1080/1072303X.2020.1859426.
15. Ron Figueroa, Travis Goode, and Dennis Massie, "Making Library Materials Available in Accessible Formats via Interlibrary Loan," SHARES Executive Subgroup on Accessibility, OCLC, www.oclc.org/content/dam/research/documents/shares/SHARES-ILL-accessibility-resources.pdf.
16. Reference & User Services Association, "ILL Code with Explanatory Text 2023," Interlibrary loan code for the United States (with explanatory text), www.ala.org/sites/default/files/rusa/content/ILL%20Code%20with%20Explanatory%20Text%202023%20%281%29.pdf.

CHAPTER 3

Principles of Web Accessibility

A blind patron from out of town visits your website wanting detailed information on the assistance they can expect when they arrive at your facility to fill out their tax forms.

A mom with a child on the autism spectrum wants to quickly know which e-books are best for her son to explore with the read-aloud option, so he can focus on them while she is in a meeting.

A young man with traumatic brain injury needs to navigate your website to find assistive technology, as well as use the online form to make an appointment with a librarian who can help him research résumé and job application tips.

The principle at the core of digital accessibility is to ensure content shared on the internet is made accessible to all users, no matter how they access websites. Given the wide variety of assistive technologies and adaptive approaches that have been developed to facilitate individuals navigating the Web, it is essential to create web content that follows consistent design principles. Over time, standardized accessibility principles and best practices have emerged to guide the development of online content so that it is widely usable and consistent. In particular, the World Wide Web Consortium (also known as the W3C) created the Web Accessibility Initiative (WAI), which is responsible for creating standards, technical specifications, documentation, and training materials to make the internet more accessible and inclusive for all. Through its work, the WAI has created the Web Content Accessibility Guidelines (WCAG), which are not only used by web developers around the world, but have also been enshrined in the accessibility laws of numerous countries.[1] Among the latter are the new rules recently released under the ADA,[2] the Accessible Rich Internet Applications (ARIA) technical specification, and other resources that have advanced web accessibility across industries as the internet has developed. Understanding these standardized methods of ensuring web accessibility is key to making online library content usable for everyone, including those who use assistive devices to navigate the Web.

▶ Web Content Accessibility Guidelines

It is difficult to overstate the influence that the WCAG have had on web accessibility. These guidelines are regularly used across industries to design accessible content and evaluate existing content. Automated testing tools are built around the guidelines and their success criteria. Moreover, the guidelines are at the center of many accessibility policies. It is imperative for those working in digital accessibility to understand these guidelines and how they should be applied. This process starts with an understanding of how the guidelines were developed and what their goals are.

The WCAG were not the earliest approach to web accessibility. Prior to the development of the first version of these guidelines, web accessibility was already a focus of those interested in the ongoing development of the internet. An early resource that emerged to help web developers design accessible content was the Unified Web Site Accessibility Guidelines, which were developed under the auspices of the Trace Research & Development Center at the University of Wisconsin at Madison. These guidelines ultimately became WCAG 1.0 after the transfer of the guidelines to the Web Accessibility Initiative in the late 1990s.[3] The first version of WCAG, WCAG 1.0, was launched in May 1999 with a focus on ensuring that disabled people could navigate web content using a range of assistive technologies and adaptive approaches to interacting with online content. The introductory text for that publication noted:

These guidelines explain how to make Web content accessible to people with disabilities. The guidelines are intended for all Web content developers (page authors and site designers) and for developers of authoring tools. The primary goal of these guidelines is to promote accessibility. However, following them will also make Web content more available to all users, whatever user agent they are using (e.g., desktop browser, voice browser, mobile phone, automobile-based personal computer, etc.) or constraints they may be operating under (e.g., noisy surroundings, under- or over-illuminated rooms, in a hands-free environment, etc.). Following these guidelines will also help people find information on the Web more quickly.[4]

To achieve these goals, the WAI has continued to update and evolve the guidelines over time, and has released multiple versions of WCAG that have responded to the changing nature of online content and our expanding understanding of what disabled users need to be able to equitably access digital content. This evolution has continued, with work starting on a new version of WCAG even before the most recent release. The maturation of the guidelines is vital in ensuring that web content is accessible. Regular reviews of any WCAG updates and the workflows to integrate them are very important to optimize access for all users.

From the very beginning of its work, the WAI has also developed training materials and guidance documents to help those at all levels to learn more about accessibility. These resources range from tutorials about how to create digital content that aligns with the guidance in WCAG,[5] to documentation on the process of creating policies[6] and accessibility statements[7] to enshrine accessibility at the center of an institution's practices. The resources also explain how to design content to serve different users, including those with cognitive and learning disabilities[8] and users who are aging.[9] Because of this commitment to providing training materials as well as guidelines, the WCAG are very influential among those who teach web accessibility as well as among practitioners.

The current iteration of the guidelines, WCAG 2.2, was released in October 2023, and, as with past updates, it aims to improve accessibility by including features that support more types of users and by responding to changing technology. These guidelines offer clear guidance on how to design various types of digital content for optimal accessibility and are written to provide a low barrier to entry for those who are new to this aspect of digital design. They are an important tool when creating new web-based digital content and are also a standard that can be used to evaluate existing online content for accessibility in libraries and beyond. In fact, the guidelines have been the basis for legal standards around the world, with many countries and jurisdictions integrating either the web content accessibility guidelines themselves or derivatives thereof into their laws.[10] For these reasons, it is important for those working on digital accessibility in libraries to have a thorough understanding of WCAG and the resources that the WAI offers for improving web access for all.

POURing Over Web Accessibility

The WCAG uses the basic principles of web accessibility as its organizing structure. It defines these principles using the acronym POUR, which stands for perceivable, operable, understandable, and robust. Each of these four words represents a key characteristic of accessible digital content. These words and the acronym they form can help developers to remember the central needs of a range of users. In addition, beginning with these principles in mind can help to make digital content accessible from the start, rather than requiring remediation or accommodations later. For this reason, it is very important for anyone responsible for creating, editing, or evaluating online materials to understand the concepts behind POUR at a minimum. Given their importance, let's look at each of these concepts in turn.

Perceivable

As the word *perceivable* suggests, this principle refers to designing digital information so that all users can perceive the material being shared. It is focused on the ability of users to take in the content that is included on a website. For many, this may immediately bring to mind the idea of being able to see (and read) the content, but it encompasses more means of perception than just vision. As with much of digital accessibility, much of this design work comes down to offering options and alternatives. Whenever flexibility can be introduced into a design, it will benefit all users by allowing them to access the content in the manner that is most convenient for them. However, beyond general flexibility, there are some specific design choices that promote perceivability.

Color contrast. At the heart of making information perceivable to those with varied needs is ensuring that certain minimal standards are met. Color contrast is a major one of these. This is, of course, important for people with color vision deficiency, but it is also helpful for those with low vision, declining vision, or even those who are simply in low-light environments. For the same reason, it is important not to use color as the only way of conveying information. A good example of this would be not using a green circle for yes and a red circle for no but, instead, using a green check mark for yes and a red X for no (because color vision deficiency makes it hard to tell the difference between red and green).

Text font style and size. Similarly, it is important to ensure that the font style and size of the text support easy reading. Selecting a font that is simple, rather than one that resembles script, and avoiding small font sizes will both improve the accessibility of the text. Research is also being done to develop specialized fonts that make text more readable for individuals with specific disabilities, such as dyslexia, though current research suggests that existing fonts of this type do not offer significant increases in accessibility.[11] As this research continues to develop, it may be another avenue for improving the accessibility of digital text. Ideally, digital content should allow users to opt to resize the font and even the word spacing, and when those choices are made, the text should re-flow to promote greater readability.

Images. Images are another major category of content that can require an alternative means of perception. Specifically, images require alternative text (typically abbreviated as alt-text) that conveys in words the meaning of the visual element. While this may initially sound straightforward, it can actually be quite complex. In fact, the same image may require different alt-text depending on the purpose for which the image is being used. Additionally, while alt-text is most often thought of with regard to images, there are other types of visual content that should also have alt-text, such as icons, buttons, diagrams, tables, and data visualizations.

Multimedia. Alternatives for multimedia content are also important to accessibility. The exact features needed will depend on the specific multimedia content being made accessible. For audio-only files, transcripts provide a text alternative that is readable by both users and assistive devices. Transcripts can also be useful for video content, as they are available in a wider range of assistive technologies than most video captions would be. For example, if a video only offers captions, users of refreshable braille displays will not be able to access the information in the captions. Transcripts can either be static files or they can scroll in sync with the multimedia file connected to them. Each of these options has advantages, but if the choice is to present automatically scrolling text, it is important to ensure that the transcripts remain accessible to assistive technologies.

A key element of video accessibility is captions. While it may initially seem as though transcripts and captions are two equivalent alternatives for making videos accessible, they do serve different needs. As mentioned, transcripts are available in a range of assistive technologies and can also be helpful for those who are better able to process information in writing. Captions, on the other hand, can help those watching the video who cannot hear the audio content, whether due to a disability or because they are in a location where they cannot play the video at full volume. Captions can either be "closed captions," which allow the user to opt to turn the captions on and off, or "open captions," which always appear as an element on the video regardless of user preference. Generally, closed captions are preferable because they offer the flexibility to opt to use captions or not. This is useful for those who may find the captions distracting while watching a video.

In addition, to ensure that video content is accessible to those who cannot see, it is important to include audio descriptions (AD)—the audible narration describing important visual elements of each scene—typically during breaks in the dialogue or other soundtrack of the video. Another option for making the audio elements of multimedia content accessible is to offer sign language interpretation of all auditory content. All these various options should be evaluated as possibilities when working with multimedia content online. The exact needs will vary depending on the characteristics of the multimedia content being made accessible and the needs of the expected audience. But the rule of thumb is flexibility.

The final element in making information perceivable is to support the presentation of content in different ways. A great example of this is the importance of dividing text content into an outline structure, and tagging each heading properly in the code so that assistive technology users can navigate between these elements to "skim" the content or skip to the section they are most interested in.

Operable

As the word *operable* suggests, the second letter in this acronym focuses on the functionality, control, and usability of the content. This relates to all aspects of the navigation and use of content being provided to users. Operability refers to both how users operate the site and how any automatic operation of the site impacts the users. While this might initially seem straightforward, there are many ways to navigate online content. Each disabled user is unique in the approach they use, so there are many combinations of tools and techniques to keep in mind while designing accessible content. As such, there are several separate topics to consider when it comes to making a site operable by all.

Operability is particularly important with respect to supporting all the ways users might navigate a site, either when using assistive technol ogies or when not using such technologies. While many web developers may assume users will be accessing their content using a mouse, this is often not the most accessible means of navigation for users with a range of disabilities, including mobility disabilities, tremors, and visual disabilities. For this reason, all content should support multiple means of navigation, including keyboard navigation, voice recognition, gesture-based navigation, and other forms of navigation using assistive technologies. Keyboard navigation, which is also sometimes referred to as *tab navigation*, refers to using keyboard features to navigate through digital content, including using the tab button to move between interactive elements, such as clickable links, expanding menus, search boxes, and fillable sections of forms. (For more information on keyboard testing, see chapter 7, "Automated and Manual Testing.") Creating content that supports keyboard navigation will also ensure that the content is accessible to users who use a variety of assistive technologies, since many of these operate in a similar manner. For example, supporting keyboard navigation will ensure that users of switch devices are able to access the content.

Clear organization, particularly at the code level, is another key component of making digital content operable. By using structural elements, such as headings and other tags, to organize the information on a page, designers ensure that users of assistive technology can quickly navigate through the content. While untagged text is read from start to finish by tools such as screen readers, offering very few ways to jump from section to section, content that has been structured using HTML tags can be navigated much like an outline, with users reading each heading-level element to get a sense of the outline of the page before reading it all or even jumping from link to link. Well-written code can also ensure that users know which page of a site they're on, through appropriate use of the page title, and can make it clear when someone using an assistive device has entered a search box, form, or other interactive element.

The concept of operability also encompasses whether the site creates conditions where the user can safely and effectively use and interact with the content. One important element of this is ensuring that individuals have enough time to interact with a page in a calm and unhurried manner. Some sites, such as e-commerce platforms, have timed elements where an individual only has a specific amount of time to complete a task. A common example of this sort of content is a theater website that allows only one minute to add your credit card information to the payment field before you lose the tickets. Many of these sites have a literal countdown clock that shows the time remaining to complete the task. While there may be situations where this functionality is needed, it is important to design it in keeping with the WCAG recommendations, or better yet, avoid it entirely.

This is because countdowns of this sort can be impossible for some users to navigate, such as those who navigate slowly through the Web due to limited mobility; and they can also be a source of confusion or stress for some users, especially those with anxiety or cognitive disabilities. For related reasons, it is helpful to allow users to have a significant amount of control over page elements that could cause distractions or interruptions, such as pop-up messages and alarms, as these can also present particular challenges for those with specific disabilities.

Finally, no discussion of operability would be complete without mentioning the need to avoid flashing content that can trigger seizures in some users. Because lights flashing at specific frequencies can cause photosensitive epilepsy, it is important that all content is tested to avoid any risk of triggering a seizure. For this same reason, it is also important to grant control over moving or flashing elements, so users can choose whether to have these play while they use a site. This is a great accessibility feature to offer with any content that plays media. Users should always be able to control when media plays and, ideally, the playback speed as well.

While these elements that are relevant to the operable portion of POUR may seem quite disparate, they are, at their core, all about control and flexibility. Designing for operability is about giving all users the ability to control their experience of digital content. The ability to independently navigate the Web is obviously at the heart of creating an accessible experience, and so focusing on the operability of a website for those with a range of disabilities is extremely important.

Understandable

Digital content is only successful if users are able to understand the information that is being presented to them, which is the heart of this element of the POUR acronym. Though a variety of disabilities can impact how well someone is able to understand the online content they navigate through, presenting *understandable* content goes beyond an accessibility consideration to become a general usability consideration. The steps taken to make content understandable can be instrumental in making content more inclusive for all users, not just those users with disabilities.

Carefully considering the language used in all digital content is one key element in making that content understandable. Many visitors to library websites are distracted, stressed, or in a hurry, so it is very important to make sure that everything is written clearly and concisely. This is true for all users, but it can also help with accessibility by making content accessible to those with cognitive or learning disabilities. A good starting point in writing for clarity and simplicity is to employ what is often referred to as *plain language*. Fortunately, thanks to the Plain Writing Act of 2010,[12] the U.S. government offers many free resources that can help everyone to learn the best practices of writing clearly, both in general and specifically for the Web. The next chapter also discusses some steps that can make content more readable. Regardless of the exact approach adopted, simplifying the language used in a digital project will make it more readable for all users.

When writing for accessibility and understandability, it is also useful to aim for text that can be read by those at a low reading level. This is beneficial for all users since it will help both those with specific reading difficulties and disabilities and those who are simply distracted or rushed in their review of the text. While this is clearly related to using plain language, it is worthwhile to keep this as a separate consideration when evaluating online content, so as to prioritize writing at a level that all members of the intended audience will find approachable and engaging. Where more complex information or technical language is needed, it is important to scaffold this information by providing definitions and other supplementary information either within the text or clearly linked from it.

Beyond the language that is used and the way the text is organized, it is also important to develop a clear navigation structure for all online content. First, it is important that the navigation options and menu be accessible to both those who are navigating visually and those who use keyboard navigation or assistive technologies. Beyond this basic requirement, it is also important that a website's contents be organized in a clear and intuitive manner; this can benefit from user testing to ensure that the site's structure is clear for a range of users. Ideally, each page should also provide a clear sense of where the user is in the larger site, for example through breadcrumbs that show the pages above the current page in the hierarchy. The content should also be predictable, meaning that the menu should remain consistent no matter where the user is on the site; the page structure should remain basically the same whenever possible; and it should be clear what will happen when a user clicks on a link or interacts with content on a page. All this will ensure that a wide range of users will find the content coherent and easy to understand.

This principle also covers how users' mistakes are handled. Errors and mistakes are a part of life, whether due to distraction, issues with entering information precisely, or confusion. Well-designed digital experiences will work to make sure that these occurrences cause minimal inconvenience or confusion for users once they've made a mistake. There are many ways to approach this work, and the best is dependent on the specific situation, but some examples of how to minimize errors are the following:

- Feature clear, accessible instructions.
- Design meaningful error messages that can help a user to recover when encountering a problem.
- Offer options to review inputs before they are submitted by the user.
- Make options easily editable and reversible.
- Integrate error-correction features, such as spell check.
- Help users to enter the correct information, by offering suggestions or requiring users to select from limited options.
- Simplify questions, instructions, and information so they are accessible to all users.

While making online content understandable has very real accessibility implications for those with cognitive disabilities, it is one aspect of accessibility that can help almost all users at some point in their use of online content. These aspects of design will help every distracted, hurried, or stressed user.

One final aspect of understandability is to ensure that assistive technologies present the content in a way that is understandable to their users. This makes it imperative that the language of the content is clearly marked on all digital content, so that tools such as screen readers know how to read that information to users. Often, this can be done at the page level, but if different sections of a page are in different languages, the "lang" attribute of the page in the HTML code can be set to the primary language and then individual elements in different languages can have their own attributes.

58　••　CHAPTER 3

This is a vital but often overlooked element of using multiple languages on a single page. Without this, screen readers may not be able to present the information in a way that users can understand.

Robust

The final letter in the POUR acronym stands for *robust*. In some ways, this is the most straightforward of the concepts covered by this acronym because it encompasses a single broad concept. The "robustness" of digital content refers to its compatibility across a wide range of scenarios. Digital content should work well in a variety of settings, such as

- across a wide range of different browsers
- when using an array of different types of assistive devices
- with a variety of different user settings and preferences enabled
- on a range of different hardware
- for both existing technologies and for optimum compatibility with technologies that will be developed in the future

Designing robust content can help to ensure accessibility for those with disabilities, but it can also be useful for others, including people who only have access to outdated equipment or software and those who navigate the Web primarily through mobile devices. Conversely, apps that are designed solely for use on mobile devices can exclude those who don't have access to a mobile device or are unable to use a mobile device due to their disability. Therefore, another aspect of robust design is to support as many ways of accessing the digital content as possible. As such, robust content will inherently be more inclusive content, making this an important design aspect to consider at all stages of a project.

When designing for robustness, it is particularly important to balance the content's compatibility with technologies that are at various stages in their life span. Designing for compatibility with older technologies, such as deprecated versions of browsers, should not prevent the content's compatibility with more modern technologies that are in the process of being adopted. At times, it may be worthwhile to survey users to determine which hardware and software are most prevalent in the community a specific library serves. Alternatively, there is research available that can help with these decisions. For example, WebAIM notes that its Screen Reader User Surveys, which it has administered a total of ten times as of this writing, "indicate that most screen reader users tend to use up-to-date browsers and screen readers, though there will always be some who lag."[13] In many cases, focusing on writing code that follows not just the WCAG success criteria but, also, the general rules and best practices of web design will help to make content more robust and compatible in more situations. Considering how digital content is presented to various agents and technologies can also help to make it compatible across a wide range of scenarios. This is where clear naming conventions and metadata can be useful. Including clear file names and descriptive, consistent metadata for all digital files and documents can contribute to a robust web presence, as well as improve search engine optimization and the usability of the content overall. While a longer discussion of user testing will appear in chapter 4, "The Accessible Library Website," it is worth noting that user testing is particularly important when determining whether a site is robust. By testing not only with automated testing tools, but also with a range of actual assistive devices that users will be using to navigate through the web content in question, it is possible to identify compatibility issues earlier in the process and correct them before they become a barrier to access.

Understanding Success Criteria

While the POUR principles provide the backbone of the Web Content Accessibility Guidelines, it is important to understand how the guidelines are organized within these principles. Within each guideline, WCAG provides a set of "success criteria." WCAG sets a two-pronged requirement for the success criteria. First, each success criterion pertains to one or more "important access issues for people with disabilities that address problems beyond the usability problems that might be faced by all users."[14] Second, each success criterion is phrased as a testable statement about the underlying content. This two-pronged requirement ensures that the WCAG remains narrowly focused on accessibility issues rather than risking scope creep to encompass more general usability issues, and it also ensures that the evaluation of content is central to the work of the guidelines.

Stating that all criteria are testable does not necessarily mean that they can all be tested via automated accessibility-testing tools. While many of the success criteria are designed to allow for automated testing, at least at an initial stage of accessibility testing, some testing cannot be automated. The requirement that criteria be "testable" simply means that it is possible to evaluate digital content and make a determination about whether it meets the requirements of each success criterion.

Moreover, each success criterion is associated with one of three levels of conformance: A, AA, or AAA. In this case, Level A conformance refers to basic levels of conformance with the guidelines; Level AA refers to intermediate conformance; and Level AAA refers to the highest level of conformance. The success criteria are associated with a conformance level by the working group responsible for WCAG, which noted that

> common factors evaluated when setting the level included:
>
> - whether the Success Criterion is essential (in other words, if the Success Criterion isn't met, then even assistive technology can't make content accessible)
> - whether it is possible to satisfy the Success Criterion for all Web sites and types of content that the Success Criteria would apply to (e.g., different topics, types of content, types of Web technology)
> - whether the Success Criterion requires skills that could reasonably be achieved by the content creators (that is, the knowledge and skill to meet the Success Criteria could be acquired in a week's training or less)
> - whether the Success Criterion would impose limits on the "look & feel" and/or function of the Web page (limits on function, presentation, freedom of expression, design, or aesthetic that the Success Criteria might place on authors)
> - whether there are no workarounds if the Success Criterion is not met.[15]

Using this process allowed the working group to offer some guidance on the relative importance of the success criteria to offering access, while still making it clear that developers and designers needed to aim beyond minimum access levels to offer truly inclusive web content that can be used by all.

In the case of Level AA or Level AAA, each conformance level includes all criteria for that level plus the lower level, unless there is an alternative criterion for a specific guideline provided for that conformance level. For example, Level AA conformance includes all Level A conformance requirements as well as all Level AA conformance requirements, except when a Level AA success criterion conflicts with a Level A success criterion. Guideline 1.2 is an example of this; it includes multiple success criteria that cover similar topics at different conformance levels, including two different and mutually incompatible approaches to audio descriptions of video content that align with separate success criteria. Here Level A conformance is associated with Success Criterion 1.2.3, which states: "An alternative for time-based media or audio description of the prerecorded video content is provided for synchronized media, except when the media is a media alternative for text and is clearly labeled as such." By contrast, Level AA conformance is associated with Success Criterion 1.2.5, which states: "Audio description is provided for all prerecorded video content in synchronized media."[16] While all of this information may lead to the assumption that it is best to aim for, or even require, complete compliance with Conformance Level AAA, the reality is more complex. This is because the inclusion of certain types of content may make it impossible for the site to be fully compliant with Level AAA. In fact, under some circumstances, strict compliance with some of the success criteria associated with Level AAA can actually decrease accessibility for users with specific disabilities. An example of a criterion that may not be possible for all digital content would be Success Criterion 2.2.3, which provides that "timing is not an essential part of the event or activity presented by the content, except for non-interactive synchronized media and real-time events."[17] In some situations, a site might need to have timed content that prevents it from meeting Level AAA conformance, which can make it difficult or impossible for institutions to achieve complete compliance with that level. Many libraries and other institutions will have policies oriented to compliance with Level AA and will aim to achieve only those Level AAA success criteria that are practical and desirable for their specific content, needs, and community.

The WAI provides additional documentation to ensure that web developers and designers have a clear understanding of the requirements to comply with the criteria, why compliance is important, who it impacts, and how to design accessible content. Though the documentation is not the same for each success criterion, generally there is information about the reason for the criterion, examples of the accessibility feature in action, and specific technical information on how to meet the criterion. This documentation is extremely helpful in making digital content more accessible, especially given that it is written to be useful to those at various levels of web development expertise. The success criteria and the documentation associated with them ensure that the web accessibility principles established in the WCAG have concrete implementation steps to guide web designers and developers in making the internet more accessible to users with a wide range of disabilities.

▶ Accessible Rich Internet Applications

Originally released in 2008,[18] Accessible Rich Internet Applications, or ARIA, is a technical specification designed to expand web accessibility guidance to interactive and dynamic digital content. It emerged in response to new technologies, such as JavaScript, which changed the way web content functioned, and specifically, how interactions are handled. These new technologies swiftly moved the internet from a collection of mostly static content to a place where individual pages could dynamically react to user interactions and inputs. This allowed users to complete much more complex tasks online. At the same time, however, it presented new barriers for assistive devices—barriers that had not been contemplated by the existing standards. These barriers exist because HTML and other relevant standardized languages don't have a means of indicating when content has changed on a page between reloads.

These developments led to the need for a new approach to fill this gap. Where the WCAG focus on content that is generally assumed to be static, with ARIA, assistive technologies can be given additional information about dynamic content and applications. Without this additional information, this dynamic content is often difficult for those using assistive devices to perceive or use, since their assistive technologies have no way of knowing when a change to the page's content has occurred unless it is somehow flagged for that technology.

ARIA is intended to fill these gaps in accessibility support that can emerge as web technology rapidly shifts and evolves. The WAI-ARIA 1.2 W3C Recommendation states that "WAI-ARIA is intended to provide missing semantics so that the intent of the author may be conveyed to assistive technologies. . . . It clarifies semantics to assistive technologies when authors create new types of objects, via style and script, that are not yet directly supported by the language of the page, because the invention of new types of objects is faster than standardized support for them appears in web languages."[19] As the recommendation also notes, it is anticipated that new approaches to accessibility will emerge within existing languages, such as HTML, which will make ARIA unnecessary, and when this occurs, ARIA should no longer be used.[20] In fact, it is generally best to use ARIA only when it is necessary to make content accessible because no other approach to accessibility exists. When other alternatives do exist, they will often be more widely usable and should therefore be preferred. However, though the exact instances in which ARIA is needed and the exact roles that ARIA plays may change over time, the goal is to continue to update ARIA, so as to ensure that it remains relevant to those newly developed objects that are not yet otherwise accessible.[21]

To ensure that assistive technologies receive the information needed to convey and interact with dynamic content, ARIA sets forth a series of "roles" and, for those roles, different states and properties. These attributes can "be used with various web technologies to expose information that is very useful to assistive technologies (such as points of a page that change dynamically) that could not be exposed otherwise, as well as providing various mechanisms to represent the semantics of various user interface controls (from basic ones such as buttons and links, to the most complex of them like treeviews and grids) to assistive technologies."[22] Roles are used to give assistive technologies more semantic information about the element to which they are attached. In some cases, HTML can convey this information. For example, the <form> tag in HTML identifies a form. However, when HTML does not offer the necessary role, ARIA can be used to indicate this information instead. The "states" indicate the current status of an element, specifically one that is changeable through user interactions or other dynamic changes. An example would be an ARIA state of "aria-checked" for a box that has already been checked by the user

64 ••• CHAPTER 3

when filling out a form. Meanwhile, "properties" give additional details about the element; for example, using aria-required="true" to indicate that a particular field in a form must be filled out for the form to validate properly. Properties are generally not applied to provide information on something that will change dynamically on the page, but instead are used to indicate information that users who were not using an assistive device would receive in some other manner, such as through a visual indicator. These examples are just some of the ways that ARIA can be used, but there are many others. Fortunately, the W3C provides documentation to support developers who are working with ARIA, including both the WAI-ARIA 1.2[23] and the ARIA Authoring Practices Guide.[24] This documentation offers specific support for best practices for making dynamic web content accessible to all users.

❱ The Future of Web Accessibility

As both the internet and assistive technologies continue to develop, so must web accessibility practices. This is why both WCAG and ARIA have already gone through revisions and different versions over the years since their debuts. And both currently have new versions under development. In particular, a working draft has been released for WCAG 3, which is expected to represent a significantly new approach to these standards. WCAG 3 is not expected to become a W3C standard for several more years, and when it is released it will not supersede WCAG 2, nor is WCAG 2 expected to be deprecated for several years after its release.[25] All of this means that designers and developers can confidently continue to work with the current version of WCAG as they create digital content and evaluate existing content.

However, it is worth considering what the future holds for WCAG 3 because it will represent a significant reimagining of the approach that has been used in previous versions of WCAG. To begin with, the expectation is that WCAG 3 will be broader in scope than WCAG 2 because it will incorporate elements that had previously been in WAI's User Agent Accessibility Guidelines 2.0 and Authoring Tool Accessibility Guidelines 2.0. Beyond this breadth, the new approach also seeks to change the way that designers and developers think about web accessibility. In the working draft of WCAG 3 released in July 2023, the goals of the new model were stated as:

1. Develop a model that encourages web sites to continue to improve accessibility (vs. stopping at the previous AA level);
2. Better reflect the lived experience of people with disabilities, who successfully use sites that have some content that does not meet WCAG 2.0 AA, or who encounter barriers with sites that meet WCAG 2.0 AA; and
3. Allow for bugs and oversight by content authors, provided the impact of them upon users with disabilities is not substantial.[26]

These goals are aimed at making practical improvements to ensure that actual usability for people with disabilities is prioritized over technically meeting specific requirements. In particular, this approach will encourage making ongoing accessibility improvement a part of the development workflow, rather than adopting a mindset of one-time achievement of Level AA compliance. This is a step forward for inclusive access to digital content, especially when taken together with the second goal, which acknowledges that the lived experiences of people with disabilities may vary.

To accomplish this purpose, the structure of WCAG 3 will also differ from that of past versions. Instead of success criteria, WCAG 3 is moving to a series of outcomes that are intended to be "in plain language; more understandable by people who are not experts in technology; more user-need oriented instead of technology-oriented; more granular, so there will be more of them; and more flexible to allow more tests than the true/false statements of WCAG 2."[27] As an overarching consideration, WCAG 3 is also intended to take into account more varied needs, meaning both the needs of individuals with different types of disabilities and also different patterns of use by individuals with the same type of disability. This will recognize that users may approach navigating content in unique ways and with their own personalized techniques. Hopefully, this will ensure that these more varied needs are better met across all types of digital content.

Because this new approach aims to change the way that accessibility and compliance are conceptualized, it has the potential to ensure that the needs of disabled users are centered more effectively in the future of web design. When WCAG 3 is released, it is certain to represent a significant change to the way web designers and developers think about accessibility. While it will be some time before WCAG 3 is finalized and even longer before it overtakes WCAG 2.2 as the dominant standard, its goals can already influence the way we think about web accessibility and how we consider who is or is not served by currently existing approaches.

Ultimately, we need to think about who those users are or might be. That blind patron who wanted to fill out their tax forms on-site? The mom who needed e-books or audiobooks for her neurodivergent son? A young man with a traumatic brain injury looking for a job? A student with a concussion? A grandmother with hearing loss? The needs of our users are varied, but the end point is the same. What are our policies and procedures around accessibility? How will we ensure that all types of digital content—whether we create, adopt, or procure it—is accessible to all our users? Using POUR and WCAG's widely accepted success criteria and standards can be useful guides in our efforts.

Accessibility and User Experience Design

Interview with **Dhruti Bhagat-Conway**, *Senior UX Designer, MIT Libraries*

How did you become interested in accessibility as part of your work as a user experience designer?

All of my web library positions were with government organizations before my current position with MIT. Government organizations (among others) have specific guidelines to follow, such as Section 508. My superiors told me to look out for basic accessibility concerns, like a lack of headings or alternative text. So, for me, it was always something I was supposed to think about.

Through training sessions, I learned there was more to accessibility than I realized. I didn't set out to become focused on accessibility. I just wanted to make sure I wasn't excluding users. In the government, our users could be anyone. Because of this, I was encouraged to keep learning and working on making content accessible.

What made you decide to pursue certification as an IAAP-Certified Professional in Accessibility Core Competencies (CPACC) and certified DHS Section 508 Trusted Tester? How has this informed your work?

I decided to pursue both of those certifications because I wanted to be confident I knew what I needed to know. You don't know what you don't know. I thought by studying for the certifications I would learn what I needed to know about accessibility. I now feel more confident that I have a better overall understanding of what I need to look for and why I need to look for it.

I think the CPACC is great for understanding the big picture of the laws and guidelines for physical and digital accessibility. I think the Section 508 Trusted Tester program is useful for digging into what the WCAG rules are and how to apply them.

What do you see as the key accessibility concepts for all library web designers and user experience designers to keep in mind when designing digital content?

I would say the most important accessibility concepts to keep in mind for library digital content are:

- Use clear writing and avoid jargon.
- Use lists wherever possible to make content easy to scan.

  - Make sure they are coded in HTML appropriately as lists.

- Check your color contrast.
- Do not use color as a way to provide meaning.

  - One common mistake is making links blue but without the underline or any other kind of visual indication.

- Use at least 16 pt font for most web content.
- Use alternative text for any meaningful icons (e.g. a hamburger menu icon).

What advice do you have for ensuring user experience testing is conducted in a way that is inclusive for users with disabilities?

There are a few ways I recommend trying to get users with disabilities represented in testing. And once they agree to test with you, there are some things you can do to help make testing more accessible.

Where to Recruit Participants with Disabilities

- Pay for testing from several companies that employ users with disabilities.
  - This is good for getting feedback from experienced users who may also be able to provide suggestions for fixing problems.
- In academic libraries:
  - Work with disability services office to recruit students or staff for testing.
  - Find older adults in your community (typically faculty or staff).
    - Many older adults struggle with disabilities, especially worsening eyesight.
    - Even if they don't use assistive technologies, they still provide valuable information.
- In public libraries:
  - Work with your local disabilities commission.
  - Work with your local older adults department.
  - Recruit older adults from your library's events for that age group.

For recruitment, I suggest having a paper signup or survey in addition to an online version.

Accommodations

- I recommend asking the user to bring their preferred device with them.
  - It allows the user to feel more comfortable.
  - It also means the user will likely not need technological accommodations if their device already has what they need.

PRINCIPLES OF WEB ACCESSIBILITY ◦●● 69

- If you cannot get any of their requested accommodations, let the user know as soon as possible.
  - You can ask if they are still willing to participate without or with partial accommodation, but do not pressure them.
- In-person testing should take place in a physically accessible location.
- Make sure everyone involved in testing understands how to assist users with disabilities in a friendly and empowering way.

What advice do you have for those who are just getting started with digital accessibility work?

Start with the Basics

- It may not seem like it, but this will have a big impact.
- Don't feel like you need to be an expert or get a certification immediately.

Learn More about Different User Perspectives

If you are able, engage with users with disabilities and learn more about their perspectives from them. Learning from actual users will give you better insight.

- This could be talking with members of your community
- It could also be training sessions where the presenter has a disability

If you can't engage with users or attend trainings, simulators can be a great way to help visualize different perspectives. I like Silktide Accessibility Checker (silktide.com/toolbar/), which is a browser extension. Here are some of the things it simulates:

- different types of color blindness
- Dyslexia
- Cataracts
- loss of contrast

Learning these things can also help you convince others to follow accessibility guidelines. In my experience, other professionals adopt accessibility into their work more when they understand its impact on users.

70 ••• CHAPTER 3

Use Browser Extensions to Help with Checking Accessibility

Especially as you're still learning, it can be helpful to have an automated tool that can check for some accessibility issues. Like with many automated tools, they can't do everything for you and will miss things and get some wrong, but they're still useful.

Recommended free browser extensions include:

- Axe Accessibility Plugin (www.deque.com/axe/)
- Accessibility Insights for Web (accessibilityinsights.io/downloads/; this tool will walk you through manual testing after it runs its automated checks.)
- ANDI (www.ssa.gov/accessibility/andi/help/install.html)
- WAVE (wave.webaim.org/)

Take Advantage of Free Resources to Further Your Education

My favorite accessibility conference is completely free, and it's online. It's called Axe-Con (www.deque.com/axe-con/), and it's hosted by Deque, a big name in accessibility. They have amazing sessions that are also recorded.

Level Access (www.levelaccess.com/resources/must-have-wcag-2-1-check list/) and Deque (dequeuniversity.com/checklists/web/) have free accessibility checklists that can help you check web pages for accessibility issues.

What do you hope to see in the future of digital accessibility in libraries and beyond?

I would like to see more positions where maintaining and furthering digital accessibility is a core part of the job. Libraries have so much content online. But, it is difficult to maintain or further accessibility part-time. Some organizations have senior-level positions in charge of accessibility. I think that's a level of commitment to accessibility we should work toward.

Another thing I want to see is having content at lower reading levels. Most people reading this will have completed a Bachelor's degree, if not a Master's degree. And our colleagues fit in that category too. I think we forget our audience may not have the same education we do, or they may not be as familiar with English as a lot of us are.

Notes

1. Kevin White, Britt Classen, Michel Hansma, Vera Lange, and Eric Velleman, eds., "Web Accessibility Laws & Policies," December 4, 2023, W3C Web Accessibility Initiative, www.w3.org/WAI/policies/.
2. U.S. Department of Justice, "Nondiscrimination on the Basis of Disability; Accessibility of Web Information and Services of State and Local Government Entities," Federal Register 89, no. 31320 (April 24, 2024).
3. Trace RERC, "History," University of Maryland, https://trace.umd.edu/history/.
4. Wendy Chisholm, Gregg Vanderheiden, and Ian Jacobs, "Web Content Accessibility Guidelines 1.0," May 5, 1999, W3C, www.w3.org/TR/1999/WAI-WEBCONTENT-19990505/.
5. Shawn Lawton Henry, "Design and Develop Overview," May 19, 2022, W3C WAI, www.w3.org/WAI/design-develop/#tutorials.
6. Kevin White and Shadi Abou-Zahra, "Developing Organizational Policies on Web Accessibility," October 2022, W3C WAI, www.w3.org/WAI/planning/org-policies/.
7. Shadi Abou-Zahra, Eric Velleman, Sanne Eendebak, Roel Antonisse, and Bas de Bruin, "Developing an Accessibility Statement," November 2018, W3C WAI, www.w3.org/WAI/planning/statements/.
8. W3C WAI, "All Supplemental Guidance: Supplemental Guidance to WCAG 2," January 2022, www.w3.org/WAI/WCAG2/supplemental/#cognitiveaccessibility guidance.
9. Andrew Arch and Shadi Abou-Zahra, Developing Websites for Older People: How Web Content Accessibility Guidelines (WCAG) 2.0 Applies. September 22, 2010, *W3C WAI*, www.w3.org/WAI/older-users/developing/.
10. Kevin White, Britt Classen, Michel Hansma, Vera Lange, and Eric Velleman, "Accessibility Laws & Policies," December 4, 2023, W3C, www.w3.org/WAI/policies/.
11. Omer Ari, "Dyslexia Fonts: What Postsecondary Instructors Need to Know," *Journal of College Reading and Learning* 52, no. 1 (2022): 64–71, doi: 10.1080/10790195.2021.1986430.
12. Plain Writing Act of 2010, 5 U.S.C. 105. (2010), www.govinfo.gov/app/details/PLAW-111publ274.
13. WebAIM, "Constructing a POUR Website: Robust," October 4, 2021, https://webaim.org/articles/pour/robust.
14. Accessibility Guidelines Working Group, "Understanding Conformance," May 7, 2024, WCAG 2.2, www.w3.org/WAI/WCAG22/Understanding/conformance#levels.
15. W3C, "Understanding WCAG 2.0: Understanding Conformance," 2023, www.w3.org/TR/UNDERSTANDING-WCAG20/conformance.html.
16. Eric Eggert, and Shadi Abou-Zahra, "How to Meet WCAG (Quick Reference)," November 12, 2023, W3C WAI, www.w3.org/WAI/WCAG22/quickref/.
17. Eggert and Abou-Zahra, "How to Meet WCAG."
18. Lisa Seeman, Michael Cooper, Rich Schwerdtfeger, and Lisa Pappas, "Accessible Rich Internet Applications (WAI-ARIA) Version 1.0.," February 4, 2008, W3C, www.w3.org/TR/2008/WD-wai-aria-20080204/.

CHAPTER 3

19. Joanmarie Diggs, James Nurthen, Michael Cooper, and Carolyn MacLeod, eds., "Accessible Rich Internet Applications (WAI-ARIA) 1.2," June 6, 2023, W3C, https://www.w3.org/TR/wai-aria-1.2/.
20. Diggs, Nurthen, Cooper, and MacLeod, eds., "Accessible Rich Internet Applications."
21. Diggs, Nurthen, Cooper, and MacLeod, eds., "Accessible Rich Internet Applications."
22. V. Rubano, "On Making Web Accessibility More Accessible: Strategy and Tools for Social Good" (doctoral dissertation, University of Bologna, 2023), https://amsdottorato.unibo.it/11023/1/tesi.pdf.
23. Diggs, Nurthen, Cooper, and MacLeod, eds., "Accessible Rich Internet Applications."
24. W3C WAI, "ARIA Authoring Practices Guide (APG)," 2024, www.w3.org/WAI/ARIA/apg/.
25. Shawn Lawton Henry, ed., "WCAG 3 Introduction," July 24, 2023, W3C WAI, www.w3.org/WAI/standards-guidelines/wcag/wcag3-intro/.
26. Jeanne Spellman, Rachael Bradley Montgomery, Michael Cooper, Shawn Lauriat, Chuck Adams, and Alastair Campbell, eds., "W3C Accessibility Guidelines (WCAG) 3.0 W3C Working Draft," July 24, 2023, W3C, www.w3.org/TR/wcag-3.0/.
27. Spellman et al., "W3C Accessibility Guidelines."

· ● ●

CHAPTER 4

The Accessible
Library Website

The library's web developer has identified accessibility issues on the library's website but isn't able to make the necessary changes due to limited access to the content management system.

A patron with cerebral palsy wants to use his own workstation to complete usability testing of the library's website with his assistive devices.

A blind patron wants to use the library's website to sign up for an upcoming book club but finds that their screen reader is incompatible with the accessibility overlay on the site.

Though an understanding of the foundations of web accessibility is key to ensuring that digital content is accessible, it can feel overwhelming to translate this into changes to existing practices or a plan for revising existing content. This chapter will offer advice on how to take the overarching accessibility principles and standards covered in the previous chapter and translate them into real change that meaningfully improves the accessibility of library websites. Though much of this can be applied to other types of digital content, the primary focus of this chapter is on library websites of all kinds, from the main library website to digital exhibits and beyond. The content in this chapter should not be considered a replacement for the WCAG or other accessibility standards or legal requirements. Instead, the aim of this chapter is to make the journey to full accessibility

74 ••• CHAPTER 4

more approachable and ensure that the early steps on this journey have the maximum impact for users. Once initial steps have been taken to ensure basic access to the library's digital content, more complicated accessibility issues can be tackled. This approach will maximize impact and can also help with advocacy, since it helps to demonstrate the outcomes that are possible when accessibility work is prioritized.

▶ Getting Started with Web Accessibility

Whether starting a new project or evaluating an existing website, it is important that accessibility is built into all aspects of the digital design workflow. If it has not been a priority historically, this can be a difficult proposition, but there are often ways to build accessibility considerations step-by-step, even when new to this type of work.

Accessibility from the Start

The best way to ensure that any digital content will be accessible is to build accessibility into the design process for a library website from the very start. Starting with a focus on accessibility can save time, minimize redesigns, and help to create content that is coherent and inclusive. Often this means thinking about accessibility even before starting a design project, at the point at which the content management system (CMS), framework, or design template is being selected. For libraries, this can be difficult if they are not involved in the decision-making process at that point, but it is important to be advocating for accessibility well before these decisions are made, so that the decision-making team asks questions about accessibility and evaluates vendors on their accessibility features. For those who do have direct control over the decision-making process, some questions to ask when making these selections are:

- Is there existing documentation about accessibility features, issues, and best practices in this CMS, framework, or design template?
- If working with an outside design team, have they included accessibility in their outline of the project plan? Do they

have team members with existing accessibility expertise?
- In the case of CMS or other similar platforms, is there a voluntary product accessibility template (VPAT) available? If so, has it been reviewed as part of the selection process?
- If design work will be done by an internal team, does that team have the necessary accessibility expertise to customize the selected CMS, framework, or design template? Will you have the ability to ask for fine-tuning after the initial site comes online?

Once a project is underway, accessibility should be built into each design stage. If a CMS or similar platform is being used, it is important to optimize the setup for accessibility by enabling any accessibility features, such as pop-up reminders about adding alternative text for images. For projects that start with use cases or personas in developing software, it is important to consider the needs of users with a variety of disabilities and those who use various types of assistive technologies within these use cases or personas. To have an authentic understanding of how users will navigate a site, user testing with a broad range of users is important (this is discussed in more depth later in this chapter). This work can be key at the early design stages to ensure that the team is asking the right questions and considering users' actual needs and use patterns. This can also be easier when the project team has a dedicated accessibility expert. While not all teams may have an expert on hand, it is useful to identify one when possible and designate an individual to primarily focus on accessibility, even if they are only just developing expertise in that area. The difference between an end product that is more inclusive and one that is not may be a simple matter of someone interested in asking the right questions. Having a specific team member focused on this work can be another means of ensuring that it is not lost in the overall project steps.

While focusing on accessibility throughout the design process is a good way to minimize the need for later remediation, it is important to test the final product to ensure that it meets at least WCAG 2.2's Level AA conformance. Automated testing is an important first step in this process, as it will identify basic issues and areas for revision. However, it is also important to test with assistive technologies before launching a project.

Walking through digital content with a screen reader can be a great way to see if the design translates to a truly usable experience for those using assistive technologies. Even for projects that have achieved Level AA compliance, it is likely that testing with a screen reader will identify places where the website's content could be reordered, restructured, or otherwise revised to provide a more inclusive experience for all. Ideally, this initial testing should be followed by a review by an expert assistive technology user, making this another excellent opportunity for user testing.

Prioritizing Change

When it comes to existing websites or other projects that were designed without taking accessibility into account, it can be challenging to know where to start on revisions, and the process can feel overwhelming. While it is important to keep full compliance as the ultimate goal, there are some steps that can be taken to maximize your initial impact and help to get the process started.

Start with user feedback. If the library has received feedback that users are encountering specific barriers when navigating the website, this is a good place to start with revisions that address those specific items. If the barriers are on a third-party site that can't be immediately remediated, this can also mean opening conversations with the vendor and planning workarounds and accommodations to meet user needs in the meantime. (For more on vendor communications, see chapter 11, "Best Practices for Working with Vendors.")

Test your existing digital presence. Starting a process of testing your content with a combination of automated accessibility testing tools and actual assistive technologies will identify where the major barriers are in your current digital content.

Look at user data. While user data may not provide a perfect picture of what your users need, particularly if some users are routinely encountering barriers, it is a good way to make some initial decisions about priority. Start with the content that is most popular and move on from there.

Consider the content that needs to be accessible. Another good way to prioritize web accessibility is to think about information that is more likely to be used by users of assistive technologies. Web pages with accessibility information, accommodation information, or other related content must be accessible for disabled users to be able to find the information they need to use the library's website and content effectively. Similarly, feedback forms should be a priority for accessibility work so that you can collect information about accessibility problems.

Ensure the accessibility of all new content. While it is important to remediate existing content, it is also important to make sure that accessibility is a priority going forward, with new content. Training everyone who edits new digital content that is being reviewed for accessibility best practices is a good way to ensure that new content won't mean that new problems are emerging all the time.

The exact process for prioritizing accessibility work is likely to vary from project to project but starting an accessibility remediation project by thoughtfully considering how the content revisions can be prioritized to maximize their impact is always worthwhile. This will ensure that users see an improved user experience sooner and can help to demonstrate that this type of remediation is impactful and can be undertaken in an efficient manner.

Inclusive User Testing

An important part of ensuring that a website is accessible is learning from real users about their personal experience navigating the content. A first step toward achieving this is to make all of the library's avenues for feedback accessible. This means that any digital or physical comment boxes, surveys, and other means of soliciting feedback should be created to be widely accessible and should specifically note what steps a user should take if they encounter a barrier. This will help to surface any accessibility barriers that may have been overlooked. However, ideally, efforts to learn from users should go beyond passively collecting feedback. One great way to gather this information is by conducting user experience tests, but unfortunately, all too often this does not happen. Even at libraries that have user experience testing programs, individuals with disabilities are frequently underrepresented in the testing populations. This can happen for a number of reasons, including the following ones:

- The outreach materials and approaches used to recruit test participants may not be accessible, may include exclusionary language,[1] or may not reach all populations within the community equitably.
- For institutions that focus on in-person user testing, their testing environments may not be accessible or may not include the assistive technologies necessary to support all users.
- Even if some assistive technologies are offered as part of an in-person testing environment, users may not have access to their preferred assistive technology or personally customized setup, which may make them reluctant to participate or may skew the results of the tests.
- Patrons with disabilities may assume that the testing environment will be inaccessible (even if efforts are made to make them accessible) without specific outreach and recruitment efforts on the library's part.

When recruiting participants for user experience tests, it is important to intentionally build a testing community that is representative of your wider community. This goes beyond disability to include considering other aspects of access, such as offering testing options in multiple languages or targeted recruiting to ensure that different segments of the community are represented. To most effectively reach individuals with disabilities, some libraries have found that it is useful to partner with other groups, such as disability services offices[2] or student groups[3] for academic libraries, to conduct outreach. For public libraries, outreach might instead focus on local groups run by and for individuals with disabilities.

The testing process should be designed to be both accessible and inclusive. Supporting remote user experience testing can be an effective step toward greater inclusion. By allowing users to participate from their own work space, it is possible to learn how users naturally approach using the site. When conducting this sort of testing, it is helpful to include interview questions that collect information about the exact technologies the user is using. This should include assistive technologies, but also other information such as the type of device they are using, the operating system it runs on, and any peripherals they use. It is also important to design tests that will be accessible, which can implicate many different aspects of the design. For example, as Karine Larose and Simon Barron note, jargon can create issues for all users but may be particularly exclusionary for those with learning disabilities.[4] More generally, building flexibility into both the testing environment and the test protocol, to accommodate the needs and preferences of a wider range of users, is key to successfully running inclusive user-testing programs, as many researchers have noted.[5] These steps will help to ensure that your user experience testing gathers authentic and meaningful data from a representative group of your users. (For more on automated and manual testing, see chapter 7, "Automated and Manual Testing.")

▶ Quick Accessibility Improvements

Getting started with web accessibility improvements can feel overwhelming, particularly if it has not been an area of focus previously. It is important to remember that there are real advantages to each improvement and step forward taken. The ultimate goal should be a website that maximizes accessibility and takes inclusive access into account during all decisions, but along the way it is key to just keep making incremental improvements. A good approach to this work is to consider the most high-impact changes you can make early in the process, so that accessibility will significantly improve for users, even if the entire site is not fully accessible. The following sections outline several types of accessibility changes that can have a significant impact without requiring the wholesale redesign of a site. These can be good places to get started at the very beginning of web accessibility projects.

Use of Structural Elements

Structuring digital content clearly can improve accessibility, usability, and readability, just by making a few changes. To achieve the full benefits of well-structured content, it is important to make sure that the structure is clear both visually and in the HTML code, so that the structural information is conveyed to assistive technologies. While almost all HTML tags contribute to the structure of the page when used correctly, when it comes to the main sections of content, the key to proper structure is the use of the different levels of the heading tags. Heading tags range from level one, which represents the highest-level content, to level six, which represents the lowest level of content. These are represented as <h1>, <h2>, <h3>, <h4>, <h5>, and <h6>. When deciding how to assign heading levels to content, it can be helpful to think of these as the levels of an outline for an essay. Level one represents the top level (of which there can only be one), with level two serving as a subsection of that topic. If there is a further subsection of level two, that is tagged with level three, and so forth. In many content management systems, each level is assigned a different style, such as a different font, text size, or color, which tempts web designers to use these headings aesthetically rather than to reflect the relative structure of the content. The problem with this choice is that this can be confusing both visually and for assistive technologies.

To best support readability for users navigating a page without assistive technologies, it is best to use style headings in a manner that visually distinguishes between the level of the content, with high-level content under larger or otherwise more prominent headings and lower-level content in subsections under smaller headings. The use of headings that are easily distinguishable from the main body text in terms of size and style can help with skimming the page visually. Properly tagged ordered and unordered lists can also help to break up the text and support organization and skimming, while still being accessible to assistive technologies.

For screen-reader users, properly ordered heading tags are particularly important to navigation. This is because many assistive technologies allow users to approximate the experience of skimming a page by skipping from heading to heading to first understand an outline of the information on the page before selecting the section that is relevant to their needs. This is also why it is important to offer clear and concise headings that will help users understand the information contained in that section of the page. Without this structure on the page, screen-reader users have limited options beyond having the entire page read to them in order from start to finish, which can significantly slow their navigation.

Improving Readability

Creating clear, easy-to-read content is another good way to improve both accessibility and usability. The use of a plain language approach to writing can help to improve overall readability. In particular, a few useful plain language guidelines are:

- Provide a logical organization for all content, which can encompass using headings, breaking material down into lists, and structuring information from more general to more specific.
- Use words that are common and widely used while avoiding jargon, abbreviations, and other specialized or complicated language.
- Keep content concise.
- Use the active voice and present tense wherever possible.
- Evaluate all text for readability, including reading level, font selection, font size, color contrast with the background the text appears on, and white space on the page.
- Know your audience and write with that audience in mind.[6]

While it may seem that using plain language will primarily help those who are reading digital content unassisted, it can also be useful for those using assistive devices, such as screen readers, since that technology may not properly pronounce jargon or uncommon technical terminology. (Read more about speech recognition in chapter 10, "Artificial Intelligence, Libraries, and Accessibility.")

Beyond using plain language, it is also useful to consider how you can convey information in multiple formats. For example, information conveyed through text might be replaced or supplemented with icons in some cases, or supplemented with images or diagrams. This is a common technique for links and other navigation tools, such as the use of social media icons that are links to an institution's account on that social media platform. For more complex information, it might be possible to include audio or video versions as well. Offering multiple ways to access the same information will meet the needs and preferences of more users. This can be helpful in conveying information and capturing users' interest.

Alt-Text

To make images, graphics, and other static visual content accessible to those using screen readers or other assistive technologies, it is vital that each visual item has alternative text (often abbreviated as alt-text) attached to it. The alt-text itself is a short, concise written description of an image or graphic that appears in a digital document or web page. The text is used to convey the nature and content of the image to users who are visually impaired or who use screen readers. When a screen reader encounters alt-text, it reads the text aloud, thus enabling the user to understand the content of the image.

Alt-text is included as part of the image tag within the HTML: <img alt="image description">. This topic was briefly discussed as part of the explanation of the "perceivable" principle of POUR in the previous chapter and is discussed in further detail in chapter 5, "Digital Media and File Accessibility." Alt-text can be complicated, so it is worth taking the time to understand the best practices about it on websites in more depth. Too often alt-text is treated as an afterthought or is written with only perfunctory information, but the reality is that detailed, concise, and relevant alt-text is vital to the accessibility of visual content.

The alt-text must convey the information that the visual item is providing to users. While it is best to describe an image or graphic as comprehensively as possible in the alt-text, it is also important to keep the alt-text as brief as possible, which causes a clear tension. Weighing these competing priorities can be difficult, but there are several ways to keep alt-text brief while also sharing enough to convey the necessary meaning. One useful approach is to cut out extraneous words of information. For example, it isn't necessary to start alt-text with "Picture of" or similar text; this can be assumed, so that the description can focus on the content of the picture. Another way to achieve this is to focus on the purpose for which the item is being shared. For example, the painting *Self-Portrait with a Straw Hat* by Vincent Van Gogh could be presented as a depiction of Van Gogh's appearance, or alternatively, from an art historical perspective, could include an explanation of his use of color or other technical elements of his approach to painting. Each of these different uses of the image could have a different alt-text that emphasizes those specific elements of the painting rather than attempting to describe all aspects of the piece equally. While there is no limit to the length of alt-text that can be included in an HTML file, some platforms, such as content management systems and social media platforms, will have a maximum character length for alt-text, often set to 125 characters, so this can be a good approximate length to aim for when creating alt-text that may be used in multiple different places.

In certain cases, it may be necessary to include more detailed and therefore longer alt-text for some types of images, such as complex data visualizations. In these situations, it is still important to focus on what key information the image is conveying and what information is extraneous and can be omitted. When it is difficult to convey all of the information from a data visualization through alt-text, it is also worth considering whether other accessibility approaches may be preferable, such as linking to the information in a more widely accessible alternative format. Alt-text is not just useful for images; it is also important for other visual content that may otherwise be invisible to assistive technologies, such as icons and buttons. A good example of this is the social media icons included in many websites' footers. All too frequently these icons lack meaningful alt-text, which can make them inaccessible to many users.

It is also important to make sure that alt-text does not merely repeat other content that is accessible to assistive technology, such as the caption for an image, or the surrounding text. Otherwise, a screen reader might read the same text multiple times in a row—first as the alt-text and then as the caption for the image—which is both inefficient and potentially confusing for users. In limited cases where an image is purely decorative, such as a logo that repeats the title of the page, it is also possible to leave the alt-text empty. This will render the image invisible to assistive technologies. For example, when the alt-text is empty, a screen reader will simply skip over the image when reading the content of a page.

Recently, AI tools designed to automatically generate alt-text have emerged. For example, Microsoft Office has integrated an AI feature that creates suggested alt-text for images across that suite of software. Some social media platforms have also integrated AI image description tools to combat the significant problem of alt-text being omitted from images shared on social media. However, at this point, most of these tools are generating generic basic descriptions of the image, at best, rather than focused, relevant descriptions of the information that the image is being used to convey in a particular context. Depending on the exact AI tool used and the complexity of the image itself, the alt-text will vary in quality; however, even in situations where it is technically correct, AI tools are not yet able to customize image descriptions for the specific context and purpose for which the image was included. For this reason, it is important to review and edit any automatically generated alt-text wherever it appears to ensure that the final alt-text is sufficient to make the image's content accessible for users of assistive technologies. (For more on AI, see chapter 10, "Artificial Intelligence, Libraries, and Accessibility.")

Unfortunately, the limitations of automated testing of alt-text are similar to those of the AI generation of alt-text itself. Though most automated accessibility testing tools will identify places where alt-text is missing, they can't tell when alt-text is of high quality. Since many platforms will automatically fill in the alt-text field with the name of the image file when no other alt-text is provided, this means that many website editors who rely on automated accessibility testing may believe that their images are properly tagged when the reality is that their "alt-text" is little more than "image3789.jpg" or some other file name. For this reason, it is necessary to train all team members who have web-editing privileges, and particularly those with image-posting responsibilities, about the importance of creating individualized and relevant alt-text for all image files. (For more on automated and manual testing, see chapter 7, "Automated and Manual Testing.")

Color Use and Contrast

Color is a huge part of the internet. It is used to develop brand associations, convey information about the success or failure of specific actions, and draw attention to specific content, among many other uses. Unfortunately, color is often used without consideration of the accessibility of these choices, which can create barriers to use for those with color vision deficiency (often popularly referred to as color blindness), for those who have low vision, and for those using some types of assistive technologies to navigate the Web. Carefully considering how color is used can help to ensure that the content of a site is accessible to a wide range of users.

When it comes to optimizing web design for accessibility, it is helpful to avoid using color as the sole means of conveying information. There are several common situations where this can occur. For example, when an interactive component of a website displays an error message, it often does so by indicating the problem in red but, to make such an indication more accessible, it is also important to indicate that information in another way as well, such as through text that explains the problem. Another common example of color being used to convey information online is the practice of making links a different color from the rest of the text. Though nowadays, links are not as frequently colored the traditional blue shade that was so often used for them in the past, many websites do still use a color to indicate that a segment of text is a clickable link. Particularly when link text is not also underlined, using color as the sole means to indicate that a specific piece of text is a clickable link can be inaccessible to users who have difficulty perceiving differences in color. When including data visualizations or other graphics on a website, it is also important to consider how color is used to convey information. A secondary means of conveying that information should always be included. Two common approaches that work for many data visualizations are to label the sections of the visualization with text as well as color, or to use both color and pattern to convey the information. While these are some examples of color use in digital content, there are countless other examples that arise, meaning that it is always important to consider how color is being used to ensure that users who may not be able to perceive those colors can still equitably access all content and features.

Another important aspect of color use is the contrast between the colors. Contrast is what allows viewers to perceive a difference between two colors, either in their hue (the basic difference between red, blue, and yellow, for instance) or in their value (how light or dark a color is, on a scale from white to black). When there is insufficient contrast between two adjacent colors, such as between text and the background it appears on, it may be difficult or impossible for users to read the text. Contrast is the subject of three different WCAG success criteria:

Success Criterion 1.4.3: Contrast (Minimum) (Level AA)[7]
Success Criterion 1.4.6: Contrast (Enhanced) (Level AAA)[8]
Success Criterion 1.4.11: Non-text Contrast (Level AA)[9]

Additionally, contrast is an element of Success Criterion 2.4.13: Focus Appearance.[10] Because of the exact standards set by these success criteria, many accessibility testing tools offer automated checks to confirm whether the contrast meets the ratios set forth by the WCAG. However, these refer to minimum contrast levels, and more contrast is always permitted. It is useful to maximize contrast to ensure that the site remains accessible to users with different vision levels and those using the content in different lighting conditions.

Accessible Links

How many times have you noticed a "click here" link on a website? For many web content creators, this is common link text that is used without too much thought and is often used multiple times on the same page, since it is a call for the specific action they want users to take. However, these links are not optimized for accessibility. The reason for this is that many assistive technologies, such as screen readers, will allow users to skip directly to the links on the page. In the case of a screen reader, this means that the text associated with each link will be read out to the user. If all of the links say "click here," there is no way for the user to know which link to select. Even worse, if the URL itself is written out on the page as the link rather than linking text, this means that the screen reader will read each character in the lengthy and rather cumbersome URL when it reaches the link. For this reason, it is important to think about accessibility when creating links. The absolute best practice is to link text that clearly states where the link will take the user. For example, the link could be the entire phrase "visit our interlibrary loan page." In the HTML code this might look like this: <a href="abclibrary.gov/ill">visit our interlibrary loan page</a>. This descriptive link is brief but will tell the user exactly where the link will take them. It is also important that each link's text is unique (unless the link takes users to the same location and there is a compelling reason to use the link twice on the same page), so that it is easy to differentiate between the links.

In some cases, it may not be possible to link text. This is the case on some social media platforms, for example. When this is the case, the best practice is to use a shortened URL, ideally with text that identifies the location the link will take users to. It is also useful to include information about the link immediately before the URL. For example, the social media post might say: "Visit our interlibrary loan website: shortenedurl.com/ILL." Using a shortened URL limits the length of time it takes for a screen reader to read it. Be sure to also include information about the destination of the link immediately before it. This ensures users are able to decide whether they want to navigate to that destination.

Where Links Open

Another aspect of link accessibility to consider is where links open when users click on them. While the default behavior for links is to navigate to the new page in the same window and tab of the browser that the user is currently in, some designers opt to have links open in a new tab or even a new window when they are clicked. While some web designers and users feel very strongly about their own personal preferences in this regard, for both good accessibility and good usability, it is important to have links open in the same tab.[11] There are several reasons why opening links in a new tab represents an accessibility issue:

- For users who are blind or have low vision, it may make navigation more difficult, particularly when going back to the previous page.
- For users with mobility disabilities, it may be more difficult to navigate between windows and tabs.
- For users with cognitive disabilities, it may be more confusing and disorienting.

With respect to the web accessibility principles, this is tied to ensuring that content is understandable by having it behave in a predictable manner. Opening in a new window or tab with no notice is the antithesis of this predictability. As such, it is not just an accessibility issue but, also, a usability issue for all users, particularly those using mobile devices.[12] While opening content in new tabs or windows should be limited, WCAG guidance does acknowledge that it may be better to default to a new tab or window in specific, limited situations where the functionality of the content in question requires it, such as situations where linking from secure content to outside content would otherwise log a user out of the platform, or situations where failure to do so will "significantly disrupt a multi-step workflow."[13] In all other situations, the default should be to open links in the same window and tab, while allowing users to decide for themselves if they wish to override this default. In certain situations, it may be worthwhile to provide guidance on how users can manually select to open in a new tab or window to ensure users know this is an option. It is worth noting that in some content management systems and learning management systems it is possible to change the default link behavior globally, which can make this a relatively quick fix for those using these types of platforms.

Proper Use of Tables

To ensure that digital content is accessible, it is also important to use tables correctly to make them accessible to assistive technologies. While it can be tempting to use tables as a means of spacing content on the site for aesthetic purposes, the first step to accessibility is to eliminate all of these uses of HTML tables. This is because of the way that assistive technologies such as screen readers will not navigate information in tables in the same way that they would if it were not in a table or in the way that would be expected based on the visual layout of the content. For content in tables, screen readers will present the information in the order that the information is listed in the HTML markup of the page. Though newer approaches to web design mean that using tables to set up a web page's design is less frequent than it was in the earlier days of the internet, the first step in reviewing the use of tables in web content is to ensure all tables are being used to convey tabular information and not simply for design purposes.

For information that is tabular in nature, such as data, tables can be used, but they must be properly labeled. This means that each row and column should have a clear header that is tagged as such in HTML. This allows those using screen readers to have these headers read aloud so that the users have context about the relationship of the columns and rows to the data. W3C-WAI also notes that "some people use alternative ways to render the data, for example by using custom stylesheets to display header cells more prominently," which is only possible when the information in the table is properly tagged.[14] These same principles apply to tables in digital documents as well. Though not all document types support HTML markup, most do allow editors to indicate the headers for each column and row, which is vital for document accessibility as well.

Allow Customization Where Possible

Allowing for flexible use and the ability to customize site properties and features is almost always a quick way to improve accessibility. Whenever this flexibility can be added to a website, it will help more people to access the content and will make the process more usable for everyone. A perfect example of this is implementing a dark mode. Dark modes flip the more standard online experience by offering a dark background with light text rather than a white or light background with dark text. This approach to web design has grown in popularity for several reasons, including personal preference, power savings when navigating the Web in dark mode, and improved accessibility for some disabled users. However, as is so often the case, dark mode is not more accessible for all users and can be inaccessible for those with other disabilities, such as astigmatism. While designing the dark mode with accessibility in mind can help to mitigate some issues, such as ensuring that all elements still have sufficiently high contrast, it is also a best practice to offer the option for users to easily select which mode they prefer. This is certainly true for dark mode, but it is also a best practice for many design choices. If it is possible to make it easier for users to opt to use web content in a customized manner, that content will be more accessible, inclusive, and usable for users with disabilities and all users. Flexibility is key.

❯ What About Accessibility Overlays?

Given that effectively designing accessible online content is an involved process, it is clear why there is an interest in tools to automate web accessibility. With the release of recent regulations with regard to ADA compliance in the United States,[15] this interest in automated solutions is almost certain to continue to grow rapidly. Some of this desire can be observed in the continued reliance on automated accessibility testing. As stated earlier, it is important to note that this can create significant blind spots and other deficiencies when institutions overly rely on these tools as the only approach to accessibility testing. Over the last several years, a new automated tool, commonly referred to as an *overlay* or a *widget,* has emerged, claiming to solve accessibility issues without the need to edit the underlying code for accessibility. For the purposes of this discussion, the term *overlay* will be used for clarity, but both of the terms are used by companies offering such tools. In deciding whether to use these tools, it is important to understand how they work and how they can be used to support inclusive access.

When considering accessibility overlays, it is important to understand how they are defined. While the exact structure of these tools can vary, generally accessibility overlays are "a tool, typically written in JavaScript, whose aim is to help users overcome accessibility issues they find on the website or app they're using. This code is added by a company, and changes are applied after the website or web app is rendered by the browser, thereby allowing it to transform its appearance, content, and behavior."[16] The exact mechanism used for this can differ, but for many of these tools, the accessibility options are a pop-up on the screen, showing the options users can select from, such as built-in screen reading functionality, the option to adjust contrast, and the ability to add features to draw focus to specific sections of the page. As these tools emerged, they were frequently used by companies that had identified a significant accessibility issue as a "stopgap" solution while their website underwent remediation.[17] In this capacity, they could offer an alternative for at least some users who would otherwise be unable to access the site's content and would therefore improve accessibility, even if only incrementally. Even to this day, many of the companies that offer accessibility overlays also offer code remediation services to their clients. This makes accessibility overlays a potentially useful element as part of a larger plan to improve web accessibility and meet legal requirements.

Though in the past accessibility overlays have been used as a short-term solution, experts argue that increasingly they are being marketed as a permanent solution to both legal compliance and actual accessibility.[18] This wouldn't be an issue if they did solve all accessibility issues and insulated libraries from lawsuits, but there is some evidence that this may not be the case. While these tools may make a site more accessible for some users, many disabled users and accessibility experts argue that, overall, some may interfere with the functioning of users' assistive technologies. When WebAIM, a web accessibility-focused nonprofit affiliated with the University of Utah, surveyed web accessibility practitioners about the effectiveness of overlays, they found that "a strong majority (67%) of respondents rate these tools as not at all or not very effective. Respondents with disabilities were even less favorable, with 72% rating them not at all or not very effective, and only 2.4% rating them as very effective."[19] Moreover, an open letter against overlays entitled the "Overlay Fact Sheet" has attracted over 800 signatories, including a wide range of accessibility practitioners, disability rights lawyers, and individuals with disabilities.[20] These concerns, especially from individuals who are disabled, suggest that overlays alone are not effectively eliminating all barriers and making websites inclusive. Moreover, these overlays may not offer the legal protection that many assume they will. In the United States, lawsuits have been filed against companies with accessibility overlays on their sites.[21] UsableNet's 2023 report on digital accessibility lawsuits found that in 2023 over 900 lawsuits were filed against companies that had already added overlays to their websites.[22] With respect to European law, in 2023 the International Association of Accessibility Professionals and the European Disability Forum issued a joint statement stating that "overlays do not make the website accessible or compliant with European accessibility legislation. They do not constitute an acceptable alternative or a substitute for fixing the website itself."[23] While none of this information can definitively answer whether or not courts in any particular country will find that an accessibility overlay is sufficient to ensure accessibility in specific situations, it does suggest that institutions should not rely on these overlays without carefully weighing their specific situation. Ultimately, it is not surprising that technology may not yet be at the point of being able to offer completely automated solutions to web accessibility.

It is possible that a day will come when this technology has advanced to the point that it can solve accessibility concerns without human intervention. But for now, as of the writing of this book, accessibility overlays are best used as a temporary piece of a larger web accessibility strategy. This strategy should also involve remediation of the site and user testing with disabled users to ensure that accessibility is optimized to meet the needs of all members of the community. While this can seem overwhelming for those who are new to designing for optimal accessibility, learning from expert assistive technology users in your community through user testing and focusing on high-impact changes at the start of your work can ensure that the accessibility of your library's digital content improves quickly and that you are serving all members of your community well.

Top 10 Legal Tips*

Eve Hill *and* **Jessica P. Weber**, *Disability Rights Lawyers at Brown, Goldstein & Levy, LLP*

1. *Start now and be proactive:* It's critical to be proactive, not reactive, in making digital content accessible from the beginning.
2. *Plan and audit for accessibility:* Have a clear plan to address gaps by testing databases and services to ensure full inclusivity.
3. *Create accessibility plans:* Have two plans: one for immediate accessibility needs and another for ongoing improvements, with the understanding that legal defenses are limited to claims of undue burden.
4. *Screen all services for accessibility:* Ensure that all services and technology are accessible to students with disabilities. In the interview, Weber noted a case in which loaner laptops lacked screen reading technology, demonstrating that the needs of disabled end users had been overlooked.
5. *They will use what you offer:* Change the mindset of assuming that people with disabilities won't use library services and instead plan as though they already are active users.
6. *Bake accessibility into procurement:* Accessibility should be integrated into procurement processes, baking it into the decision-making process, just as security is.
7. *Transparency is key:* If something can't be made accessible immediately, such as databases, institutions should be clear about the issue, provide a timeline for resolution, and offer clear contact points for support.

8. *Use AI carefully:* The growing use of AI for accessibility tasks (e.g., document remediation, captioning) can assist us, but human checks are still necessary to ensure accuracy.

9. *Train faculty and plan for course materials:* Faculty members must create accessible materials or submit them for remediation well in advance. Relying on last-minute fixes when a student with disabilities enrolls is not sustainable. The same could be applied to participants in a public library workshop.

10. *Litigation is a last resort:* When institutions have a clear plan for improving accessibility and are making progress, plaintiffs and courts are less likely to pursue lawsuits. Having a plan and acting on it is a strong defense against legal action.

* The editors acknowledge using ChatGPT to organize this list by pulling their transcript interview with Eve Hill and Jessica P. Weber, stripping the text of any identifying information, and using the prompt, "Please summarize the main points the speakers made (as close to their own words as you can). Arrange their main points in a top ten list where 1 is the most common point." The editors then edited the text for content and clarity.

Notes

1. K. Larose and S. Barron, "How White Is Your UX Practice? Inclusion and Diversity in Critical UX Research," in *User Experience in Libraries: Yearbook 2017* (CreateSpace Independent Publishing Platform, 2017), 27–28.

2. C. Pontoriero and G. Zippo-Mazur, "Evaluating the User Experience of Patrons with Disabilities at a Community College Library," *Library Trends* 67, no. 3 (2019): 497–515; A. Marcaccio, S. Clarke, and A. Wetheral, "Learning about Real Experiences from Real Users: A Blueprint for Participatory Accessibility Testing," *Partnership* 17, no. 1 (2022): 1–21; L. B. Campbell and B. Kester, "Centering Students with Disabilities: An Accessible User Experience Study of a Library Research Guide," *Weave: Journal of Library User Experience* 6, no. 1 (2023), doi: https://doi.org/10.3998/weaveux.1067.

3. K. Brown, A. de Bie, A. Aggarwal, R. Joslin, S. Williams-Habibi, and V. Sivanesanathan, "Students with Disabilities as Partners: A Case Study on User Testing an Accessibility Website," *International Journal for Students as Partners* 4, no. 2 (2020), https://doi.org/10.15173/ijsap.v4i2.4051.

4. Larose and Barron, "How White Is Your UX Practice?"

5. See, for example, Brown et al., "Students with Disabilities as Partners," https://doi.org/10.15173/ijsap.v4i2.4051; and Campbell and Kester, "Centering Students with Disabilities," doi: https://doi.org/10.3998/weaveux.1067.

6. These guidelines are adapted from the more extensive guidelines and materials provided on PlainLanguage.gov, at www.plainlanguage.gov/.
7. Accessibility Guidelines Working Group, "Understanding SC 1.4.3: Contrast (Minimum) (Level AA)," WCAG 2.2: Understanding Docs, May 2, 2024, www.w3.org/WAI/WCAG22/Understanding/contrast-minimum.html.
8. Accessibility Guidelines Working Group. "Understanding SC 1.4.6: Contrast (Enhanced) (Level AAA)," WCAG 2.2: Understanding Docs, May 2, 2024, www.w3.org/WAI/WCAG22/Understanding/contrast-enhanced.html.
9. Accessibility Guidelines Working Group, "Understanding SC 1.4.11: Non-text Contrast (Level AA)," WCAG 2.2: Understanding Docs, May 2, 2024, www.w3.org/WAI/WCAG22/Understanding/non-text-contrast.html.
10. Alastair Campbell, Chuck Adams, Rachael Bradley Montgomery, Michael Cooper, and Andrew Kirkpatrick, "Web Content Accessibility Guidelines (WCAG) 2.2," October 5, 2023, W3C, www.w3.org/TR/WCAG22/.
11. Jakob Nielsen and Anna Kaley, "Opening Links in New Browser Windows and Tabs," September 27, 2020, Nielsen Norman Group, www.nngroup.com/articles/new-browser-windows-and-tabs/.
12. Nielsen and Kaley, "Opening Links in New Browser Windows and Tabs," www.nngroup.com/articles/new-browser-windows-and-tabs/.
13. Accessibility Guidelines Working Group, "Technique G200: Opening New Windows and Tabs from a Link Only When Necessary," WCAG 2.1 Techniques, June 20, 2023, www.w3.org/WAI/WCAG21/Techniques/general/G200.
14. Eric Eggert, Shadi Abou-Zahra, and Brian Elton, "Tables Tutorial," February 16, 2023, W3C-WAI, www.w3.org/WAI/tutorials/tables/.
15. U.S. Department of Justice, Civil Rights Division, "Fact Sheet: New Rule on the Accessibility of Web Content and Mobile Apps Provided by State and Local Governments," March 8, 2024, ADA.gov, www.ada.gov/resources/2024-03-08-web-rule/.
16. Ashley Firth, "Outsourcing Accessibility," in *Practical Web Accessibility: A Comprehensive Guide to Digital Inclusion* (Berkeley, CA: Apress, 2024), 354.
17. A11Y Project Team, "Should I Use an Accessibility Overlay?" March 8, 2021, The A11Y Project, www.a11yproject.com/posts/should-i-use-an-accessibility-overlay/.
18. A11Y Project Team, "Should I Use an Accessibility Overlay?" www.a11yproject.com/posts/should-i-use-an-accessibility-overlay/.
19. WebAIM, "Survey of Web Accessibility Practitioners #3 Results," January 26, 2021, https://webaim.org/projects/practitionersurvey3/.
20. Overlay Fact Sheet, https://overlayfactsheet.com/en/.
21. See, for example, Murphy v. EyeBobs, LLC. 638 F. Supp. 3d 463 (W.D. Pa. 2021). Lawyer Lainey Feingold tracks additional cases on her website: see Lainey Feingold, "Legal Update: Accessibility Overlay Edition," December 7, 2023, Law Office of Lainey Feingold, www.lflegal.com/2021/11/overlay-legal-update/.
22. Jason Taylor, "Decoding Digital Accessibility Lawsuits 2023: Key Trends & Insights," December 27, 2023, *UsableNet* (blog), https://blog.usablenet.com/decoding-digital-accessibility-lawsuits-in-2023-key-trends-strategic-insights.
23. Andre Felix, "European Disability Forum and International Association of Accessibility Professionals, Joint Statement on Accessibility Overlays," May 17, 2023, European Disability Forum, www.edf-feph.org/publications/joint-statement-on-accessibility-overlays/.

• • •

CHAPTER 5

Digital Media and File Accessibility

A blind library employee navigating between
shared files wants to collaborate with colleagues
on revised cataloging documentation.

A school librarian who supports the needs of
deaf students in grades 6–12 wants to mount
online tutorials for all the students but is
frustrated with poor automated captioning.

A student with dyslexia needs an accessible
chapter of a book assigned for their sociology
course so they can read it using Kurzweil 3000.

While thoughts of digital accessibility often focus on websites and databases, media files are also an important part of libraries' digital footprint. As such, files must be designed to optimize accessibility for all. Any time this content is included on a website, shared on social media, distributed via e-mail, or otherwise distributed online, it should be designed and reviewed to confirm that it will be accessible to those with a variety of disabilities and for users of a range of assistive technologies. This is a frequently overlooked piece of digital accessibility but, fortunately, accessibility for these types of files has been an increasing area of focus, and more file creation software has integrated accessibility features now than ever before. While many of the techniques around accessibility vary between the type of media and the authoring software used, the general principles of accessibility continue through to this content. One

96 ••• CHAPTER 5

universally applicable accessibility best practice for digital files is to name the file with each word in the file name capitalized, so as to ease the process of finding and opening the appropriate file for all users. Beyond that, the focus is on offering different ways of accessing the information shared so that it is available to all users equitably and inclusively.

▶ Audio Files

Proper captioning is important for all audio content. However, there are special considerations for audio files created by the library, such as introductions to resources, podcasts on upcoming events, or interviews with authors. For these "born library" resources, careful planning is key. For many born-library resources, librarians have clear plans and often begin with a script. That script is a crucial asset in your accessibility planning. It can be used to form the basis of your transcript and as a touchstone in checking any automated products you receive so that you can edit them accordingly. Even if you don't follow the script to the letter, so long as the sense of what you are saying matches the words in your transcript, it captures the message and meaning. For example, if you intended to say "employees" and instead say "staff," it is sufficient.

When we speak of captioning and transcripts, we must distinguish between what is doable and what is ideal at different stages of your accessibility journey. Practical considerations may include the time, expertise, training, speaker, and potential learning curve you might have. Consider, however, that a transcript is not equivalent to captions. The drawback of transcripts is that they are not time-coded, so those who are d/Deaf or hard-of-hearing don't get real-time information that is available to the rest of the audience. We should note that transcripts are useful as a supplement to your media. A major benefit for libraries to ensure that transcripts are posted along with audio files is that this allows them to be searchable on the Web, which may increase your reach.

An example might be the audio component of a library tour. Much like the kind of audio tours you might find in a museum, library tours are likely intentional and deliberate. Your storyboard, script, environment, and equipment are key to ensuring that the audio itself is of high quality,

DIGITAL MEDIA AND FILE ACCESSIBILITY ● ● ● **97**

with low background noise, a high-quality microphone, and a speaker who can enunciate, speaking slowly and clearly and pausing between lines and sections. Clear enunciation is not always a given. Speakers may have a disability that impedes clear speech, or they might be non-native speakers who use English as a second language, or they could just have braces or new dentures. In all of these cases, automated captioning (and even live captioners) might struggle to capture their words and thereby their meaning. In this situation, it might be important to rely on the written script created at the start of the project as a basis for the captions, with edits manually added as necessary.

❱ Video Files

For video content, we know that our born-library videos need proper captioning. If we know that is our end point, how many of these videos should begin with a script or very detailed outline as discussed in the audio files section? For longer or more complex videos, captioning the file manually may be too labor-intensive or time-consuming. In a case like that, you could try to auto-caption using YouTube, for example. However, the results might not meet the accuracy level needed for accessibility and won't include any nonverbal sounds. In addition, the visual information in the video will remain inaccessible, even with captions.

Captions alone don't suffice if we want to include everyone. Those who have low or no vision will depend on the description of visual information to be included. For example, if a security training video shows people in ski masks carrying guns, this would be important information to explain for those who cannot see the video. For films and documentaries, this is extremely costly and labor-intensive, but for the kinds of videos we create in libraries to help our users, it may be less so

Often library tutorials lend themselves well to pairing with a step-by-step document based on clear directions. We have control over how we approach these and what information we include. For database navigation, for example, we might say, "Look carefully at how your results list changes," as it is paired with visual information we rely on the user to see. However, we might change this to "Notice that, before applying limiters of date and subject, we had 2,152 results and after applying criteria we narrowed that to 31." With proper description in all we do, we can take our visually impaired users with us on that journey more seamlessly. Depending on the database, it is also important to consider whether users of specific types of assistive technologies will encounter different navigation options and then include that information when relevant.

While this strategy is doable in most contexts, there may be situations in which the description of visual information takes enough time to be disruptive to the sighted user. In these cases, providing an alternative asset with audio descriptions may suffice. Though the best practice is to have a toggle switch that allows users to choose the version they prefer, most libraries and library systems don't have ready access to a platform that supports this, or the expertise to create a file with embedded audio descriptions. More often than not, libraries will need to engage a vendor for such work. (See chapter 11 on "Best Practices for Working with Vendors" for an in-depth discussion of managing those relationships.)

Sign Language

Many would not think of sign language as part of digital accessibility because it doesn't feel digital to see signing with hands. Today, we see sign language used by churches to reach congregants, by government agencies to convey emergency information to everyone in their community, and at large-scale political events to engage voters. Even the 2024 Super Bowl pregame and halftime shows included American Sign Language (ASL) to reach a wider audience. Large library systems like the New York Public Library include ASL and captioning services in their budgets. ASL is very much a viable and important option and is included in the WCAG AAA standards as 1.2.6: Sign Language. While it is not required in most web accessibility policies, video and live stream events can be enhanced with the use of sign language. For many hearing-impaired people, sign language is their first language, while English is secondary and not as comprehensible to them. If your library system offers large-scale events, training, and meetings, consider sign language as an option for patrons to request, whether they attend in person or remotely. In these cases, it is important to provide clear instructions on how patrons can request this service and also give a timeline for the amount of advanced notice the library needs to provide it.

In the future, look for enhancements to sign language integration that include a video overlay of AI-generated signing avatars, translation tools, and gesture-recognition technology. All of these emerging technologies can be harnessed by libraries to increase communication and create alternative content at lower costs when needed. But we should also keep in mind that the risks of depending on these technologies include incorrect translations and AI systems' hallucinations.

For those for whom sign language is their primary language, captioning might be a complementary tool to increase comprehension, but it won't take center stage unless they have no other choice. Libraries are always finding a balance between budgets and services, but for those whose first language is ASL, for instance, nothing compares or is truly equal to offering live sign language interpretation. Libraries should aspire to provide it as an option when possible. At the same time, it is important to remember that this is not an alternative to captions, as those are a necessity for many who do not communicate with sign language.

❱ Text Files

Libraries share text files in countless different ways and for many different purposes. Promotional fliers, class handouts, internal policies, forms, reading lists, and more are shared as text files. Whether sent in an e-mail or linked on the website, these files must be designed with accessibility in mind, so that they're accessible to assistive technology users and are easy for all users to read. Fortunately, many of the best practices that will make a document accessible are the same regardless of the software used to create the document. Better yet, many of these practices are similar to those applied to other web design projects. An understanding of these practices will be applicable to virtually all document-creation tools.

Clear Structure
Just as with websites, documents need to have a clear structure. Given the length of many documents, it is even more important that structural elements are included to allow those using assistive technologies to navigate through the document efficiently. When a document has a clear

outline structure that is properly tagged, a screen reader will be able to read that outline to the user, allowing them to understand the overall structure and contents of the document and facilitating their jumping to specific sections. Effectively, this structure is very similar to the structural tags in HTML. While the style formatting tools vary slightly across authoring tools, the underlying principle is to use these built-in style formatting tools to create an outline for the document. This means indicating the title, sections, and subsections at a minimum, as well as tagging images with clear alt-text. All page structure should be indicated with these tags and not with styles, such as bold text, italics, or other stylistic elements that are not indicated by screen readers. If the document includes footnotes or endnotes, it is also important to use the built-in tools to create these so that users can access them seamlessly with assistive technologies. For document creation tools that have an automatically generated table of contents or outline feature, it can be useful to see if these match the document's intended structure, since these tools generally rely on the same style of formatting. If a section is left out of the table of contents or outline, it is probably not properly tagged.

For documents that will be converted to PDF, document structure can be carried over into the PDF, but only if the document is converted in the proper way. Any conversion process that strips out the formatting will generate a PDF without tags. An example of an inappropriate conversion process is using the print to PDF option for a Microsoft Word document, which results in an untagged PDF. Instead, in this case, it would be a better practice to save the document as a PDF from the Microsoft Word document. Because of the risk that conversion will lead to an improperly tagged document, any document created in one authoring software and converted to another file type should be tested for proper tagging before distribution.

Reading Order

When designing a document for accessibility, it is important to make sure that the content will be read by screen readers in the appropriate order. For documents that only contain text in a single column, this is not generally going to be a problem. However, if the text includes images, callout boxes, or multiple columns, it is important to ensure that the content will be read by a screen reader in the intended order. This becomes even more of a consideration for file types that involve more complicated layouts, such as slide decks, flyers, and newsletters. One way to test this is by using a screen reader to confirm the reading order. Also, in many document-authoring tools, the tab key can be used to move the focus from element to element in the order a screen reader would read the content. Finally, as discussed further in a later section, this is one element of accessibility that is included in many built-in accessibility testing tools within individual document-authoring tools.

Design Documents for Readability

Just as when writing content for websites, it is important to consider readability when creating documents. This will improve the accessibility of the document and also make it more user-friendly for all readers. Some approaches to consider are simple font, color contrast, and reading level.

Simple Font

All text fonts used in the document should maximize readability. This means selecting a standard font that is not overly stylized. In particular, any fonts that mimic script will be more difficult to read. While stylized fonts can be tempting, particularly for documents with graphic design elements, such as flyers or newsletters, they will make the document more difficult to read for those with low vision or some types of learning disabilities. Particularly for blocks of text, it is generally preferable to use a sans serif font to promote readability for all. As mentioned in chapter 3, "Principles of Web Accessibility," there is currently little evidence that the fonts designed to improve reading for dyslexic readers have much impact. This is an ongoing area of research, so it is a topic to watch. Font size should also be considered as part of the accessibility determination, particularly for documents in which readers will not be able to adjust the font size for themselves.

Color Contrast

As with other digital content, color contrast is imperative for accessible document design. This applies to all files, but it is particularly important for those with more visual elements. WCAG standards around color contrast can also be used when selecting colors for documents. While text color is, of course, a priority, all the elements of the design should also meet color contrast standards. When choosing document themes or designing the graphic elements for a file, color contrast should not be assumed. Checking all of the colors and erring on the side of high-contrast color choices will maximize accessibility and ensure that readability is optimized for all users. (For more on color contrast, see chapter 3, "Principles of Web Accessibility.")

Reading Level
No matter the type of document, it is important to write with the audience in mind. This means writing at the reading level of the audience and avoiding unnecessary jargon or complicated syntax. The same basic principles used for writing successful web content apply here. However, with documents there is more opportunity to write for a specialized audience, meaning that it is possible to target writing specifically to the recipients of the document in some cases. When a document is designed to be read quickly, such as the text of an outreach e-mail or on a slide that will only be displayed for a limited time, the text should be simplified and written at the lowest reading level possible to make it easier to scan the document and retain the necessary information. At the other extreme, when documents are lengthy or complicated, it is useful to offer a brief summary written for a more general audience.

Specific File Types

It is beyond the scope of this book to detail the accessibility features and issues of every single file type and application. However, it is worth noting that there are specialty applications to assist those with disabilities, as well as content creators. These applications ensure that the content and creation of materials for use in discrete intellectual disciplines are fully accessible. Each of these disciplines might have associated file type outputs. For example, MathType and EquatIO enable users to make math and chemistry equations accessible, ensuring that formulas are displayed correctly and read appropriately by screen readers. EquatIO even allows a user to take a photo of an equation written on a whiteboard, turning it into usable characters for an accessible equation. Integrations of MathType are available for HTML editors, XML editors, content management systems, Windows and Mac, and so on. MathType can ingest files in LaTeX or SVG format. SVGs (Scalable Vector Graphics) can be used to display two-dimensional charts, illustrations, and graphics. While this file type is text-based, making it readable by screen readers, it can also be responsive, and SVGs can be customized so that they don't get distorted when resized and will maintain proper ratio when scaled to any size.[1]

Other programs like Noteflight, an online music notation program accessible for screen readers, and Soundbeam, which uses ultrasonic sensors to detect movements, allow users to compose, perform, and express themselves. This type of technology is on the rise in use with the elderly and those with dementia, in addition to those with fine motor impairments. MusicSharpeye is a specialty program for scanning sheet music into music notion files, MusicXML, or MIDI (Musical Instrument Digital Interface) files. These programs can allow for the same kind of processing that OCR technology allows, making the files usable in musical notation or sequencing software like Sibelius. Alternatively, users might use magnification programs like Lime Lighter or software like Lime Aloud, Lime, or Goodfeel to allow for braille notation of music.

Programs like ArcGIS will integrate with screen-reading software like JAWS to allow users with visual impairments to access and analyze spatial data, while other programs like the SAS Graphics Accelerator are designed to help visually disabled users create and connect with data visualizations by using sonification and tactile feedback. Whether it is architecture, engineering, coding, or art history, librarians need to keep in mind that specific specialty programs and file types exist and are in the pipeline to allow every discipline to be fully inclusive. While we may not be familiar with all the various file types in existence, the information we need is often only a simple search away. Our responsibility is to determine the needs of our patrons and determine which programs users most need access to.

ePub

An ePub, or "electronic publication," is a file type that is used for storing books and other written content. Because it is compatible with many different e-readers, ePub is the most widely used file format for storing e-books and related materials. This is a file type that can be accessible for many users with visual impairments if it is created correctly. The W3C is currently responsible for accessibility standards pertaining to ePub, and these standards pertain both to the document content and to the metadata offered to make the documents discoverable.[2] Because ePub authoring uses many of the same technologies as web design, such as XHTML and CSS, many WCAG success criteria are relevant to the design of accessible ePub files, and the standard directly refers to WCAG for this reason. However, the standard includes other requirements around page navigation and media overlays that are more specific to ePubs. The standard's metadata requirements ensure that users know what senses are required to use the file (i.e., is the content visual or tactile), the accessibility features included in the file, and any known barriers to use, among other information pertaining to accessibility. Whether creating or evaluating ePub documents, it is important to factor in these requirements to ensure that the resulting file will be accessible to the widest possible group of users.

DAISY

Another important technical standard to know about when designing for accessibility is the "digital accessible information system," or DAISY. This is not technically a file type but, instead, a collection of files that, taken together, provide access to the content of a book both as text and as audio. Unlike other types of audiobooks, DAISY provides synchronized access to both an audio version of the content and the text. When relevant, images can also be included. DAISY relies on MP3 and XML as the basis of these related files. The user experience with a DAISY version of a book or periodical is meant to align more closely with that of a print book, including offering the ability to search through the content, to bookmark specific sections, navigate through sections, and control the speed at which the audio is played. One of the advantages of DAISY is that it offers a lot of flexibility in how users access the materials, as they can select the method that works best for them. For example, different users of the same DAISY book could opt to listen to the book as audio, read it using a refreshable braille display, or view an enlarged version using a screen magnification tool. DAISY format books are available through several sources, including the National Library Service for the Blind and Print Disabled and its affiliate libraries in the United States.

Data Files

Many of the accessibility principles that apply to text files also apply to data files. However, there are some unique considerations that come up when working with data. Most assistive technologies can navigate comma-separated values (CSV) files when they are formatted clearly, so the first step in the process is to select a data file software that will result in this type of document. From there, formatting is particularly important. The following best practices will help to optimize the accessibility of CSV files:

- Give the file and all sheets and tables within the file a specific title that will give the user a clear sense of what is included in the file, sheet, or table. This will facilitate use by everyone, but it is particularly useful for those who are not able to visually skim the content to determine what is in the file or sheet.
- Since screen readers will start reading in the first cell of the document, be sure to include some content in that location, such as the title of the sheet or special instructions for navigating the data.
- Do not use color as the sole means of conveying information, and select colors that are sufficiently high in contrast for all users.
- Avoid features that are primarily visual in nature, such as splitting, freezing, or hiding rows, columns, or sections, because this may not be indicated by assistive devices and could create unnecessary confusion.
- If filters must be used, they should be accompanied by adjacent explanatory text.
- Though features that track changes may be useful for modification and collaboration, they may not be accessible, so it is important to consider the impact they will have when deciding whether to use them for a specific project.
- When using formulas or any other features that may not be immediately clear, it is helpful to add explanatory text in adjacent cells.

106 ••• CHAPTER 5

As with other file types, the last step should always be to use the built-in accessibility checker to identify and fix any problems. Though not all tools will have a built-in accessibility checker, the number that do is increasing all the time, so it is always worth checking to see if one is available, and if you are selecting which program to use for spreadsheet creation, it is worth using a tool that offers this feature.

▶ Images

Libraries share digital images in many different places, from digital photo archives to book covers in the library catalog, to social media posts and beyond. As a purely visual medium, these files are only accessible to all if they are accompanied by alternative text that accurately and completely conveys the information in the image. As mentioned previously, alternative text, or alt-text, is a brief, concise text description of an image that is available to assistive technologies such as screen readers. The name comes from the fact that this text description should provide a thorough alternative to the image itself. This text appears in the "alt" HTML attribute, which fits within the "img" image tag. As an example of this, an image of a refreshable braille display could be represented in HTML with this code:

```
<img src="img/braille.jpg" alt="refreshable braille display">
```

For those using screen readers, everything appearing between the quotation marks in the alt-text tag will be read aloud. If no alt-tag is present, the screen reader will instead read out the file name of the image. Since file names often do not offer a complete picture of the content of the image, this is not sufficient to make the image accessible. Moreover, many image file names don't convey any information about the image itself, with some being an automatically generated lengthy series of characters. These file names can be particularly problematic for screen readers because they don't explain the content of the image but do take a relatively long time to be read aloud.

To avoid these issues, it is important to be intentional with alt-text for all images. However, this can be more complicated than it first appears because there is an art to writing alt-text that is clear, concise, and serves as a thorough alternative for the image itself. The key qualities of effective alt-text are:

- **Keep it brief.** Short alt-text is preferable, and some platforms may place a fairly stringent character limit on alt-text. Try to distill the important information about the image down to the shortest length of text possible.
- **Use simple language.** Just as with other web content, alt-text should be written in plain language that is at a reading level that will be clear to all members of the site's audience.
- **Create unique descriptions.** Each image should have a unique text description to allow users to differentiate among the images. If there are many similar images, it is important to focus on their differences in the alt-text.
- **Consider why the image is being included.** The best alt-text for a specific image may vary considerably, depending on the context in which the image is shared. For example, an image of a painted portrait of Abraham Lincoln could be shared to show Lincoln's appearance or to illustrate the technique used by the artist, among other possible uses. Understanding what the image is meant to convey is vital to writing effective and relevant alt-text for the image.
- **Avoid repetition.** Any information that is conveyed in the surrounding text around the image can be omitted from the alt-text to help keep it brief.
- **Remember that alt-text is read aloud.** It is often mentioned that an added benefit of alt-text is that it can help with search engine optimization (SEO). While this can be true in some cases, this does not mean that the alt-text tag is the place to list a variety of synonyms for SEO that are not visible on the page. The primary purpose of alt-text should always be accessibility for those who will have the alt-text read to them by a screen reader or other assistive technology.

Fundamentally, it is important to remember that the alt-text should replace the image as a complete alternative. This means that a person accessing the alt-text without access to the image would have the same experience as a person seeing the image. Alt-text that does not achieve this level of description will not offer an equitable experience for those using assistive technologies and may actually create barriers to using the site.

Decorative Images

Images that do not convey any additional information related to the content of the page are a separate case when it comes to alt-text. Decorative images fall into two main categories. First, there are images that are visually decorative and are present purely for visual interest rather than to share information. Examples of this include background images that are not tied to the topic of the page and are just meant to offer visual interest, or company or organization logos. Second, there are images where a text alternative is already present. Some images may already have nearby text that serves as an alternative, such as a caption or a passage of text in the surrounding paragraphs that fully describes the image. Alt-text for these images would be repetitive, which is why they are considered decorative, though this is only the case when the caption or other text fully describes the content of the image. These images should have an empty alt-text tag, which is sometimes referred to as null alt-text. This is achieved by putting two quotation marks without a space between them in the alt-tag:

alt=""

An empty alt-text tag will be skipped by screen readers. It is particularly important to make sure that the quotation marks are adjacent without a space between them. If there is a space, it is possible that the image will not be skipped by screen readers. Even if an image is decorative, it is very important to include the alt-tag to prevent the screen reader from reading the file name in its place. Correctly using empty or null alt-tags will allow those using assistive technologies to more seamlessly and efficiently navigate through the content, making this an important part of creating appropriate alt-text.

Detailed or Complicated Images

Alt-text is particularly difficult for images that are detailed, convey complex information, or include a large amount of text. These images cannot be fully described in the short amount of text that should be used in an alt-text tag, and this is particularly problematic when the platform imposes a character limit for alt-text. Examples of such images are data visualizations, flow charts, and diagrams, though this same approach applies to any complicated images that cannot be described in a typical alt-text tag. In this case, including a longer description of the image in the surrounding text is generally the best approach. This has the dual advantages of making the image accessible to those using assistive technologies and also offering a different point of access for the information for those with cognitive disabilities and even for those who simply prefer to read information rather than interpret an image. If the longer description is not able to be immediately adjacent to the image, the alt-text tag can include an indication of where the longer description appears. This allows screen-reader users to understand the connection between the image and the longer description and facilitates efficient navigation to this additional information.

In cases where this is not a possibility, one alternative is to link to another page with a longer description of the image. This link should be immediately after the image, if possible, and the text of the link should clearly indicate that it will take users to the longer description of the image. In this case, the image should almost always still have brief alt-text, though there may be some cases where it is more effective to mark the image as decorative instead. This option allows all users to access the extended description without taking space on the same page as the image. For data-intensive images, it can also be useful to link out to the data in an accessible format, but it is important that this is in addition to the description of the visualization and not instead of that description.

As an alternative to having a visible link adjacent to the image, there is also the "longdesc" attribute, which appears within the image tag and contains a link to the location of the long description. An example of this would be:

```
<img src="orgchart.png" alt="library's org chart"
    longdesc="abc.edu/orgchartdesc">
```

However, it is important to know that the longdesc attribute is not supported by all browsers or by mobile platforms, and it is generally only accessible to screen readers rather than all assistive technologies. For this reason, this is not necessarily the most inclusive approach to providing a text alternative for an image.

▶ Using Built-in Accessibility Features and Checkers

Many authoring tools offer built-in accessibility features and, in particular, automated accessibility checkers. One of the most common features across different platforms is the ability to add alternative text to images that are integrated into text files, but there is an array of other features, depending on the type of file being created. Microsoft PowerPoint, for one, includes a feature that can add automatic captions to the screen as a presentation is being delivered. When adopting an authoring tool, a review of the accessibility features and the related documentation should be made a standard practice to ensure that creators are taking advantage of all available features.

Even when using all of the built-in accessibility features and following best practices for accessible design, automated accessibility checkers help verify that a document will be usable for everyone. Not all authoring tools include these checkers, but many Microsoft Office and Adobe Acrobat tools feature robust accessibility checkers that can identify and, in some cases, even propose fixes for accessibility issues. Using these tools should be a standard step in the document creation workflow whenever they are available.

▶ When in Doubt, Offer Alternatives

While it is essential to design files for accessibility, it is also true that the precise user experience of each individual will vary significantly based on the assistive technology they use. For this reason, it is often desirable to offer multiple file types where possible. If a document is designed in Microsoft Word and then converted into a PDF, for example, it is worth considering whether it is possible to share both options side-by-side. In cases where this is not possible, it is helpful to offer a way for those with specific accessibility needs to contact the library to request alternative file types. As is always the case with accessibility, it is essential to remember that everyone's needs are unique, so supporting a process for these requests is important for full accessibility. This is particularly true when the library is sharing long or complicated documents, such as in the case of institutional repositories or sharing documents in non-standard file types.

With libraries creating and providing access to a wide range of digital file types, it is critical to ensure that accessibility is at the forefront of all file creation. By developing workflows that prioritize designing for accessibility and by offering training for those who create documents, it is possible to ensure that all patrons and employees will have equitable access to these materials. As is often the case in accessibility work, creating documents with accessibility in mind from the start is much more efficient and effective than remediating them at a later date. Still, for libraries that already have a large number of inaccessible materials, materials can be remediated on request to help with prioritization. Because many of the principles of file accessibility align with the principles of web accessibility, this work can also be part of a larger move toward accessible design at the library.

A Digital Media Vendor's Perspective on Partnering

Interview with **Stacie Taylor,** *Operations Manager, Swank Motion Pictures, Inc.*

How long have you had a Swank Digital Campus Advisory Committee, and what were the visions or goals for that?

The Swank Digital Campus Advisory Committee was first established back in early 2021 with the intent of gathering feedback from schools that actively use our service. Since the Digital Campus was established sixteen years ago, we've gained valuable knowledge regarding how schools use streaming media and what they're looking for in a platform. Prior to the committee being formed, our feedback loop was rather informal within our partner schools, and to a certain extent, we became very reactive to feedback. Now, we're able to present our ideas for enhancements proactively before they hit production or release and use the suggestions and feedback from real-life users to help better prioritize our initiatives. This has helped drive our bigger, more long-term development projects for the portal and has led to a better product and user experience.

While the Digital Advisory Committee was not created for accessibility purposes alone, how has accessibility come into play and has that changed any of your plans?

Accessibility has always played an important role in developing enhancements within the Swank streaming platform. When we first started the Advisory Committee, captions were the main topic of conversation when it came to accessibility, which has obviously evolved significantly since then. Through our meetings and the feedback received, we have been able to validate the significance of accessibility within our partner schools and continue enhancing all our accessibility components. We've since implemented internal and external accessibility audits that have led to a more accessible website and portal for all, and we're currently developing the technology within our portal to make audio descriptions available for movies that offer this feature.

What do you see as the key accessibility changes or improvements on the horizon for e-resources?

We're hearing more and more about the importance of audio descriptions and believe this will become the next standard for videos, much like closed captioning has.

What would you like librarians to understand about a vendor's perspective on meeting accessibility standards? What challenges do you face?

For streaming video, specifically regarding accessibility, one of our challenges is the limitation of resources available for films. With a library as vast as ours, with films dating back to the early 1900s, accessibility features such as closed captioning and audio description files don't exist for all films. As a provider rather than a producer of film, we're dependent upon what resources have already been created for many of the films we offer. Additionally, balancing the need to maintain a digital platform that takes into account not only providing accessibility but also enhancing other feature sets used in the academic space, overall user experience, and equitable access—all while keeping it affordable for schools—can be challenging.

How does your team identify accessibility issues and collect feedback about these topics?

We've had several accessibility audits and reviews done on our streaming portal, and we review the feedback provided with our IT and Development teams to identify what we can do to improve upon the areas that need attention.

What are your top tips for communicating with vendors and ensuring that accessibility issues rise in priority?

Open communication between schools and vendors is key. We often find out about issues or areas where improvement is needed well after they've been raised by faculty and students.

Notes

1. Nils Binder, "Responsive SVGs," 12 Days of Web, https://12daysofweb.dev/2023/responsive-svgs/.
2. Matt Garrish, George Kerscher, Charles LaPierre, and Avneesh Singh, eds., "EPUB Accessibility 1.0," January 25, 2017, W3C, www.w3.org/submissions/epub-a11y/.

· · ·

CHAPTER 6

Accessible Communications and Events

A father using VoiceOver on his iPhone struggles to navigate through the online form required to register his child for the library's STEM program series.

A librarian who manages a digital archive at the state library must ensure that all communications with the public are accessible.

A Deaf patron with a mobility disability preventing them from leaving their home wants to keep up with library events via the library's YouTube channel.

C ommunications are of vital importance in libraries. Whether they involve outreach newsletters to patrons about library services, social media posts about upcoming events, or internal e-mails to ensure that the whole team is on the same page, a library's communications are at the center of virtually every aspect of its work, and digital communications make up an ever-increasing percentage of the messages involved. Almost all audiences your communications reach will include people with a disability. While accessibility is often perceived as a feature that is only needed in messages specifically aimed at patrons with disabilities, the reality is that disabled people are part of the library team, and they are recipients of all types of library services. For this reason, accessibility should be at the core of the library's communications efforts to reach all

116 ••• CHAPTER 6

members of both the internal and external community. While this may initially seem overwhelming, many of the same principles of other accessible digital design apply to digital communications across platforms, and those principles that are specialized are relatively easy to integrate into existing communications workflows. This chapter will offer tips related to all types of a library's digital communications.

▶ Social Media

Social media are a key part of many libraries' outreach strategies, with many libraries maintaining a presence on a variety of platforms. Notably, some libraries are eager to test out the potential of newly released platforms while they are still in their infancy, even though these often have underdeveloped and untested accessibility features and policies. Given that social media can encompass a wide range of different types of platforms and can support a variety of types of media, there are many different accessibility issues at play. Though the exact features vary significantly across platforms, there are a series of best practices that apply generally and can help to improve the accessibility of even those social media platforms that have not yet released a full range of accessibility features.

Capitalization Matters

While some memes and jokes on social media may rely on using non-standard capitalization, such as capitalizing every letter in a word, capitalizing every other letter, or capitalizing random letters within a word, these can present barriers for some users. For those with disabilities that impact reading, including some vision disabilities and dyslexia, this text may be significantly more difficult to read. In addition, screen readers may not be able to read this text clearly. Some screen readers may read everything that is capitalized letter by letter. Though many screen readers will be able to read the words, the pronunciation can still be impacted, depending on the settings the user has enabled. For these reasons, using capitalization for visual effect can make the content of the posts less accessible.

Appropriate capitalization is also the key to making hashtags accessible. This can be done by capitalizing the first letter of all words in the hashtag or all but the first word in the hashtag. Capitalizing all words is referred to as Pascal case (e.g., #PublicLibrary). Capitalizing each word other than the first is referred to as camel case (e.g., #publicLibrary). This process of capitalizing the first letter of each individual word in a hashtag can significantly improve accessibility for many users. It makes hashtags easier to read for those who may have low vision or a reading disability. But beyond that, it is even more important for screen reader users. Screen readers can't distinguish separate words when a hashtag has no capital letters. Instead, they will read the hashtag as a single word, which can be difficult or impossible to understand. Capitalizing each word in the hashtag differentiates them for screen readers so that each word will be pronounced correctly. Though a seemingly minor change to the hashtag, this makes for a very significant impact on the accessibility of social media posts.

Minimize the Use of Emojis

Emojis can be a lot of fun, so it's understandable that libraries want to use them to participate in popular trends. Unfortunately, most emojis are read in a very awkward manner, if at all, by screen readers and other assistive devices. Many emojis have descriptions or titles associated with them that will be read out when they are encountered by an assistive device, and the exact nature of that description or title can vary by platform. When used in moderation, emojis don't present a major problem for those using assistive technologies. For example, if you post "Happy 100th birthday to the public library! 🎂 ," the single instance of the cake emoji will be read by most devices as "Birthday Cake Emoji."

Problems and inconveniences can arise in a few situations. First, if emojis are used repetitively, this can make navigating the content much slower and more cumbersome. It is not uncommon to see users posting multiple identical emojis to convey emphasis, but when this happens, the same text will be read over and over as many times as there are emojis. This can be compounded when the repetitive string of emojis itself recurs, such as when it is part of a user's screen name on the social media platform. Another issue that can arise is that emojis are often used colloquially in a way that does not literally align with the official name for the emoji. An illustration of this type of emoji slang would be the symbol of a 100 with two lines under it (💯) being used to mean agreement. When hearing the title of this emoji, which is "Hundred Points," it might be difficult to understand this alternate meaning. Additionally, some people may have a hard time understanding the emoji they are looking at, either because they cannot see the details of the image or because they have a hard time interpreting the meaning of particular facial expressions or poses.

For these reasons, it is best to make limited use of emojis in social media posts. It is a best practice to not have any emoji in the screen name of the account. When using emojis in the posts themselves, avoid unnecessary repetition, make sure that the text can be understood even if the emojis are not fully understood, and consider the placement of the emojis so that they don't break up the flow of the text when read aloud. When using emojis, placing them at the end of the text will lead to the best results for most people using assistive technologies. These practices will help to make social media content more inclusive and accessible for all.

Use Shortened Links

For accessibility purposes, it is best to hyperlink text that describes the destination of the link rather than simply pasting the URL into the text. Regrettably, many social media platforms do not allow this. Instead, users can only paste URLs into their posts. Given that these URLs will be read letter by letter by screen readers, it is best to use shortened URLs. If it is possible to create a vanity link that indicates some information about the destination, this can also be a more usable experience. When including a URL in a post, it is also helpful to include it after the main text of the post so that users can opt to skip to the next post when the screen reader starts to read the URL if they are not interested in using it.

Don't Use Text Layout to Convey Meaning

While most social media posts follow standard formatting for the text, some memes and jokes rely on formatting to convey their meaning on social media. One very common example of this type of post involves two photos side by side. Above the first image is the text "If you don't love me at my," broken across three lines. Above the second image is the text "Then you don't deserve me at my," also broken across three lines. To create the appearance of the text being divided into two columns above each photo, each line has a tab to split the text up.[1] With a screen reader, this means that the post would be read as "If you don't Then you don't love me deserve me at my at my," followed by the alt-text for each image in turn. Needless to say, this would be fairly difficult to understand without the benefit of seeing the layout. Since screen readers do not generally indicate spaces or tabs, users have no way of knowing how the text was laid out. This is just one instance of the way layout has been used in memes on social media, but there have been others, including some that include emojis, leading to even more potential for inaccessibility. The key to avoiding this problem is to remember to read word by word from left to right on each line to determine how the content will be read by screen readers.

A related type of content that relies on layout and spacing is ASCII art, which refers to graphic designs that make patterns or pictures using ASCII characters. Simple examples are sometimes referred to as emoticons. A classic example is the emoticon of a figure shrugging made entirely out of ASCII characters: ¯_(ツ)_/¯. While this example is simple, ASCII art can also be large and involved, with scenes that take up one or more pages. These do not have alternative text or titles associated with them, so their meaning is not understood by assistive devices. In addition, depending on the size of the ASCII art, it might be difficult for users of screen magnification software to determine the overall pattern while viewing small magnified sections individually. While ASCII art is not as popular as it once was, it is still seen sometimes on social media, and it is generally a good idea to avoid these trends unless the same information is conveyed in another accessible manner at the same time.

Offer Alternate Methods of Perceiving Information

As in other settings, it is important to always offer multiple ways to understand any information being presented, particularly when it is in a format that cannot be converted easily by an assistive device such as a screen reader or refreshable braille display. This means that any audio or visual content should have alternatives, as in other settings. Ideally, this would mean alt-text for images and captions and audio descriptions for videos. However, some platforms debut without support for these accessibility features. In those cases, it is crucial to be thoughtful about how the platform is used to promote accessibility. So, if the text description of an image cannot be added to an alt-text field, it can be included in the text of the post with the image. This is often done at the end of the post and starts with an indication that it is the description of the image. For image-focused platforms, such as Instagram, if the image in the post contains text, it is important to include all of that text in an accessible location. In most cases, it will probably make the most sense to include that text in the caption rather than in the alt-text field.

For videos, if captions or audio descriptions are not fully supported on the social media platform, this information could be included in the text posted alongside the video, or it might be possible to link to a version of the video on a platform that supports these features. Of course, avoiding posting anything that can't be made accessible is another option. This means de-prioritizing social media platforms that do not feature robust accessibility features, or simply opting to only post content that is accessible.

Along with these approaches, it is also worthwhile to advocate with social media companies about the importance of accessibility features. The reality is that a combination of all these approaches will likely be necessary for all libraries that aim to have a robust and accessible social media presence. Keeping accessibility in mind when designing the library's social media strategy can be a helpful way to make sure that inclusion is never sacrificed in this type of online outreach.

▶ GIFs

The Graphics Interchange Format, or GIF file format, is popular on social media. These brief video clips without sound, which often loop, are typically used to share clips of films or TV shows, animation, artwork, or jokes. For people with photosensitive epilepsy, which can include seizures triggered by rapid flashes of light, GIFs can present a danger if they continue to rapidly flash. To avoid this potential hazard, GIFs should be set up to pause after no more than five seconds and should ideally allow the user to pause the content. Many platforms have this option to promote accessibility, but it is important to test for this when using GIFs on a new publishing platform.

Beyond this, GIFs can also present accessibility barriers for those with visual disabilities. To avoid this, each GIF must have appropriate alt-text and should be sufficiently high contrast. If text is included, it should have that text in a readable font of reasonable size and remain visible for a reasonable amount of time to be read. For this reason, it is important to only use GIFs that have been reviewed for these features or were created with accessibility in mind. Many of the available GIFs on the internet are inaccessible for one or more reasons, so it is best to proceed with caution when using them.

▶ E-Mail

Accessibility is often overlooked when creating e-mails, but it is equally critical in this setting. Many of the same principles from general web design and social media accessibility carry through to creating accessible e-mails, particularly as it relates to formatting and the handling of non-standard content like emojis and GIFs. There are also a few items that are worth specifically considering when it comes to e-mail communications.

As with other types of digital text, a lot of e-mail accessibility comes down to usable, readable design. This means that it is still important to choose simple fonts, select a readable font size, use the built-in layout options such as heading tags, and include ample white space. In e-mails, this guidance also applies to any signatures or boilerplate text that is added to all e-mails at your institution, so it is important to review all components of the e-mail.

While it is often overlooked, alt-text is, of course, equally significant in e-mails as in other digital settings, and many e-mail providers do provide support for adding alt-text after an image has been added to the body of an e-mail. It is important to understand what the library's e-mail provider allows, and to integrate creating either alt-text or an image description in the text of the e-mail into the workflow for creating e-mail messages. Images with alt-text should also be formatted as in-line images to ensure that the alt-text is read in the correct place in the text.

Additional considerations that are specific to e-mail include the following ones:

- Write subject headings that are descriptive of the contents while still being brief.

- Name attached files with descriptive file names.
- Use the default HTML format whenever possible to maximize accessibility for those using assistive technologies.
- Offer a plaintext alternative for those who have trouble with the formatting for any reason.

Creating e-mails following these best practices will ensure that your content is usable for everyone who receives the e-mail, and it will also help to make the e-mail content more engaging and usable for all recipients.

Newsletters

E-mail newsletters can be a great way to get the word out, particularly to patrons who can opt in to subscribing. To make these communications engaging and useful to all members of your community, it is important to remember a few specific points.

Choose Accessible Platforms

Many libraries maintain and send their e-mail newsletters through outside platforms that are specifically designed for this work. Not all of these are equally accessible, however. Look for documentation about their accessibility, and consider whether the product will allow the library to send an accessible final product to its subscribers.

Keep Layouts Simple

The most accessible and readable option will always be a single-column layout. This will make the content clearer to those using screen readers and those with certain reading disabilities, but it will also make the user experience more consistent for those reading on mobile devices and generally offers a sleeker final product.

Offer Alternatives

Offer access to the information contained in the newsletter on a separate website if there are any concerns about e-mail accessibility (or just for those who prefer it). When adopting this approach, include a link to this alternative version at the top of the e-mail for those who would prefer to access the content that way.

▶ Forms

Digital forms are a great way to collect information from people online, whether collecting feedback from patrons or work-related information from employees. But these forms can easily present barriers to disabled users if they are not designed with accessibility in mind. For this reason, it is very important to confirm the accessibility of any form the library creates.

Provide Clear Instructions

Digital forms should provide clear instructions about their intended purpose and the steps the user must take to fill out the form. This sounds straightforward, but often the instructions for the form or the individual fields can be difficult to understand and interpret, leading to frustration and incorrect responses. This can disproportionately impact users with disabilities, particularly those with cognitive disabilities or learning disabilities. For this reason, review all instructions for clarity and simplicity. Ideally, it is good to have someone who is not responsible for writing the instructions and questions review them to see if they are able to complete the form without issues.

Create Forms That Are Tagged for Accessibility

As with all online content, properly tagging forms is vital to their accessibility. In the case of forms, this means properly identifying each element of the form with either labels or ARIA attributes, as well as grouping segments of the form with the appropriate tags. All of this will make the form navigable by screen readers and other assistive technologies. Without this, a user may not be able to associate a specific prompt with a form field or may not be able to take certain actions, such as submitting the form. Many libraries use WYSIWYG form-creation tools. These often limit user access to these accessibility-related tags and automatically generate the code for the form. When using tools of this sort, review the documentation about accessibility to use it in the most accessible manner possible. It is also important to test the resulting form for accessibility, and it is best to offer an alternative means of submitting the information for those who encounter accessibility barriers.

All Notifications Must Be Accessible

Forms can involve a few types of notifications. Some will have pop-up visuals that indicate when an entry in one or more of the fields cannot be validated. This is common in fields that are requesting a number when non-numeric characters are entered in the field. When such a notification is part of a form, it must be accessible, meaning that it must be readable by assistive technologies and that it must also be accessible to those who have color vision deficiency. This is why many online forms will have red text appear that also has an X mark next to it. Another type of notification is that of successful submission. When there is a page or a pop-up window indicating that the form has been submitted, this information should be available to assistive devices as well.

Allow Mistakes to Be Corrected

Making it easy to correct any errors on a form is a general usability best practice, but it is especially important in making the form accessible. People with a wide range of disabilities, including motor disabilities, low vision, and cognitive disabilities, may all be more likely to need to correct problems with their form. For this reason, it should be easy to go back to earlier content to make corrections at all points in the form, and there should be a final option to confirm the information being submitted, particularly for any high-stakes forms. Ideally, it is also helpful to offer a way to get in touch with the library if a mistake is discovered later for information that has lasting importance.

Avoid Time Limits

Some online forms, such as those related to purchasing or reserving event tickets, will include a countdown clock with a time limit to complete the process or risk having to start over. While there can be reasons to limit how long a user has to complete a specific transaction, these time limits should be avoided as much as possible, and when they are absolutely necessary, they should offer as much time as possible to complete the transaction. This is true for a couple of reasons. First, these time limits and countdown clocks can be unnecessarily stressful or confusing for those with anxiety or cognitive disabilities, or for users who are distracted or otherwise not able to fully focus on the form. Second, users of certain types of assistive technologies or users with fine motor disabilities may need longer than the average person to complete the transaction. In both of these cases, a strict time limit could prevent the person from using the service. When using a form that must have a time limit, such as when using an outside vendor for event ticketing, it is good to offer an alternative way to complete the transaction, such as calling the library or sending an e-mail.

▶ A Note on Accessible Online Events

Over the last several years, the number of online events has increased rapidly. From online programming for patrons to digital meetings, online events are a great opportunity to reach a wider audience and offer participation options for those who can't come to the library or meeting location. But without focusing on accessibility, these online events can exclude people with many types of disabilities. When planning an online event, make sure to consider how to optimize it for accessibility.

Select an Accessible Platform and Enable Relevant Features

Not all online event platforms are equally accessible. Whether you are looking for a platform to host a major conference, an online meeting platform, or a platform for author events, you should evaluate the accessibility features before making a final decision. It is increasingly common for platforms to offer accessibility features and to be designed for compatibility with assistive technologies, but significant differences still exist. Consider several features, such as:

- Their compliance with WCAG 2.1 or higher
- The availability and accuracy of automated captions
- An option for each attendee to choose to turn on or off captions
- The ability to integrate human-generated captions
- Options for including sign language interpreters in an easily visible space on the screen
- Accessible interactive features, such as polling

Once an accessible platform is in place, it also has to be used in an accessible manner. For example, in many platforms that offer automated captions, the event organizer must enable this feature before users can turn on these captions. In this situation, turning on captions should be a standardized and default step in the workflow for all events. If the platform has other accessibility features that attendees can make use of, it can also be helpful to offer documentation about these in the initial outreach about the event.

Offer a Way to Request Accommodations

For all events, have a means of requesting accommodations. Information about how to do this can be included in the program advertisement for events or in the invitation for meetings. Each person's needs are different; even if you already have a plan for making the event accessible, offer a way to make customized requests. It can also help to explain what features will be available for the event so that attendees can decide whether an accommodation is needed. Common accommodations that might be requested include sign language interpretation, advanced access to slides or other materials, the provision of accessible versions of ancillary materials like handouts, and CART captioning. Particularly for larger events, budget for the possibility that an accommodation will be requested.

Support Multiple Ways of Participating

For events that involve attendee participation, there should be many ways to interact with the group. Many online events create structures for communication, such as asking participants to place questions in a specific queue or raise their hands digitally. When possible, it is helpful to offer support for alternate uses. Some individuals with cognitive disabilities may find it confusing to navigate between the event chat and the question queue, and attendees with fine motor disabilities may find it difficult to click a small button to raise their hands. By allowing everyone to communicate in the way that works best for them, the event organizer can create a more inclusive environment for all. Along the same lines, letting participants choose between typing their comments or turning on their microphones to speak can offer more usable options for all attendees. Wherever possible, events should also have an option to dial in for those without computers and should avoid requiring users to have their cameras on. Considering all of these possibilities will help to develop an inclusive event for users with all types of needs and preferences.

Share the Agenda and Materials in Advance

Distributing both an agenda and any materials for the event to attendees in advance can increase accessibility for everyone. For those who use screen readers, sharing these materials in advance can offer users time to review them with their screen reader before the event, so they can focus on the speaker during the event. Attendees with cognitive disabilities or learning disabilities having access to the materials in advance can offer an opportunity to consider the content at their own pace and can offer more time for developing questions and responses. Doing this can offer a better experience and more thoughtful conversation for all attendees. All of the materials shared should be designed for accessibility. (See chapter 5, "Digital Media and File Accessibility," for more information on designing accessible digital files.)

Describe Visual Content

To offer equitable access for blind and low-vision attendees, as well as those who have dialed into the event, it is helpful to describe visual content during the event. If the materials are distributed in advance, this can help to limit the amount of description necessary, but it is still important to make sure that everyone can follow along with the visual elements on the screen. Describing the appearance of any speakers who appear on the screen can also create a more inclusive environment for all and is a necessity if that appearance is important to the introduction or overall content.

Make Space for Everyone to Participate

Even when an event is designed with accessibility at its core, there is still a need to carve out space for meaningful participation by all. Attendees with cognitive disabilities and those who use AACs (augmentative and alternative communication) may need more time to participate in the conversation. Make them feel welcome and encouraged to participate both during the event and after, if that works better for them. In addition, people with some disabilities, such as anxiety, may be uncomfortable with speaking in front of a group. To involve those who prefer to present their contribution in writing, it can be helpful for a moderator to verbalize these sorts of questions or comments. Moderators should be sure to check the chat and question queue frequently. As a moderator, it is also useful to pay attention to whether certain attendees seem to be excluded, especially from collaborative or conversation-based events, so that they can be offered opportunities to contribute.

The exact accessibility needs and priorities will vary between events, so there are a lot of different features and options to consider when developing an accessible and inclusive event. This will help to involve more attendees in events at all times and build an even larger audience for meetings and events of all kinds.

❱ Digital Displays and Signage

Given their physical form, it can be easy to forget that digital signs are still a part of the library's digital presence. In terms of accessibility, the content on digital screens exists at the intersection of digital accessibility principles and physical signage design principles. Because digital signs are increasingly common in libraries, it is good to keep some basic best practices in mind.

Choose the Best Device for the Job

There are many different types of digital displays on the market, so be sure to evaluate options for the specific location where the device will be placed. Check that the sign has sufficient screen resolution, a surface that will work with the space's lighting conditions and is at a size that will be readable from where most users will see the display.

Emphasize Clarity

Clarity is extremely important for digital signage, particularly because viewers will often be standing at a distance from the signage and may be viewing it at unusual angles or with glare from the surrounding lighting. The design should be simple, any text should be large, and all elements should be high contrast.

Make Interaction Easy

If the goal is for viewers to navigate to a website or complete an action, make that process easy by using a QR code paired with a shortened URL.

For Moving Images, Avoid Flashing Lights

If a video or animation is displayed on a digital sign, it is important to make sure that it does not flash rapidly as this can trigger seizures for those with photosensitive epilepsy.

Offer an Alternative

Even if the digital display is designed to be as accessible as possible, offer alternate ways to receive the same information. This could be done by posting the information on the library's website, providing a braille or tactile alternative, or having a team member nearby to answer questions.

Inclusive communications and outreach must center accessibility at each stage of the process. In many cases, the general principles of digital accessibility applied to web design will apply to outreach and publicity materials as well, but there are some unique considerations depending on the type of communications being done. Libraries must ensure that everyone who conducts outreach on behalf of the library understands how to make those activities accessible and inclusive so that the library reaches the whole community with its communications.

Online Events and Archives

Interview with **Lydia Tang**, *Senior Outreach and Engagement Coordinator, Lyrasis*

Having taught online workshops and worked on outreach and engagement, what do you see as the key accessibility considerations for those offering digital events to library employees or patrons?
Some key accessibility considerations include:

1. Flexibility in accessing content. Recording the session and providing a transcript or summary can help people who wanted to attend but were unable to attend at the specific time.

2. During the online event, it's important to make sure the session itself is as accessible as possible. It's nearly impossible to be "fully accessible" for all types of disabilities, so ensuring that the registration page has a way to request accommodations is key. This way, it can be helpful to know whether ASL or CART captions are needed (some groups benefit from various accommodations more than others) and to be transparent on what accommodations are planned already.
3. If you are using slides, create your slides according to accessibility best practices.
   - Use unique slide titles.
   - Use alt text for any images.
   - Pay attention to the reading order of text boxes in your slide deck.
   - Use a sans serif font for readability.
   - Use sufficient color contrast and avoid visually busy or animated gifs that could be distracting.
4. If you are trying to do an online event on a shoestring, here are some imperfect ideas for advancing accessibility:
   - Make sure that captions can be toggled on, whether it's through the web conferencing platform or through the slide software.
   - Use headphones with a microphone to ensure that the audio quality is good. If you are presenting in an acoustically over reverberant or loud ambience environment, it can be harder to hear you.
   - At the beginning of the event, welcome guests and orient them to how captions can be toggled on. Share a link to your slide deck in the chat to allow anyone to follow along with your slide deck using any assistive technology needed.
   - During the presentation, describe any visual content in your slides to allow anyone who might have low vision/blind to understand your content.

Do you see any key distinctions between an event aimed at library employees and one offered for patrons?

The care, attention, and respect for accessibility should be the same between patrons and library employees. Sometimes institutions might consider cutting corners for accessibility for staff events, but the root of that impulse may be embedded ableism. It is always a good idea to model and normalize accessibility best practices, including for internal audiences.

What are common accessibility challenges for online events? Do you have any recommendations on how to approach these challenges?

Some common accessibility challenges are:

1. Infrastructure failure. Some people just won't have reliable access to technology and the internet to be able to access the event. This is why an online event can expand accessibility in some ways but also can be another source of exposing haves and have nots within society.
2. Not providing captions is a big easy fail. AI-generated captions will be imperfect but can be a baseline. Remember when speaking to speak slower and very clearly to help with comprehension and caption generation. If the event is being recorded for asynchronous access, be sure to review and correct the caption files. Names, jargon, capitalizations, and punctuation often aren't transcribed correctly with AI.
3. Not sharing slides is another big easy fail. If someone uses a screen reader, there may be little to no way that they can actually access the slide deck content being presented to them. Allowing them the chance ahead of time (ideally), during, or afterward is good to allow users to access and digest the content.

You have worked extensively on best practices for archives working to make their digital collections and online programming more accessible and inclusive. What do you see as the first steps for archivists who want to start this work at their institution?

The first step would be to explore the content of the Society of American Archivists's "Guidelines for Accessible Archives for People with Disabilities."[i] The next step is to get started! Doing and adding one more accessible thing is the way to get started.

For digital collections, ask questions from your team and the platform that you pick for hosting your digital collections:

- Does your digital collection platform have a VPAT (Voluntary Product Accessibility Template) that documents their level of compliance? Do they have accessibility factored into their development road map?

- Does your website have an accessibility statement? This statement should underscore your institution's commitment to accessibility and offer contact information for a person or committee that can receive and respond to any accessibility questions or feedback.
- What workflows are being done to advance accessibility, such as OCR, tagging PDFs for navigation, adding alt-text to visual images, and adding captions/transcripts for audiovisual or audio content?

What advice do you have for those interested in learning more about digital accessibility?

Deque University has online training, and they offer full scholarships for people with disabilities.[ii] The International Association of Accessibility Professionals has several certification tracks, with the foundational one being the Certified Professional in Accessibility Core Competencies.[iii] Begin to experiment with built-in screen readers and other accessibility tools to see how it can be experienced (or not). Listen and learn from people with disabilities by inviting them into your spaces, services, and online resources and pay them to provide user feedback.

Notes

i. SAA Task Force to Revise Best Practices on Accessibility, "Guidelines for Accessible Archives for People with Disabilities," Society of American Archivists, 2019, www2.archivists.org/groups/reference-access-and-outreach-section/guidelines-for-accessible-archives-for-people-with-disabilities.

ii. Deque University, "Deque University Scholarships for People with Disabilities," https://dequeuniversity.com/scholarships.

iii. International Association of Accessibility Professionals, "Certified Professional in Accessibility Core Competencies (CPACC)," 2024, www.accessibilityassociation.org/s/certified-professional.

Note

1. See, for example, Minnesota Twins (@Twins), "If you don't Then you don't love me deserve me at my me at my," Twitter, April 4, 2018, 3:35 p.m., https://x.com/Twins/status/981620744374415360.

• ● ●

CHAPTER 7

Automated and Manual Testing

A graduate student in library school wonders "Who am I to test content?" when completing a web audit in their internship.

An e-resource librarian wants to verify the accessibility of a new database the library is considering subscribing to, but questions her knowledge and training in this area.

An ILL staff member fears that he will fail his users if he misses issues when testing document accessibility.

Most librarians we've encountered and worked with feel these same doubts regularly, and perhaps especially when we test our libraries' products, platforms, and services for their conformance to accessibility standards. The problem is that, as librarians, we are trained to admit what we don't know and we fear getting things wrong. All of this is a normal part of the imposter syndrome we feel when we approach technical tasks that deeply affect our users and over which we think we have little dominion. Having a checklist or approach to conformance testing is one thing. Using that approach is another. And there is only one way to get more comfortable with it: by forging ahead and doing it, bit by bit.

One helpful approach is to define what you are doing and what you're not doing. What exactly will you be testing: the top level of a library catalog (or some other digital platform)? The records within that catalog? The items provided within those records? If you are testing a website, which browser(s) are you testing with? Are you testing desktop and mobile sites? You may not be able to do everything. How will you choose? A variety of random selection? Only text documents? Only multimedia?

Think of this kind of task like casual sandlot baseball. Kids place the bases where they can be based on the size of the lot or how much of it they want to use. Basically, a player determines how far to run by where the bases are placed. None of it is bad or good. Sometimes, a player starts small and gets more ambitious as they build confidence. This approach works well for testing. Test in stages, beginning with a top-level conformance review. Your web pages should spell out, as best as possible, what your accessibility goals and priorities are. What efforts are you making to achieve these goals? And how will you be testing to ensure those goals are met? When it comes to testing, the only way you truly fail is by not trying at all or by not explaining your approach.

▶ Ensuring the Accessibility of Licensed Content

The reality of digital content in libraries is that most of the platforms libraries use are licensed from vendors. From their online public access catalog (OPAC) to individual databases, most libraries have at least some digital platforms that are created and maintained by outside vendors. Because the library team will have fewer opportunities to make changes and edits to these platforms, it is important to understand any accessibility features or barriers in those platforms as early in the process as possible. A significant component of this process is working effectively with the product's vendor, as discussed further in chapter 11, "Best Practices for Working with Vendors."

There are other important steps that can be taken to help understand a platform's accessibility, and then integrate that information into the library's workflows and decisions. Noah Roth, an electronic resources librarian, successfully created and implemented an electronic information technology (EIT) accessibility policy as part of a team at SUNY Broome Community College. Roth notes that the evaluation process does get better:

The process for a short-staffed library might be more truncated but equally effective if:

- emphasis was placed on purchasing primarily accessible products. Staff who purchased [products] would need to develop a greater understanding of WCAG standards and be willing to review a product VPAT before initiating the purchase, and decline to move forward in most instances if the product was inaccessible.
- triage: focus on high-impact products first and then move to evaluation of lower-impact products.
- cross-train staff to handle several aspects of the process, and
- develop a knowledge base/templates of common accessibility issues and solutions to speed up the process.[1]

▶ Understanding VPATs

One of the best tools for evaluating digital content from vendors is the VPAT, or Voluntary Product Accessibility Template. Developed by the Information Technology Industry Council in collaboration with the U.S. government, the VPAT is a tool for reporting on the degree to which a product does or does not adhere to specific accessibility standards. There are four versions of the VPAT currently available: one each for compliance with the requirements of the WCAG, U.S. Revised Section 508, and EN 301 549, as well as a fourth international version that details compliance with all three of these standards in a single document. Reviewing any of the four versions of the template can be useful, but most libraries, especially those in the United States, will probably benefit the most from reviewing the WCAG version of the document. This will be especially true after the newly adopted rules under the ADA that are specifically tied to WCAG 2.1 go into effect. While the different versions of the template have separate criteria, overall they all offer a picture of the usability of the product for users with differing needs. So even if the preferred version of the template is not available for a specific platform, it is still worth reviewing any available VPAT for that platform. The template is completed for each individual product. One advantage of the VPAT is that it can be completed either by the vendor responsible for the product or by any outside party reviewing the product. A completed VPAT is technically referred to as an Accessibility Conformance Report (ACR), but colloquially many refer to both the blank template and a completed version of it as a VPAT.

Since the development of the VPAT, it has become the dominant means of communicating the level of accessibility of digital products, particularly for vendors who work with U.S. or European governmental entities or those who work closely with other entities that prioritize accessibility. An increasing number of vendors will make VPATs for their products publicly available on their website, but even if that is not the case, many are able to produce them upon request when their product is being evaluated by a potential licensee or subscriber. When a VPAT is not available from the vendor, it is worth looking to see if any third parties have evaluated the platform using the template. To be useful, a VPAT must be completely filled out and updated to reflect the most current version of the platform. Any time there is a significant update to a platform, there should be a corresponding revision to the VPAT to reflect all the current features of the platform. For this reason, it can be useful to make requesting an updated VPAT, or at least inquiring whether there is an update, a part of the renewal workflow for subscriptions.

For all four types of VPAT, the document features tables with the criteria relevant to the type of compliance documented in that version. The tables start with a column for the criteria, followed by a column for the conformance level, and then finally followed by a column for additional remarks and explanations. The conformance level can be listed as one of five options: Supports, Partially Supports, Does Not Support, Not Applicable, and Not Evaluated. Because these options don't offer the opportunity for much nuance, a thorough document will generally include a significant amount of additional information in the final column to explain any criteria that do not reach a conformance level of "Supports." This additional information is arguably the most valuable component of the VPAT because it will offer a clear picture of any barriers that will exist for users. Since very few platforms are able to achieve complete accessibility, particularly in the case of newer platforms still undergoing active development, it is important to review all of these additional notes when evaluating a platform. This information will clarify if there are elements of the platform that will require accommodations and will help in planning the expected accommodations for most users.

▶ Evaluating Platform Accessibility

The process of determining the accessibility of a platform is a multi-stage one. A relatively straightforward first step in evaluating a platform is to request a VPAT from the vendor but, unfortunately, this is not sufficient to ensure accessibility. Many VPATs will list only known issues, so the presence of a VPAT does not necessarily mean that a product is fully compliant with the relevant accessibility standard. In such cases, the VPAT is still useful information that can help in evaluating a product to decide whether to subscribe to it and make plans for remediation or accommodations but recognize that a VPAT may not be the end point of the accessibility work the library must do. In addition, research indicates that VPATs are not always accurate, which points to the reason why the VPAT is only one piece of an overarching workflow for evaluating a platform.[2] Accessibility evaluation and testing have vital roles to play in verifying the accessibility of the digital platforms that libraries license. This process can help to fill in any gaps in information provided in the VPAT, identify any errors, and establish the overall accessibility level of the platform in cases where no VPAT is available. While the independent evaluation of platforms is still not a standard part of the evaluation process for licensed content at many libraries, it is worthwhile to integrate these steps into the process of evaluating such content.

Conformance Review

One of the best ways to begin testing is to start with a top-level conformance review. This kind of testing seeks to confirm that the product conforms to the basic web accessibility standards outlined in the WCAG. (See chapter 3, "Principles of Web Accessibility," for more information on the WCAG.) At a minimum, a top-level conformance review would look, for example, at a platform's home page, run sample searches, and evaluate a few records, generally covering discrete types of representative content. Conformance review reports should specify the WCAG standard level, test assets using this standard, identify compliance and gaps, and provide a clear path forward with recommendations. Reviews may respond to an existing VPAT but need not have a VPAT to establish conformance. Remember that the VPAT is voluntary. Often, companies attempt to complete them in-house, or they farm them out. Sometimes the VPATs provided are of limited value to libraries, which means that actually checking the content's conformance is crucial.

The entire review process can feel overwhelming if you are not comfortable with your level of expertise. A simple strategy to get some practice doing conformance reviews and meet your goals can be to create a buddy system. In the State University of New York (SUNY) system (where both authors currently work), the system itself provides myriad opportunities for collaboration. One such opportunity was the Library Accessibility Cohort. Co-chaired by the authors, this group started with a focus on evaluating the accessibility of the subscription databases to which many libraries across SUNY subscribed. With the cohort, participating librarians set out to do conformance reviews for these top databases. In this effort, we were able to lean on each other for support, work through our imposter syndrome issues, and check each other's work. Not every librarian will have such a built-in network. Still, you probably belong to a professional development group, are part of a consortium with interest groups, or perhaps have several library branches in your local area. The way you seek conformance review companionship is up to you and your relationships, but forming these collaborations will pay off in a multitude of ways. Many cohort members reported finding this collaboration to be a useful way of forging bonds that otherwise would not have flourished.

Additionally, libraries that have learned from OCR complaints and from library systems often partner to complete some conformance reviews like the SUNY cohort did. Consider the Library Accessibility Alliance, an effort composed of the Big Ten Academic Alliance and other partners like the Association of Southeastern Research Libraries. Many of these groups will not only report on the accessibility of their resources but will also provide guidance, tools, and resources for contract language and communications with vendors, as well as checklists to help you get started. There are many of these resources, and they are widely available. Try looking at the toolkits from these collaborations or from large universities before downloading any vendor or third-party "free checklists." Once you sign up to receive these free checklists, which might be of varying quality and usefulness, you will then be contacted by the vendors enticing you to engage their products and services. This can be a nuisance.

If you choose, another approach to confirming the conformance of platforms is to hire one of those third-party experts or companies to complete the testing. This approach may be out of reach for most libraries' budgets, but it can be useful to consider when working with a larger organization, such as a consortium. For libraries or vendors that create new platforms for use by other institutions, this can be a good way to check the accessibility of the platform and share this information with potential users. When hiring a third-party expert, the following factors can be useful for evaluating potential experts:

- Will the evaluation be completed by someone who regularly uses assistive technology in their day-to-day life?
- What process and tools are used in the review process?
- Has this expert or team previously completed conformance reviews?
- Is the expert able to guarantee independence from the vendor(s) being reviewed?
- Will there be any restrictions on how you can use the testing report? Is there any prohibition on posting the report for internal or external use?

Whichever approach you adopt to review the conformance of digital platforms, it is important to document your findings and monitor updates to the platform to determine when a new review will need to be completed.

Given the number and scope of available testing resources, it might be tempting to take up a report done by one of these external groups. One of the most crucial warnings when using reports done by other libraries or consortia is to ensure that they are current and thorough. Even if you adopt an approach based on existing conformance reviews, the onus is on you to double-check before adopting them. What problems highlighted in the report remain to this day? Has the vendor provided a road map to address gaps in compliance? Are there workflows to ameliorate barriers

140 ●●● CHAPTER 7

discovered? What feedback can you gather from recent online forum concerns? Remember that third-party applications and databases must always be vetted.

Manual Testing

No matter what tools you employ, every content creator, adopter, or curator must familiarize themselves with manual testing principles and skills. There are simple things that all librarians can do to check files in the course of their work. (Much of the information here will mirror what is found in chapter 4, "The Accessible Library Website.")

Many libraries will benefit from a structured approach to accessibility conformance review that involves a combination of manual and automated testing. The reason why this combination is important is that automated testing is often a useful starting place, but it cannot catch all the problems. For example, it is not capable of understanding that some obscure file name that got added automatically as alt-text is not useful as alt-text on an image. While the automated checkers might pick up some things, they will probably fail often enough to create an obstacle to achieving the goal of fully inclusive content.

Content Testing and Resizing

One of the first manual tests is to look at your content and ensure that it is at the appropriate reading level and is organized in a clear, usable, and predictable way. Content should follow the POUR principles discussed in chapter 3, "Principles of Web Accessibility."

Next, you should look at how the information reflows when you change the percentage and zoom in. Is everything available at 100 percent still visible at 200 percent? We want to ensure that the content is still in a logical order and available with no omissions. This kind of test is easy enough for anyone to do. Simply zoom in by choosing Ctrl and + on a PC or Command and + on a Mac. Can you read the page text without having to scroll across horizontally? Does content suddenly seem off, layered on top of one another, or did crucial navigation elements disappear or move unpredictably? Do the links work? Are all links created properly using semantic HTML and not spelled out so that a screen-reader user will hear "H T T P colon slash slash w w w dot"?

Keyboard Testing

A simple way to begin is with some basic keyboard testing. Unplug or disconnect your mouse and attempt the following:

- Use **Tab** to navigate the page (Shift + Tab will navigate backward).
- Use **Enter** to activate buttons or links.
- Use **arrow keys** to select menus, radio buttons, and autocomplete.
- Use the **Spacebar** to activate buttons, check boxes, and expand menus.
- Use **Escape** to close dialog boxes.

As you move around the page, if you are sighted, look for visual focus indicators around each element you activate. Note where visual focus indicators (see WCAG 2.4.7 and refer to chapter 3, "Principles of Web Accessibility") are nonexistent or out of order (see WCAG 2.4.3). Does the navigation make sense and is it in a logical order? Are you able to get out of dialog boxes or skip content as needed?

Mobile Testing

What about the mobile site? Are you testing on iOS and Android? How does it fare when you change the display? Does everything still make sense? Mobile testing can be just as intimidating as keyboard testing feels when you first start out, but it is one way to hone your skills and integrate testing into so many more situations than you may have anticipated. That is, once you know the shortcuts, you may find yourself curious about sites and documents not originally in your purview.

If you are creating born-library applications for mobile use, it is important to note that both iOS and Android offer some limited accessibility-testing support. These should be used in conjunction with basic accessible web-design principles and manual testing. Guidance on manual testing in each platform is widely available, but knowing simple shortcuts can be a great way to get comfortable experiencing where barriers exist in the development phase before you launch. If you are not developing these tools yourself, but instead have delegated that task to a vendor, remember

142 ••• CHAPTER 7

that the responsibility lies with the institution purchasing and adopting the goods and services.

Testing Tips

Apple iOS

- Press the iPhone side button three times to activate VoiceOver. This shortcut is customizable under Settings> Control Center if pressing the side button becomes an issue.
  - Swipe right to move forward, swipe left to move backward.
- Set up a Bluetooth keyboard and try to navigate your mobile site using the keyboard alone, as one might do if they had a motor impairment like arthritis or a tremor.
- Set the speech rate under Settings > Accessibility > VoiceOver > Speaking rate.
- Practice using Voiceover Practice mode. When you turn on VoiceOver, tap Practice and then double tap to start.

Android

- Open the Settings > navigate to Accessibility > select TalkBack.
- At the top Talkback, use On/Off to activate TalkBack.
- Set the speech rate under Settings > Text to Speech > Speech rate.
- Practice using TalkBack's Tutorial and help under Talkback settings.

Automated Testing Tools

There are many automated testing tools out there (for a full list of available tools, see WAI's Evaluation Tools List).[3] These might appear as software, external websites, or plug-ins that scan documents or websites. Some are built into applications, like the Check Accessibility tool in the Microsoft Office suite. Some tools offer a suite of testing for overall web accessibility or PDF accessibility. Others focus on a discrete element of accessibility, like checking the color contrast. Some tools are free, and some are paid. For libraries that are part of a larger institution, it is valuable to check whether your IT department or another department already subscribes to a paid tool the library could also use at no additional cost. The most important thing to remember about automated testing tools is they are not a silver bullet. They are a great starting place to discover the most common issues affecting users, but they don't take the place of manual testing and basic user testing. Normally, automated tools are part of a larger process for conformance testing that may begin with them but does not end with them.

Automated tools are useful for web designers and developers. But what about the average person? How can we each use automated tools to check accessibility in our own documents or other content we create in the process of creating guides, tutorials, web pages, event announcements, and more? There are some simple and reliable resources freely available. The following section is a list of some widely accepted testing tools to help you get started.

Free Tools for Testing

WebAIM's WAVE Accessibility Evaluation Tool

- A browser-based option that works for those who cannot install new software on their computer.
- A plug-in is available for Chrome, Firefox, and Edge.
- The tabs of information for each page will include a Summary, Details, and Information, among other things like Order, Structure, and Contrast.
- It prioritizes issues into categories of Errors, Alerts, Features, and Elements. For each, WAVE will define the issues if you click on the i for more information.
- WAVE does overall testing of various issues, including contrast-checking, and focuses on WCAG 2.2.

Silktide Accessibility Checker

- It has a plug-in tool for automated checking in Chrome, Firefox, Safari, Edge, and Opera.
- Gives pass/fail scoring for all levels of WCAG 2.0 to 2.2.

144 ••• CHAPTER 7

- Includes simulators for screen reading and a variety of disabilities, including cognitive ones.

SiteImprove

- Includes extension for Chrome, Edge, Firefox, and Opera.
- Prioritizes information based on WCAG level by errors, warnings, and review items and even specifies which role might be responsible for the issue (editor, webmaster, or developer).
- Tells you what WCAG standard was missed and how you can meet the criteria.

There are also testing tools specific to particular issues, like dedicated contrast checkers or disability simulators.

We have listed the most popular automated overall testing tools. These are but a sample of the many tools that are freely available, and the ones you choose should be evaluated for clarity and ease of use. While tools evolve and more become available, remember that these are just one part of your approach to testing. Manual testing will remain central to ensuring access, as will user experience testing. And nothing can beat a web designer who understands the basic principles of accessibility. It might be tempting to engage with a vendor who promises to take care of all your issues using an overlay, but overlays may create different barriers so additional testing should still be a part of your workflow when adopting an overlay. (For a fuller discussion of overlays, see chapter 4, "The Accessible Library Website.") All testing (manual and automated) must be frequent and iterative. The website is an ever-changing asset. A sound testing plan will respect this fact by ensuring that regular checks are performed.

Creating an EIT Exception and Alternative Access Process

Noah Roth, *Electronic Resources Librarian, SUNY Broome Community College*

- You will always have the challenges of time, training, and staffing constraints, including turnover.
- Manage the documentation and tracking of exceptions and alternative access solutions by tracking and storing your documentation/communication in a shared space.
- The process is as important as the product. The process leads to an increased awareness of accessibility on campus, especially among those charged with procurement.
- Universal appeal: the benefit of purchasing more accessible products is enhanced usability for all, as accessible products usually improve access for users in general.
- It gets even better. When a purchase is initiated, a flag is sent by an IT/EIT approver that starts the review process. A product is reviewed, and if the VPAT and/or follow-up testing reveals significant accessibility problems, the group convenes again after receiving a purchaser's narrative explaining both why an exception is needed and how equally effective alternate access will be provided.

Notes

1. Noah Roth, personal interview, "Electronic Information Accessibility Exception Process," September 18, 2024.
2. Anna Sturgill and Elyssa M. Gould, "Trends in VPATs over Time," *Journal of Electronic Resources Librarianship* 35, no. 4 (2023): 249–59; Melina Zavala and Matthew Reidsma, "Trust, but Verify: Auditing Vendor-Supplied Accessibility Claims," *Code4Lib Journal* 48 (2020); Samuel Kent Willis and Faye O'Reilly, "Filling

the Gap in Database Usability: Putting Vendor Accessibility Compliance to the Test," *Information Technology and Libraries* 39, no. 4 (2020).

3. W3C Web Accessibility Initiative (WAI), "Web Accessibility Evaluation Tools List," www.w3.org/WAI/test-evaluate/tools/list/.

• • •

CHAPTER 8

Accessibility of Emerging Technologies

The library director suggests buying a PlayStation 5 Pro and some games to offer for circulation or use for programming but isn't sure whether special equipment would be needed to make it accessible.

The library system your library belongs to is in the early stages of adopting a new shared discovery system and needs to develop a process for evaluating the accessibility of each of the options being considered.

A vendor is marketing a new software option for staff scheduling, and you have been tasked with evaluating whether the library should start using it.

Given the speed with which new technologies emerge and existing technologies evolve, it can be difficult to keep up with all of the changes. As libraries seek to serve their patrons and improve the efficiency of their operations, new technologies are almost always rapidly adopted to create engaging programming for patrons or to refine behind-the-scenes workflows. But while evaluating and adopting new tools or features, it is important to ensure accessibility is never lost in the process. This work is crucial as new technologies are developed, since accessibility barriers often exist in the initial iterations. It can be tempting to assume the developers of new technologies will always be on top of accessibility needs, especially at a time when so many libraries are stretched thin in terms of staffing and budgets. But, there are many reasons why this is not a safe assumption.

148 ••• CHAPTER 8

Countless examples exist of new tools, games, and devices debuting with significant accessibility issues that were overlooked in the initial rush to market. For this reason, library workers must have strategies in place for considering accessibility as new technologies emerge. This chapter will introduce the techniques and strategies that can help with this process.

❱ Ensuring the Accessibility of New Technologies

New technologies can jump from a mere idea to a popular reality with surprising speed. With many libraries eager to be early adopters of these new technologies to support patrons and employees alike, it is imperative to have a clear plan for how accessibility evaluation will fit into these decisions. Depending on the nature of the new technology, identifying an accessibility issue might lead to delaying the timeline for adoption, developing a plan for how to accommodate those who are unable to use the tool, or negotiating changes with the creator of the new technology. Regardless of what will be done if an issue is identified, it is vital to evaluate the technology's accessibility and learn about any barriers as part of the adoption process. This will allow for informed decision-making and can protect the library from future complaints from users, whether in the form of legal action or simply dissatisfaction with the services offered by the library. Fortunately, there are overarching principles and best practices that can guide the process of evaluating new technologies, even if these technologies feel completely different from anything that has come before them.

Review Existing Documentation

When considering the adoption of any new digital resource, one of the first steps in the workflow should be to determine what accessibility documentation already exists for the resource. This documentation can take many forms, from formal evaluations done by the company producing the item or by outside groups, to more informal information provided on the company's website. All of this information can be useful in building a full picture of how accessible the product is and what remediation or accommodations the library might be responsible for if the tool is adopted.

As discussed in chapter 7, "Automated and Manual Testing," an internationally recognized standard for reporting on the accessibility features and issues of a product is the VPAT. This is most frequently used to evaluate the accessibility of OPACs, databases, and social media platforms. One significant advantage of the VPAT is the degree to which it is standardized, which can make it easier to compare across products and quickly identify issues. This can be particularly helpful in the case of newer products, where the VPAT's structure can make it easier to understand accessibility issues and features. It is also helpful that the VPAT can be used both by the company responsible for the product and by outside parties. Nonetheless, a disadvantage of VPATs is that they are not always filled out completely or accurately (as discussed in chapter 7), which makes it important to ensure they are only one piece of an accessibility review process. If a company does provide a VPAT for a product, it needs to be reviewed thoroughly, both to determine whether it seems complete and accurate and to identify where the company has highlighted potential issues with the product. Providing a VPAT does not mean that the company is assuring users there are no accessibility barriers present. It is simply a structured way of reporting on known issues as well as accessibility features. A VPAT can be particularly helpful for identifying issues that might change the way the item is used at the library, and it might facilitate any planning for possible accommodations, or for outreach about the item to inform users of potential barriers.

Many vendors also provide accessibility documentation about their products as part of their public online presence. This might be information about how to use built-in accessibility features or information about known issues. For example, many social media platforms have online documentation available about their platform's features, and this documentation often has a section on accessibility features and issues. Beyond social media platforms, many products will either have a section about accessibility or at least describe the product in a way that identifies accessibility features and barriers on their website. When deciding whether or not to use a new software tool, it is helpful to review this information with a particular focus on accessibility. The information can also be a useful training resource if there are accessibility features that need to be enabled, or if there are best practices for using the product in a more accessible manner. As with a VPAT, this information may not always be complete, but it is a good starting place for learning more about the accessibility landscape of any new technology that is being considered for adoption, particularly before the library has set up a trial or purchased the product.

One specific type of accessibility documentation that is particularly important is the accessibility road map. This is a statement about the company's future plans for accessibility, which is often available in databases but can also be found in any number of hardware and software products. Though such documentation may indicate that there are existing problems with the product, it is useful to know the development team is aware of these issues and there is a timeline for these issues to be resolved. Such a road map also demonstrates that accessibility is a priority for the development team. For technologies where the library is working directly with a company through a contractual relationship, this can also be a helpful guide to negotiation about accessibility features and plans for the future (as discussed further in chapter 11, "Best Practices for Working with Vendors").

In situations where the company has not developed any of its own documentation or where the existing official documentation is lacking, it is also useful to look for outside documentation. A great source of this is government entities that are using the platform, such as a new social media application, for example. In the United States, accessibility requirements placed on governmental departments have led some of these departments to develop their own accessibility best practices around new technologies they are adopting. These can explain known barriers or set out the preferred workflow for maximizing the accessibility of the platform. This guidance is sometimes publicly posted, and when it is, it can serve as a helpful guide to using the tool in a way that is inclusive for as many users as possible. In some cases, this sort of documentation is developed by other third parties. Examples of this include the work done by the Library Accessibility Alliance and the IT and Development Subgroup of the Digital Library Federation's Digital Accessibility Working Group,[1] both of which audit digital resources and share the results of their reviews for free on their websites. These resources can be invaluable when evaluating products for adoption that are already being used in other libraries, though they are not as readily available for technologies not yet adopted in many libraries.

Look to Standards for Comparable Technologies

Though new technologies can feel completely fresh and different, they are, at least in some ways, usually an evolution of past technologies. They may integrate existing accessibility features in new ways or build on technologies already in use for years. This means that existing standards can be useful when evaluating new technologies even if they are not directly applicable to them. A good example of this is the captions used to make audio content accessible to those who are d/Deaf or hard of hearing. While an early use of captions allowed television content to be accessible, since then captions have been used on a wide range of types of content, ranging from online videos to the audio component of XR (extended reality) experiences. (Chapter 9, "Accessibility of eXtended Reality," covers the latter in detail.) In cases where new standards have not yet been developed for new technologies, the standards applied to older technologies can be instructive. In the case of captions, many have looked to the Federal Communications Commission's rules about closed captioning for television to guide approaches to creating usable captions in other settings, and to evaluate whether existing captions in new technologies are sufficient.

Similarly, many of the concepts at the heart of the WCAG can apply beyond the Web as well. Though the WCAG's specific success criteria are written with web content in mind, the principles and explanations can be applied to other types of software and emerging technologies in the absence of other standards. While this might not catch every possible issue, using existing standards to evaluate new technologies is a good starting point for those who may not feel they have the level of accessibility expertise necessary to evaluate these new technologies in a vacuum. These standards can also suggest ways of structuring guidance and best practices to make a new technology usable by a broad range of potential users, which is helpful for those who are working on an evaluation workflow that will be applied by many different members of their library team.

Rely on the General Principles Underlying Accessible Design

When the existing documentation and standards are not sufficient to fully evaluate the accessibility of a new technology, the general principles of accessible design can provide guidance. There are several different sets of accessible design principles, all of which can be useful in evaluating new technologies. Two prominent examples are inclusive design and universal design,[2] both of which have principles that can guide the evaluation of new technologies. Regardless of which approach to design is adopted, a few guiding principles that can apply to a wide range of newly emerging technologies are provided in the following sections.

Always Consider the Needs of a Range of Users
Understanding the end user is an essential component of all design, but too often the needs of the user are boiled down to an average that designers work toward. Both universal design and inclusive design prompt us to consider the full diversity of those who will be using any product. They point to a type of design that doesn't just recognize not all users are the same, but embraces the need for a product or service to be usable and welcoming for the full range of potential users, no matter their needs. Recognizing the needs of people with a variety of disabilities and those who use any of the assistive devices available on the market is a key component of this, but it is also important to recognize the needs of users vary regardless of whether they have a disability or not. The same features that can benefit disabled users can have advantages for others as well, for example, the rising popularity of captions and the number of people who use the voice control features of their mobile devices to enable a hands-free experience. Whether designing a new product or evaluating an existing product, recognizing the full range of user needs and preferences is vital to inclusion and usability.

Evaluate Optimization for Assistive Technologies
For users who work with assistive technologies, these technologies must function with the products they are using. Some products offer assistive technologies, such as a built-in text-to-speech option, but in almost all cases, it is preferable that users be able to use their own assistive technology for two reasons. First of all, users will have developed expertise with their preferred assistive technology and may have a workstation that combines multiple assistive technologies. Second, if a digital platform blocks assistive devices, users may not be able to navigate to use the built-in features meant to replace the functionality. It is best, then, for new technologies to be designed to accommodate a range of assistive technologies. At the core

of this is a design that is structured in a way that information is shared with assistive technologies and can be processed effectively, for example, in properly labeling digital elements for use by assistive technologies. When evaluating a new technology, consider how users of assistive technologies would be able to work with it, think about the structure of its content, and test it with a range of assistive technologies to determine whether there are barriers.

Focus on Flexibility and Support for Adaptation
Flexibility is one of the principles of universal design for good reason. Technologies that are flexible allow users to adapt them to their needs and preferences, which makes them easier to use and more accessible. Flexibility also supports individual choice about how to interact with the technology, which can be key for those with a disability that prevents certain types of interactions. When evaluating new technologies, bear in mind how many options and choices the user has for interacting with the product. For example, digital platforms that allow users to read an article on the screen, change font size, print it to read on paper, or opt to have the content read aloud with a screen reader, offer multiple ways for the user to reach the same end point of understanding the content of the article. Options for customization and personalization should always be considered as part of evaluating a new technology.

Work with Users

While the principles of accessibility offer vital guidance, keep in mind that at the end of the day, the purpose of all accessibility work is to ensure a wide range of people can use the tools being created. If a tool somehow meets the technical requirements but is still unusable by those who use assistive technologies and those who have disabilities, then it is still inaccessible. For this reason, working with disabled users is a key part of the evaluation process. And this work can be useful even when there is no existing guidance or documentation to fall back on for a new technology.

When considering if there are accessibility barriers inherent in a newly adopted technology, user testing can be a great approach. For libraries that already have robust user-testing resources, make sure users with a range of disabilities and users who employ a variety of assistive technologies are included in the testing population. Arrange the tests so as to allow participants to use their own technology setups, including preferred assistive technologies, whenever possible. For those new to working with users in this way, there are many ways members of the community can be integrated into the evaluation of new tools, from formal user testing to feedback surveys or comment boxes that are accessibly designed and shared in ways that will reach the whole community and encourage them to share their views.

When recruiting users to provide feedback on new tools, think about ways to reach everyone in your community, from those who use the library on a daily basis to those who rarely use its resources. It is possible some of the people who are not regular library users are actually encountering barriers to use that can be resolved to better meet their needs. As part of recruiting participants, remember that patrons and employees both use library technologies in different ways. Including employees, and particularly employees with disabilities, in the user testing population will identify different issues and help to prevent future problems for a group that uses these tools on a day-to-day basis.

For new technologies, particularly those with limited accessibility information available, running user experience tests with disabled individuals can help to identify both barriers and helpful features, as well as offering insights into the advice of real users about possible accommodations or approaches to remediation. While users may not be able to provide guidance on the technical aspects of how to fix issues that arise, they can demonstrate needs and pain points that may otherwise go unnoticed. If it is not possible to run user testing on a new product during the evaluation process, it is worthwhile to seek out existing feedback from disabled users, such as product reviews written by them. Including the perspectives of disabled users can be invaluable when evaluating all technologies, but especially those that are newly emerging.

Find or Build Community

Community is a necessity for effective accessibility work, particularly for newly emerging technologies. It is impossible for any one person to be an expert on all aspects of accessibility, and being part of a community of like-minded practitioners is a wonderful way to learn from others and combine expertise together for a greater impact. There are many examples of the way community is at the center of accessibility work, from the efforts of the groups that create and continually update the WCAG and other resources available from W3C's WAI to new communities arising around the accessibility of XR and AI technologies. When it comes to emerging technologies, community can be particularly valuable because it offers a variety of perspectives and skills, as well as the ability to divide up tasks.

Though some of those working in libraries may be the only employee responsible for accessibility at their library, this need not be a barrier to finding a strong community. For those working at a library that is part of a larger institution, whether that is a university or a local government, there are opportunities to find accessibility experts and advocates in other departments who are facing similar questions and challenges. Additional opportunities exist in library systems and consortia. This can range from groups like the SUNY Library Accessibility Cohort, which had members from across the State University of New York campuses working together to achieve digital accessibility goals, to the work of organizations like the Library Accessibility Alliance, which grew out of work by the Big Ten Academic Alliance and now includes dozens of institutions. Professional organizations can also offer an avenue for this type of collaboration. Many professional groups for librarians have subcommittees or interest groups for members who are interested in various aspects of accessibility. Some of these groups are open to all librarians who are interested in contributing to their work, and not just those who work at member institutions. For example, the Digital Library Federation welcomes involvement from all interested participants regardless of membership status, and its Digital Accessibility Working Group offers opportunities to develop skills while making a real impact. Forming committees or interest groups through systems, consortia, or professional organizations can have the added benefit of bringing together professionals from different sizes and types of libraries, which is useful in brainstorming ideas and developing broadly applicable initiatives and resources.

There are opportunities for community beyond libraries as well. These can be found in related professional organizations for user experience and IT professionals. Even beyond these organizations, informal groups related to accessibility meet both virtually and in many cities around the world. Connecting with these groups can be a good way to find out about both technologies that are not yet common in libraries and new use cases that have not yet been introduced to libraries. There is a wealth of online forums, such as GitHub or Facebook groups, devoted to specific aspects of accessibility that can provide resources and support on both accessibility and emerging technologies. All of these opportunities for community have a lot to offer, particularly for those who are interested in expanding their accessibility skills.

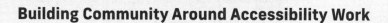

Building Community Around Accessibility Work

Interview with **Laura Harris**, *Web Services and Distance Learning Librarian, SUNY Oswego*

What drew you to accessibility work in libraries?

When I first got involved with accessibility work at the university level, I didn't have a strong interest in it. I was asked to join a workgroup focused on improving accessibility of course materials in online courses because of my role in supporting online learning. While I understood the importance of accessibility work, I didn't feel passionate about it in the beginning.

About a year or so later, my university received a complaint through the federal Office of Civil Rights—as did several other schools in the SUNY system. As a result, our campus workgroup began to grow, and our focus changed to providing education about accessibility practices to various campus constituencies.

One result of these complaints is that the SUNY system required campuses to complete IT-related accessibility plans. Campus libraries were required to complete a portion of this plan. I worked on that part of the campus accessibility plan with my library director, Sarah Weisman, and that was the start of my accessibility work in libraries specifically. Since then, I've continued to work with my library director and other people in the library to increase accessibility. I've also been able to connect with other librarians interested in accessibility through a SUNY-wide group that began in 2020.

While all of this was going on, there was another factor fueling my knowledge of, and interest in, accessibility work. For most of my nine years at SUNY Oswego, I have been the liaison to our teacher education programs. Almost every fall and spring semester, I have provided library instruction to a class focused on special education. This has provided me with many opportunities to learn more about specific disabilities.

My path into accessibility work wasn't intentional, but it's become an important part of both my personal and professional lives.

How have you built community around accessibility work in your library, on campus, and across SUNY?

As I mentioned previously, I was invited to join both campus-wide and SUNY-wide groups focused on accessibility work. In those cases, I benefited from the initiative of others. I hope I've contributed to those communities, but I didn't start them.

In 2023, my library director and I started a library-wide accessibility committee. We asked several librarians to be part of the committee because each of them had job responsibilities that we felt should include accessibility work. For example, our e-resources librarian was included because she is our primary contact with database vendors, and if we have accessibility needs related to those databases, she would be the person to contact the vendors. I'm a member of the committee in part because I manage the library's website, and it's my responsibility to make sure it follows web accessibility guidelines.

How has participating in the SUNY-wide library accessibility committee helped you to improve accessibility at your institution?

The SUNY-wide library accessibility committee is made up of librarians with a variety of different roles. This helped me to understand that accessibility work cannot be the work of just one librarian—it needs to be the work of many. This informed the creation of my library's accessibility committee.

The SUNY-wide library accessibility committee members have a broad base of expertise, which has been an invaluable resource for me. My colleagues have also

158 ●●● CHAPTER 8

shared outside professional development opportunities that have contributed to my understanding of disability and accessibility.

Describe the 10-Day Campus Accessibility Challenge that your institution created. What was the result of this work? Has it had a lasting impact?

Note: the following response draws from M. L. Thornton et al., "10-Day Campus Accessibility Challenge," *Journal of Postsecondary Education and Disability*, 36, no. 1 (2023): 23–39.

At SUNY Oswego, we have a series of professional development sessions that are offered before Spring semester, which are collectively called "Winter Breakout." We have a similar series offered after Spring semester, called "Spring Breakout." These sessions are provided for faculty and staff, by faculty and staff.

The campus accessibility workgroup has been offering Breakout sessions on accessibility topics for several years. During the fall 2020 semester, the workgroup started talking about what we could do differently for Winter Breakout 2021—we knew people were dealing with stress and burnout due to the pandemic. We were inspired by fitness challenges that are popular on social media; people are challenged to be consistent in an activity over a set period of time (often 30 days), and that activity may get progressively harder or more complex over the challenge period. They're also meant to be fun! Our challenge was two weeks (10 business days) and covered a variety of different accessibility topics. It was also open to students as well as faculty and staff.

Based on pre- and post-challenge surveys, we found that participants felt more confident in their accessibility skills after completing the challenge. Participants also commented that the challenge helped them to feel a sense of community around, and commitment to, accessibility work. While I hope we have had a lasting impact on the participants of the challenge, it definitely impacted the campus accessibility workgroup as well. We have continued to look for new ways to educate others on disability and accessibility, and we were inspired to create a full course. We are currently piloting this course, titled "Access: A Quest Toward Inclusion," and it will be available across SUNY campuses.

What advice do you have for those interested in finding their own supportive community to support accessibility work?

If you're very new to accessibility work, I think there are a lot of learning and networking opportunities within the librarian profession. You'll find many librarians with expertise in different areas of accessibility work. For example, there are many librarians who have written or presented about universal design for learning, a framework for inclusive instruction. Look for topics that interest you, or that are relevant to your work, and reach out to these experts if you have questions.

In some ways, I think accessibility work naturally leads to community-building. There are so many different disabilities, different accommodations, and different roles (students, faculty, staff, etc.) that it's impossible for one office or department to meet every need. It's important to learn what services are available on your campus, and to communicate what services the library can offer—so that offices can refer to one another to help meet people's accessibility needs. This will also illuminate gaps in services, and areas for potential advocacy.

Notes

1. Library Accessibility Alliance, www.libraryaccessibility.org; Digital Library Federation, "IT and Development," DLF Wiki, https://wiki.diglib.org/IT_and _Development.
2. Microsoft Inclusive Design, https://inclusive.microsoft.design/; GSA, "Universal Design and Accessibility," August 2023, www.section508.gov/develop/universal -design/.

CHAPTER 9

Accessibility of eXtended Reality

A child who uses a wheelchair attends the library's program built around a popular new augmented reality app.

A job seeker signs up for the library's virtual reality job-training program.

A blind student enrolls in a class that features a virtual reality tour of an archeological site as one of the course activities.

Over the past several years, eXtended reality, often abbreviated XR, has become an increasingly influential technology, including in library settings. XR refers to an array of technologies including augmented reality (AR), mixed reality (MR), and virtual reality (VR). All of these technologies create an altered reality for users, with AR adding elements to the existing environment; VR offering immersive elements, typically for multiple senses, to offer a completely new reality; and MR existing at a point on the spectrum between these two options. Collectively these technologies are sometimes also referred to as "immersive technologies." Throughout the last decade, XR has become more prevalent across sectors, including industry, education, and leisure, to name just a few. As its popularity has increased, libraries have also taken notice, with XR impacting programming and collections at all types of libraries. As libraries begin to explore the role they have in bringing XR to their communities, it is vital

162 ●●● CHAPTER 9

that accessibility is considered from the very start, just as it must be for other technologies, so that the library patrons in these scenarios are able to participate equitably. While approaches to XR accessibility are still developing, there are ways libraries can maximize inclusion at the same time as they adopt these new technologies.

▶ A Brief Background on XR

A complete discussion of XR technologies should be grounded in an understanding of the definitions and current status of each of the three technologies in turn. This helps to demonstrate the increasingly central role these technologies promise to play in the future in a host of fields. The similarities and differences among these three types of technologies can have significant implications for both their uses in libraries and efforts to ensure their accessibility.

Virtual Reality

Virtual reality (VR) can be used to refer to any means of immersing a person in a created reality that is different than their own. While current technologies may come to mind when thinking of VR, some have made compelling arguments that even stereoscopic photo viewers and panoramic paintings could be considered early attempts at creating these immersive virtual realities.[1] With the march forward of technology, virtual reality has become higher-tech and more immersive over time. Many of the current VR tools available to consumers consist of headsets but, despite the fact that visual information is typically central to VR experiences, this is far from the only sensory mode that can be included in such an experience. VR often provides other sensory inputs, such as immersive sound experiences and haptic feedback through gloves, vests, or even full-body suits. Newer technologies are even adding scents to virtual worlds through a device worn on or near the user's face.[2]

VR experiences can be used for a variety of purposes, from gaming and space or product design to training a wide range of professionals on technologies or interactions that are difficult to practice in the real world. In fact, flight simulator training was an early use of VR technologies,[3] and more recently VR's training applications have been expanded to include training for medical professionals, retail experiences for consumers, and much more.[4] Embodied Labs, a company founded by former librarian Erin Washington and her sister, offers "an immersive training platform that uses virtual reality technology to embody the perspectives and conditions of others" so as to allow medical students, caregivers, employees at companies serving disabled individuals, and others to simulatively experience a variety of health conditions, such as dementia, Parkinson's disease, vision loss, and more.[5] Research is also being conducted into its use in the treatment of some medical conditions.[6] With the continued interest in VR among researchers, corporations, and consumers, the uses of the technology are likely to continue to proliferate over time.

Augmented Reality

Unlike VR, *augmented reality (AR)* does not attempt to immerse users in an environment. Instead, AR seeks to add elements to the existing environment. The result is interactive digital content that is overlaid on top of the user's existing environment. This can be achieved through a variety of digital devices, including glasses, tablets, and smartphones. Typically, the digital content does not directly interact with the physical environment and is instead simply superimposed on top of the user's location. Frequently, AR experiences for tablets and smartphones are associated with specific apps, such as Pokémon GO. As with VR, AR can add content that interacts with a variety of senses. While visual content is commonly used by many of the most famous AR applications, auditory, haptic, and olfactory inputs are also possible.

And like VR, AR can be used in a wide variety of different ways. In addition to uses such as gaming and education, common consumer AR uses are navigation, such as in smartphone apps that superimpose arrows over a view of the user's current location; and marketing and retail uses, such as IKEA's augmented reality app that allows users to see furniture "in" their home.[7] In professional settings, AR can be used to help a variety of workers complete their tasks more efficiently, such as applications that help medical professionals find patients' veins or that help library workers shelf-read to find misplaced books.[8] Because AR applications can make use of technologies already owned by many consumers, such as smartphones and tablets, or those that can be used without obstructing views of the local environment, such as AR-enabled glasses, AR's uses have outstripped those of virtual reality. This more widespread adoption makes it likely that AR will continue to be influential across a variety of fields.

Mixed Reality

Researchers have noted that there is no single, universal definition of *mixed reality (MR)* and the terms *AR* and *MR* are used interchangeably by some, particularly those who are not technical experts,[9] which may cause confusion about this type of technology. For the purposes of a basic understanding of this technology, MR can be thought of as those applications that feature both VR and AR elements in a single product. The distinguishing feature of MR applications is that they allow the digital elements to interact with the physical world in a way that is generally absent in VR and AR applications. As with AR and VR, MR applications are most often focused on visual content, but they can feature content directed at any sense. An example of MR would be an app that allows users to create virtual content that they then associate with a specific location in their environment.

Classifying applications as AR, MR, or VR can be difficult, which is one reason why the overarching term *XR* is frequently used. As the W3C's Accessible Platform Architectures Working Group has noted of these technologies, "the important commonality between them [is] that they all offer some degree of spatial tracking with which to simulate a view of virtual content, as well as navigation and interaction with the objects within these environments."[10] This brings them together technologically and means that the lines between the separate technologies can blur in individual examples. It also leads to overlapping accessibility issues, barriers, and best practices that can apply to the technologies regardless of their exact point on the XR spectrum.

For libraries, many different types of XR applications can have applications for programming, collections, and more. Because such a wide range of experiences can include XR and because all of these types of XR can include the stimulation of various senses, different XR experiences may be inaccessible to different groups of users. For example, XR experiences that include sound as a key component could be inaccessible to users who are d/Deaf or hard of hearing, while another VR experience might not include sound but may instead require specific motions, presenting an issue for users with mobility impairments. In addition, the nature of XR means that both the software and hardware must be accessible for all users to have equitable access to everything that the experience has to offer. This means it is important to carefully evaluate individual XR experiences, tools, and resources to make sure they are widely accessible before adopting them in the library. This will only become more important as XR makes further inroads into fields like education, health care, and job training. Given the diverse uses being developed for XR technology, it is critical that it be inclusive and accessible to all users so that no one is excluded from the benefits this technology can bring.

▶ XR in Libraries

As XR has grown in popularity, a wide range of use cases have emerged for it. Many different types of libraries have integrated XR applications into their work in various ways. They range from supporting researchers and designers working on XR projects, to using XR to share their collections in new ways, to hosting programming centered around XR experiences. The many ways libraries have integrated this technology to better serve their communities demonstrate the diverse uses of XR and the varied ways libraries can support their patrons. This also gives a sense of the importance of designing these efforts for accessibility, given that it can touch on so many priorities and services libraries offer for their communities. As XR continues to develop, the number of ways libraries find to integrate these technologies into their offerings will also continue to expand. It is vital that accessibility is integrated from the beginning of these efforts so all users can have the same opportunities to be entertained, educated, and supported by XR technology.

XR and Programming

For libraries of all types, XR technologies open new avenues for programming that can appeal to a wide swath of the community. AR apps have proved particularly popular as the basis for library programming at all levels.

When the game Pokémon GO first emerged, many libraries jumped at the opportunity to embrace this new technology to engage patrons of all ages. The Skokie (IL) Public Library designed Pokémon GO Safaris for elementary school students that combined playing the game with learning about local landmarks.[11] Beyond this popular app, there are other apps and tools that can serve as the basis of fun programs. The White Plains (NY) Public Library used Quiver to allow patrons to "make physical coloring-book pages become fully animated, three-dimensional models," which combined a creative element with learning about AR technology.[12] These are only two examples of the creative ways libraries have built programming around a variety of XR applications and software. AR apps for mobile devices have been particularly popular for this purpose because many libraries offer tablets and devices for checkout that can support these apps. Plus, a wide range of patrons have their own smartphones and devices that support these types of apps. XR technologies can also help libraries in offering programming around job preparedness. For example, the North Las Vegas Library District and the Carson City Library, both in Nevada, are launching a new program of virtual reality field trips by which adults working on job training and re-skilling can learn about in-demand jobs across the state.[13]

Even academic libraries have gotten in on the fun. A number of academic libraries have experimented with using XR tools for one specific type of library programming: library orientations. At Florida Southern College, these efforts were inspired by the enormous popularity of Pokémon GO.[14] Their library event ultimately incorporated both AR, using the Aurasma app to allow students to complete a scavenger hunt featuring augmented reality elements created by the library team; and VR, using Google Cardboard to view one of two *New York Times* VR videos.[15] The team at Cal Poly Pomona was more than just inspired by Pokémon GO; they actually redesigned their existing paper-based orientation to instead require students to complete tasks aligned with the ACRL's Framework for Information Literacy in order to find Pokestops in the library, making an orientation experience that was completely Pokémon-themed.[16] A small-scale research project conducted at Rutgers University–Camden found some evidence that library orientations that integrate AR may result in an increase in "students' perception that librarians and staff want to help them,"[17] which suggests that these efforts may be worth further exploration in the future. XR technologies can open new avenues to engage students and build their excitement about the library's offerings.

XR and Collections

Beyond library programs, XR can also be used to connect patrons with collections. In a high school library environment, for example, Kai Rush researched using AR to connect reluctant readers to book trailers and additional content about books to help them connect with books to read for pleasure.[18] Connecting patrons with items in the collection can even extend to rare, fragile, and historical materials that might not be widely usable by patrons. AR has been used by many libraries to add new dimensions to library exhibitions. The National Library of Medicine in the United States, the National Library of Korea, and the National Library of Sweden have all used AR technologies to offer supplemental information and, in particular, multimedia content that connects users with historical events and items in new ways.[19] For these organizations, the use of AR technology can help them to achieve their public education goals by making historical materials and media interpreting those materials more widely available and engaging. At Washington College's Archives and Special Collections, the team took this idea a step further in creating their Augmented Archives project. Rather than simply adding AR to exhibitions, they offered opportunities for students to "receive training in both the investigative curation skills and technological proficiencies needed to plan and execute an AR-enhanced exhibit."[20] These are only a few examples of the ways that AR has been used by libraries in exhibitions. Beyond these, XR technologies have been used at different types of museums and libraries to offer new ways to experience time periods, locations, and items that would otherwise be impossible to experience. New approaches to these applications are emerging all the time, which suggests that these sorts of opportunities to use XR technologies to interact with, curate, and share archival and special materials in libraries are only getting started.

XR and Research

Libraries can also become integrated into the research that their communities are undertaking with XR technologies. A great example of this is the Therapeutic Games and Applications Laboratory (The GApp Lab), which

168 ••• CHAPTER 9

is a collaborative effort between the Entertainment Arts & Engineering program, the Center for Medical Innovation, and the Spencer S. Eccles Health Sciences Library at the University of Utah.[21] The librarians are integrated into multiple aspects of this work and contribute to grant-writing, literature reviews, research study design, data management, and even teaching.[22] By embracing the newly emerging technology of VR, librarians are able to embed themselves within patron research and support this work in a multifaceted way. For campuses with faculty working on XR research, design, and development, this can be an important way of staying relevant to new types of academic work.

These examples are only a few of the ways XR technologies might be used in libraries in the future to educate, engage, and excite patrons of all ages. While these current and upcoming applications are exciting, it is important to ensure that those who adopt these applications in libraries consider how many patrons will be able to participate in the experiences. This is why it is imperative to keep accessibility at the top of mind when working on XR projects in libraries. As XR touches more different library programs and services, including those that are foundational to library use, such as orientations, the tools used must ensure that all patrons will be able to participate in these experiences regardless of ability.

❯ Accessibility Practices for XR

In order to ensure that XR is developed in a way that is inclusive of people with a variety of disabilities and who use various assistive technologies, it is vital to consider accessibility throughout the process of creating XR hardware and software. Because XR can involve different senses and can require greater manual dexterity than other types of software interactions, there are many ways that it can be inaccessible if inclusion is not a focus during the development process. The authors of the IEEE's (Institute of Electrical and Electronics Engineers') Global Initiative on Ethics of Extended Reality report summarized these issues clearly:

> XR technologies are especially at risk for the exclusion of people with disabilities based on their immersive nature. For example, consider an

adventure game with a sword-wielding hero. With a traditional 2D interface, a player might press a button to swing their sword; in an XR version, they might physically swing their controller, an act requiring much more physical dexterity. If the designers do not consider an accessible alternative, many disabled gamers would be excluded.

XR also requires rethinking existing accessibility features for immersive formats. Features like captions are well understood on rectangular 2D screens but present many new challenges in XR. For example, how should a user be cued to a speaker behind them? Should captions appear at a set distance and risk being occluded by other content, or render in front and risk disorienting the user?[23]

While the general principles of accessible design, such as designing with a range of assistive technologies in mind and designing so that there are multiple ways to interact with a program using different senses, remain the same, accessibility is nevertheless often overlooked. Examples of this inaccessibility exist across different types of XR experiences. For instance, Pokémon GO had significant accessibility issues when it was first released, including its lack of support for Apple's VoiceOver screen reader,[24] its features that were not accessible to those with color perception disabilities,[25] and its offering of limited options for those who cannot walk long distances.[26] While these examples come from a single game, they are hardly limited to only this one AR app. In fact, the reason why Pokémon GO did not support Apple's VoiceOver screen reader at launch was that the Unity Engine used by the developers to create the game was incompatible with mobile screen readers.[27] Fortunately, since the debut of Unity 2023.2 Tech Stream, this problem has been addressed and screen reader compatibility continues to improve with new releases of the Unity Engine.[28] But this is just a single tool, and it is imperative that the accessibility of the final product becomes a priority across development tools. Moreover, the development tools can also have barriers that prevent users with disabilities from designing and creating their own XR experiences.

To avoid these potential problems for both creators and users, experts in the field have been working on tools that will make XR accessibility more straightforward for all developers and designers. This process has been somewhat similar to the process through which WCAG emerged, in that experts in both the field of accessibility and the field of XR have come together to consider what accessibility and inclusion require for XR experiences and environments. Currently, there are W3C working groups that produce resources to improve the accessibility of XR. The Accessible Platform Architectures Working Group is responsible for developing a document entitled the XR Accessibility User Requirements, which outlines what individuals with disabilities need to be able to fully interact with any type of XR technology.[29] This list of requirements is not the same as the guidelines or success criteria found in WCAG 2.2, but is instead designed to inform developers about the needs of disabled users. Since these needs have often been overlooked in XR design, this resource is intended to offer a basic understanding of the existing, often unmet needs as a first step to greater accessibility. When individuals with disabilities and other accessibility experts are not included in the design team, this type of resource can be vital to raising awareness of common accessibility barriers and approaches for inclusive development.

The W3C is far from the only group working on this topic. XR Access, a research consortium based at Cornell Tech, has also taken the lead in both conducting research and curating resources in this area.[30] Founded in 2019 by Shiri Azenkot, a faculty member at Cornell Tech, and Larry Goldberg, the former head of accessibility at Verizon Media, the consortium has worked to create a strong community around the accessibility of XR technologies, including through an annual conference focused on this topic.[31] Their Prototype for the People program "aims to fix the lack of accessible open-source solutions for XR by creating a grassroots campaign to accelerate open-source development and prototyping," and specifically urges developers to involve individuals with disabilities both as co-designers and testers.[32] This approach is a particularly important aspect of their work because inclusion throughout the design process is key to optimizing the final product for accessibility and is also a necessary step toward making the community of XR developers more inclusive for those with disabilities. XR Access has partnered with the XR Association, an industry group to promote the development and adoption of XR, to create the XRAccessibility Project on GitHub. This project is an open-source repository that collects standards, guidelines, and resources that help XR developers to make their products inclusive and accessible.[33]

Of particular note, this GitHub project includes resources that are specifically aimed at disabled developers,[34] to improve the accessibility of the creation of XR experiences as well as the accessibility of these products for end users. Through this work, XR Access is helping to make sure that individuals with disabilities have access at all points in the development ecosystem, from serving as the creators of XR experiences to making use of these experiences as consumers. Not only will this lead to expanded opportunities for these disabled individuals, but it will also help to integrate inclusion into the industry in ways that are more authentic and better meet the needs of users with disabilities.

More informal opportunities for the community have also emerged for those working in the XR field in the form of groups like the A11yVR group, which brings together practitioners from around the world to better understand XR accessibility.[35] Resources from adjacent areas can also be useful in working toward more inclusive design for immersive technologies. An excellent example of this is the Game Accessibility Guidelines, which provides for accessible design in all types of digital gaming.[36] Many of these guidelines are broad enough to be applicable even to immersive experiences without gaming elements. Taken together, all of these formal and informal resources can help those who want to work on improved XR accessibility at all levels, from developing new hardware and software to evaluating immersive technologies for use in libraries.

▶ XR Accessibility Work in Libraries

Because libraries primarily use XR technologies to collect, share, and teach, it is often difficult for librarians to directly impact the accessibility of those technologies. For librarians working on the creation of XR resources, it is vital to integrate accessibility into all stages of the development process, just as with other technologies. Yet, even those who do not develop XR resources can still have an impact on accessibility. When collecting XR applications and building programming around them, accessibility and inclusion must be central considerations. And there is definitely evidence that some institutions are starting to consider these issues. The team at Florida Southern College's Roux Library acknowledged the potential issues presented by their

XR-based orientation activity and noted the potential to develop a process for having "student employees available as 'buddies' to assist patrons with visual or other impairments" in future iterations of the event, though they did not integrate this accessibility feature into their initial program.[37]

Beyond this example, the adoption of XR technologies in libraries has not always been accompanied by a corresponding attention to accessibility. Research done by Zack Lischer-Katz and Jasmine Clark found a "majority of institutions surveyed do not have policies or dedicated staff to support accessibility for XR technologies," and only about a quarter of those surveyed were "very familiar" or "extremely familiar" with the accessibility challenges presented by XR technologies.[38] This suggests that there is significant work still to be done to ensure all immersive technologies in libraries are accompanied by appropriate support for accessibility.

Thankfully, this work is starting to be done, and those who are working in this area have developed practices that can be applied at other institutions. Jasmine Clark's work with the team at Temple University's Loretta C. Duckworth Scholars Studio is a central example of this.[39] She has not only conducted user testing with disabled users to develop an understanding of the accessibility challenges present in VR technologies, but has also used the results of these tests to develop and implement practices to improve accessibility. In particular, this information led to the development of "an auditing workflow that would allow any staff member or student worker to examine newly licensed VR experiences and produce an accessibility report," along with an exploration of how this could inform collection development choices.[40] This not only demonstrates the value in conducting tests with users with various disabilities and needs to evaluate new technologies, but also shows how this testing can immediately translate to improved practices. For those who are not able to conduct user tests, an alternative approach is to bring in an outside accessibility expert to evaluate VR practices for opportunities to improve accessibility, as has been done at the University of Oklahoma Libraries.[41] These two examples also point to the value of developing connections within libraries working on accessibility improvements for immersive technologies to share best practices and collaborate on these improvements.

In the future, immersive technologies and their uses in libraries are certain to continue to evolve quickly. It is vital libraries set a foundation for accessibility at all stages in the workflows around the purchase and use of XR technologies in libraries. Carefully considering these topics now and integrating accessibility into decision-making processes will ensure that inclusive choices are made. In addition, helping to advance the accessibility of immersive technologies can have a real impact on their future development trajectory by conveying the importance of accessibility to students learning about XR, researchers studying these technologies, and vendors selling the related hardware and software.

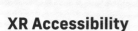

XR Accessibility

Interview with **Jasmine Clark**, *Digital Scholarship Librarian, Temple University*

What do you see as the accessibility opportunities provided by XR in general and XR in libraries?
I think that the opportunities offered by XR technologies greatly differ depending on the technology. While there have been promising tests with VR around spatial orientation for visually impaired users, as well as interesting therapeutic applications for users with neurological/psychological disabilities, I believe that most of the feasible, immediate opportunities in accessibility lie in AR. AR is already being widely used in commerce (e.g., options to view furniture in your space virtually before purchasing), guided tours (e.g., tours that overlay 3D models of historic buildings and structures onto current environments), and gaming (e.g., Pokémon Go!). AR can be used with a smartphone, which many users already have, and avoids issues with having to learn new accessibility features on a separate, and often expensive, new device. In addition, the ability to take the virtual into the physical expands the opportunities for users to receive assistance in their day-to-day lives. For example, suppose a patron visiting your library needs things like additional signage or real-time warnings about physical accessibility barriers. In that case, they can have those things pop up in an AR app without

174 ••• CHAPTER 9

obstructing their view or slowing them down. They can zoom in on signage, bring it to eye height, or otherwise interact with it without navigating crowds or physical barriers. I am not saying that technologies like VR, 360-degree video, or CAVEs (Cave Automatic Virtual Environments) don't have accessibility applications. However, AR has a lower barrier to entry.

What do you see as the biggest accessibility challenges around XR in libraries?

Development support is a major barrier for most libraries. Most XR isn't designed with accessibility in mind, so libraries will often need to develop their own experiences, find existing extensions and kits to correct specific issues, or develop their own workarounds for their users. Whether they contract a company or hire a developer, developer time is expensive, and development is more than coding. UX testing, experiential design, and project management for XR are all pretty specialized and necessary. Having access to all of this will only be feasible for libraries with a certain level of funding. In addition to all of this, XR accessibility standards aren't particularly well developed yet. This means that librarians have to have enough knowledge to audit and address XR accessibility problems with very little guidance. This is another barrier as well.

What is your advice for librarians who want to make their XR collections more accessible?

The first thing librarians will have to do is familiarize themselves with existing accessibility guidelines and design principles. There are not well-developed standards for XR, which covers a range of technologies and devices. Librarians will have to familiarize themselves with what exists and adapt it to what they have. Standards like the Game Accessibility Guidelines (gameaccessibilityguidelines.com), Xbox Accessibility Guidelines (learn.microsoft.com/en-us/gaming/accessibility/guidelines), XR Accessibility User Requirements (www.w3.org/TR/xaur/), and Web Content Accessibility Guidelines (www.w3.org/TR/WCAG22/) are all useful starting points for those looking to learn more. Once familiar with accessibility guidelines, librarians will need to do some basic auditing of their XR collections. This means playing any games/going through any experiences, watching playthroughs/walkthroughs, and keeping a list of important warnings for patrons. Training volunteers, student workers, and other staff will also be necessary because all of this is more feasible when the work is split.

What are the best resources for librarians who want to learn more about XR accessibility and advocate for accessibility in XR work at their institution?

The guidelines I've listed above are a good place to start. In addition, community groups are always a good place to learn, ask questions, and keep up to date with efforts in the space. Some great starting options are:

- The Big Ten Library Accessibility Alliance often hosts webinars and does a lot of advocacy work (btaa.org/library/programs-and-services/reports)
- Educause—Games and Learning (connect.educause.edu/community -home?CommunityKey=87949950-e350-4ce3-9b77-3a3429e96cd4)
- Educause—IT Accessibility (connect.educause.edu/community-home? CommunityKey=cbf79115-53ad-4797-a495-285ee543c95d)
- Educause—XR (Extended Reality) Community Group (www.educause.edu/ community/xr-extended-reality-community-group)
- W3C—Immersive Web Working Group (www.w3.org/groups/wg/immersive-web/)
- XR Access (xraccess.org)

What are your hopes for future improvements around XR accessibility, particularly in libraries?

I would like to see more collaboration across libraries. Libraries have always functioned via consortia and shared agreements. However, that hasn't extended to the emerging technology space yet. Pushes for shared licensing, funding, and knowledge would greatly develop XR for the public and education.

Notes

1. Virtual Reality Society, "History of Virtual Reality," 2017, www.vrs.org.uk/virtual -reality/history.html.
2. Simon Makin, "Virtual Reality System Lets You Stop and Smell the Roses," *Scientific American*, May 9, 2023, www.scientificamerican.com/article/virtual-reality-system -lets-you-stop-and-smell-the-roses/.

3. H. Pope, "Introduction to Virtual and Augmented Reality," *Library Technology Reports* 54, no. 6 (2018): 6.
4. Randi Q. Mao, Lucy Lan, Jeffrey Kay, Ryan Lohre, Olufemi R. Ayeni, and Danny P. Goel, "Immersive Virtual Reality for Surgical Training: A Systematic Review," *Journal of Surgical Research* 268 (2021): 40–58; Kate Schaefer, "Exterior Displays," in *Swipe, Scan, Shop: Interactive Visual Merchandising* (London: Bloomsbury Visual Arts, 2021), 156–75, http://dx.doi.org/10.5040/9781350092891.ch-007.
5. Hayleigh Moore, "MLIS Alumni Spotlight: The Joys of Aging Using VR – Erin Washington, MLIS '09," University of Maryland, College of Information, April 13, 2022, https://ischool.umd.edu/news/mlis-alumni-spotlight-the-joys-of-aging-using-vr-erin-washington-mlis-09/; Embodied Labs, www.embodiedlabs.com/.
6. See, for example, Maria V. Nararro-Haro et al., "The Use of Virtual Reality to Facilitate Mindfulness Skills Training in Dialectical Behavioral Therapy for Borderline Personality Disorder: A Case Study," *Frontiers in Psychology* 7 (2016): 1573; Fengfeng Ke, Jewoong Moon, and Zlatko Sokolikj, "Virtual Reality-Based Social Skills Training for Children with Autism Spectrum Disorder," *Journal of Special Education Technology* 37, no. 1 (2022): 49–62; Anita Gupta, Kevin Scott, and Matthew Dukewich, "Innovative Technology Using Virtual Reality in the Treatment of Pain: Does It Reduce Pain via Distraction, or Is There More to It?" *Pain Medicine* 19, no. 1 (2018): 151–59.
7. Selcen Ozturkcan, "Service Innovation: Using Augmented Reality in the IKEA Place App," *Journal of Information Technology Teaching Cases* 11, no. 1 (2021): 8–13.
8. M. Taha, M. Ibrahim, and H. H. Zayed, "Digital Vein Mapping Using Augmented Reality," *International Journal of Intelligent Engineering & Systems* 13, no. 6 (2020); L. Aaronson, "Video: Augmented Reality App for Librarians Instantly Shows Which Books Are Misfiled," *Popular Science*, April 21, 2011, www.popsci.com/technology/article/2011-04/augmented-reality-app-librarians-instantly-shows-which-books-are-misfiled/.
9. Maximilian Speicher, Brian D. Hall, and Michael Nebeling, "What Is Mixed Reality?" in "Proceedings of the 2019 CHI Conference on Human Factors in Computing Systems," 2019, 4, https://dl.acm.org/doi/10.1145/3290605.3300767.
10. Joshue O'Connor et al., eds., "XR Accessibility User Requirements," August 25, 2021, W3C, www.w3.org/TR/xaur/.
11. Carli Spina, "Pokémon GO: What Do Librarians Need to Know?" *School Library Journal*, July 12, 2016. www.libraryjournal.com/story/pokemon-go-what-do-librarians-need-to-know.
12. Austin Olney, "Augmented Reality: All about Holograms," in *Beyond Reality: Augmented, Virtual, and Mixed Reality in the Library*, ed. Kenneth J. Varnum (Chicago: American Library Association, 2019), 6.
13. Matt Enis, "Nevada Libraries Launch Workforce Development Program with VR, Librarians-in-Residence," *Library Journal*, July 25, 2024, www.libraryjournal.com/story/news/nevada-libraries-launch-workforce-development-program-with-vr-librarians-in-residence.
14. J. N. Hornick and S. Wade, "Augmenting Orientation: Animating an Interactive Welcome Event at an Academic Library with AR and VR," in *Augmented and Virtual*

Reality in Libraries, ed. J. P. Van Arnhem, C. Elliott, and M. Rose (Rowman & Littlefield, 2018), 74.

15. Hornick and Wade, "Augmenting Orientation," 74.

16. K. A. Smith and P. R. Hottinger, "Gotta Catch 'em All: A Case Study about Cal Poly Pomona's Pokémon GO AR Orientation," in *Augmented and Virtual Reality in Libraries*, ed. J. P. Van Arnhem, C. Elliott, and M. Rose (Rowman & Littlefield, 2018), 145–58.

17. S. Kannegiser, "Effects of an Augmented Reality Library Orientation on Anxiety and Self-Efficacy: An Exploratory Study," *College & Research Libraries* 82, no. 3 (2021): 361.

18. Kai Rush, "Augmented Reality (AR): A School Library App to Engage High School Reluctant Readers to Read for Pleasure" (Graduate Research Theses & Dissertations, 2017), 1586, https://huskiecommons.lib.niu.edu/allgraduate -thesesdissertations/1586.

19. Ellora Barman, "Augmented Reality in Libraries," IFLA, June 5, 2023, www.ifla.org/ news/augmented-reality-in-libraries/.

20. Heather Calloway and Raven Bishop, "Augmented Archives: Engaging Students in Archives and Special Collections through Augmented Reality Technology," in *Augmented and Virtual Reality in Libraries*, ed. J. P. Van Arnhem, C. Elliott, and M. Rose (Rowman & Littlefield, 2018), 94.

21. Spencer S. Eccles Health Sciences Library, GApp Lab, University of Utah, https:// library.med.utah.edu/synapse/gapp/.

22. Brandon Patterson et al., "Play, Education, and Research: Exploring Virtual Reality through Libraries," in *Beyond Reality: Augmented, Virtual, and Mixed Reality in the Library*, ed. Kenneth J. Varnum (Chicago: American Library Association, 2019), 54.

23. Dylan Fox and Isabel Guenette Thornton, "Extended Reality (XR) Ethics and Diversity, Inclusion, and Accessibility," IEEE Standards Association, 2022, https:// standards.ieee.org/wp-content/uploads/2022/04/Ethics_Diversity_Inclusion _Accessibility.pdf.

24. Lee Huffman and Aaron Preece, "Pokemon GO: Elevating the Conversation around Accessible Gaming," American Foundation for the Blind, www.afb.org/ aw/17/9/15295.

25. Alex Barker, "Pokémon Go: Are Incense and Street View the Key to More Inclusivity for Disabled People?" AbilityNet, September 4, 2016, https://abilitynet.org.uk/ news-blogs/pok%C3%A9mon-go-are-incense-and-street-view-key-more- inclusivity-disabled-people.

26. Kittypokemonsalot, "Let's Talk About Accessibility and Pokémon GO," GOHub. May 29, 2021, https://pokemongohub.net/post/article/opinion/lets-talk-about -accessibility-and-pokemon-go/.

27. Julia Perdigueiro, "A Look at Mobile Screen Reader Support in the Unity Engine," Unity, January 19, 2024, https://unity.com/blog/engine-platform/mobile-screen -reader-support-in-unity.

28. Perdigueiro, "Mobile Screen Reader Support."

29. O'Connor et al., eds., "XR Accessibility User Requirements."

30. XR Access, "About XR Access," https://live-xraccess.pantheonsite.io/about/.

31. XR Access, "About XR Access," https://live-xraccess.pantheonsite.io/.

32. XR Access, "Prototype for the People," https://xraccess.org/workstreams/prototype-for-the-people/.
33. XR Association and XR Access, "The XRAccessibility Project," https://github.com/XRAccessibility/xraccessibility.github.io.
34. XR Association and XR Access, "Resources for Disabled Developers," The XRAccessibility Project, https://github.com/XRAccessibility/xraccessibility.github.io?tab=readme-ov-file#resources-for-disabled-developers.
35. A11yVR Accessibility Virtual Reality Group, www.meetup.com/a11yvr/.
36. Game Accessibility Guidelines, https://gameaccessibilityguidelines.com/.
37. Hornick and Wade, "Augmenting Orientation," 89.
38. Zack Lischer-Katz and Jasmine Clark, "XR Accessibility Initiatives in Academic Libraries," *Proceedings of the Association for Information Science and Technology* 58, no. 1 (2021): 780–83.
39. Lischer-Katz and Clark, "XR Accessibility Initiatives."
40. Lischer-Katz and Clark, "XR Accessibility Initiatives."
41. Lischer-Katz and Clark, "XR Accessibility Initiatives."

●●●

CHAPTER 10

Artificial Intelligence, Libraries, and Accessibility

A recent library science grad is asked to complete a task for which she needs Python. While she knows code, she isn't an expert on accessibility. She wonders if she can get help on coding from ChatGPT.

A local art historian is applying for a grant. His application must be fully accessible if he hopes to receive government funding. He thinks about how AI can help him create alt-text for his images.

A local group wants to partner with the public library for a League of Women Voters event. They want the widest possible audience to participate, but they are not able to fund a sign language interpreter. They suggest using AI to live caption the event.

Artificial intelligence (AI) is growing at an unprecedented rate. Back in 1982, Buckminster Fuller noted that "until 1900, human knowledge doubled approximately every century. By the end of World War II knowledge was doubling every 25 years."[1] The rise of artificial intelligence that is generative in nature compounds this acceleration beyond any predictions or calculations. The current momentum is dizzying. According to Statista, the adoption of ChatGPT was exponentially faster than any main online service, including Instagram, which took only 2.5 months to reach one million users. By contrast, ChatGPT launched in November 2022, and in only five days had reached that same threshold.[2]

180 ●●● CHAPTER 10

While ChatGPT reflects a new era of AI development, AI itself is nothing new. It has existed for decades and most of us depend on it daily: facial and voice recognition for phones, streaming recommendations, and even personal AI DJs to mix your daily vibe based on "liked" songs. AI holds tremendous potential; yet it is also regarded as an existential threat. The way models are trained can be rife with issues of bias or even risks to human health. The result is an AI tool that may lack discretion when carrying out a task, or one which compounds bias and stereotypes. Furthermore, ingested texts and information (even when used to discover potential pitfalls) become inextricably part of the AI corpus, leaving vulnerabilities that creators don't yet understand but which certainly involve privacy and intellectual property rights.

This chapter focuses on how librarians might use AI technology to ensure that our libraries, collections, and services are more accessible while staying aware of its potential risks.

❱ What Is AI?

Artificial intelligence (AI) is a machine or computer's ability to learn, problem-solve, and act in ways that would typically require human intelligence. These technologies can replace human effort in completing time-consuming, labor-intensive, or complex tasks. A system that learns from input and predicts based on what it has learned would qualify as AI. The term *intelligence* is largely colloquial and not entirely accurate. Tools that automate (performing tasks based on instructions) alone are not considered AI. The tool must learn and adapt to the users' needs to be considered AI. Plenty of AI tools exist in our everyday lives that accurately predict based on the large language models that form the basis for those predictions. That said, natural language processing is not yet completely reliable. Queries written in natural language often fail to provide robust and relevant results unless the natural language includes specific and unique terms defined for the tool.

Virtual assistants like Siri, Alexa, and Google Assistant fall under several categories and are partially AI (through the subset of machine learning) and partially automation. Asking a virtual assistant to put an item on your grocery list is mere automation (you are telling the tool what to do). Asking that virtual assistant to predict what groceries you might need based on past purchases is predictive based on an algorithm (perhaps the average time it takes to consume a good and the amount of time passed since that good was last purchased). Asking the virtual assistant to create a grocery list focused on Portuguese delicacies, taking into account your health restrictions and what you likely have in your pantry and based on past purchases, is a more complex, time-consuming task that would qualify as AI with a dash of machine learning (ML). Here the system learns from the input data and considers a set of criteria you provide, resulting in a more robust answer based on your interactions, behavior, needs, and past purchases. And it does all this in seconds, saving you, the user, the twenty minutes (or more) it might have taken you to create the same list with the same criteria. The possibilities are infinite.

Why is it important to understand what AI is and isn't? This distinction is crucial for librarians to understand so that we can appropriately leverage this technology. As AI becomes more informed and nuanced, librarians could use AI to create, correct, catalog, and manage information in ways that, before AI, would have been nearly impossible given staffing levels and diminished budgets. Could the technology help us with staffing issues at service desks or streamline vacation schedules in mere moments? Could the deep learning that AI is capable of help us predict or correct biased subject headings as our language shifts over time? As new AI products become available, could we use them to increase accessibility and level the playing field for all our users? All these things are possible if librarians weigh the risks and head off potential issues of privacy and bias.

❯ Risks of AI

We mention the risks of AI throughout this chapter, but it bears further and deeper explanation. Certainly, there is a great deal of discussion around this topic as part of the zeitgeist

Job Risks

As AI replaces some of our processes, administrators might be lulled into complacency about the wider work of librarianship. While AI might be able to analyze and create metadata for large volumes of archival records,

182 ••• CHAPTER 10

for example, the fundamental value a trained archivist brings in contextualizing the collection might be at risk.[3] As institutions tout the ability of AI to replace employees, they also often overlook the skills needed to create successful prompts to get the desired output from AI. Where AI is adopted in libraries, it is important to ensure that it is used to support employees and not to replace them.

Hiring Risks

AI is being used as a frontline tool for hiring when there is a large pool of candidates. This technology still misses a lot and can have built-in biases. Some hiring tools require the user to speak to the camera head-on. However, if the algorithm is set to rank lower anyone with "shifty eyes," for example, nystagmus may be more to blame than any perceived avoidant behavior. The candidate might be a perfect match and still be passed over because of this. The same could be said for someone who is neurodivergent. They may be the perfect candidate but be unable to present well for the camera.

Hallucination Risks

Most AI systems still hallucinate, making up information such as citations, words, and even additional limbs in some generative AI examples. This is more common than most users realize. As librarians employ AI to help with tasks such as coding, we need to consider the risks of hallucinations and how we can test to ensure that we are not including them in the final product of whatever we do.

Bias Risks

Many large language models carry over the biases included in the corpus of that model. If there is cultural bias, for example, on what constitutes beauty as a concept, how might that carry over into the generative images, translations, or alt-text descriptions that AI might be used to create?

Overreliance Risks

Librarians may come to depend on AI to streamline processes, like accessibility testing or remediation. Most of the literature focuses on risks such as privacy or bias, but there is a human risk here of complacency in over-relying on technology to replace human judgment, particularly when employees are stretched thin.

Privacy, Data Security, and Intellectual Property Risks

When librarians engage AI for tasks, are they thinking carefully about the kinds of tasks and the risks taken with user privacy, intellectual property, or data security? Where are the servers holding the data you have inputted? Does everything automatically become part of the corpus for the model? If we are working to use AI to write alternative text for a local author's images for their new book, are we risking that author's intellectual property when we feed the images into the AI tool? These and many other questions will need to be considered. Currently, there are a number of ongoing lawsuits regarding the intellectual property issues around AI.[4]

Environmental Risks

In addition to the risks previously outlined, many have raised environmental concerns about AI as well. From the construction of the equipment and data centers that house the servers hosting AI tools to the energy it takes to run these data centers, there are several ways AI can have a negative impact on the environment, as the UN Environment Programme has highlighted.[5] This impact can have disproportionate effects across the globe, which magnifies these concerns.[6] It is difficult to generalize about this impact, since it can be significantly different depending on the type of AI application used,[7] but it is an important factor to consider when discussing AI.

▶ Benefits of AI

Of course, artificial intelligence can be useful for automating services in areas where a lack of subject-specific training, or even a lack of coding knowledge, can be bolstered. Given that librarians are at the forefront of information equity, centered on usability, and are in tune with user needs, Martin Frické notes of librarians:

> They are ideal partners to AI to bring out the best in this information with all its aspects, challenges, and facets. And, on the other side of this,

there are many AI and ML technologies that have the potential to improve librarianship. There is an opportunity for synergy or symbiosis.[8]

While the proponents and creators of current AI models acknowledge the potential drawbacks, they hold fast to the idea that "AI may well be a bridge to a newly prosperous era of greatly reduced human suffering."[9] AI holds a great deal of potential to improve our work and our processes. In the book *Artificial Intelligence and Librarianship*, Frické projects that AI can be useful to libraries in myriad ways. Frické explores how AI technologies can streamline back-end processes, a benefit that means our time and energy could be invested more in issues like accessibility. He cautions that we "need to check that the improvements are available to all, including people with disabilities."[10] (See chapter 8, "Accessibility of Emerging Technologies," for a fuller discussion of how to approach adopting new technologies.)

▶ Large-Scale OCR Projects

Recent efforts to use AI to reduce workload and increase accessibility include OCR at scale on documents that previously remained unreadable. Project Gutenberg makes thousands of books in the public domain available in audiobook format using AI-enhanced processes. Clearly, using AI to scan inaccessible texts allows more materials to be available to our patrons than ever before. It is still the case, though, that newer content will mostly be available as an audiobook through specific disability-related efforts like the Talking Book Library, a free library service for New Yorkers who can't use print materials "due to a visual, physical or reading disability."[11]

Leveraging AI technology can speed up the pace of making more materials accessible. The time savings can allow librarians to promote relevant accessible text and audiobook projects, ensuring higher adoption and even integration with curricula, giving users choices where none had existed before. Librarians must know which large-scale OCR projects exist, what level of accessibility they attain, and whether there are known barriers. Crafting guides replete with accessible resources that are appropriate to the population being served can reduce barriers for patrons in ways we may never fully realize simply because fewer barriers need to be reported.

When accessibility goes well, things are quiet. When there are barriers, more and more, patrons should feel empowered to report those. Librarians need to be ready to field these issues and understand where they can attain equal access to the items or determine equivalent alternatives. Even as AI feels like an existential threat, it seems like a delayed one as librarians will always have a great deal to do in learning about, beta-testing, curating, and promoting such resources.

▶ AI-Enhanced OCR and Alternative Text

Much like Project Gutenberg has used AI to scan and "read" items on a large scale, there may suddenly be fresh options for creating new remediation processes using AI. Another way librarians can leverage it is by using tools to improve older content in-house as part of the workflow when an accessibility barrier is reported. Lots of tools exist for this, but some are costly either in terms of time, learning curve, or money.

Projects (both commercial and not-for-profit) are underway to meet this immediate need, or at least reduce the workload throughout the process. One such project, BeMyAI, is an enhancement to the BeMyEyes project. BeMyAI sets out to act as a "virtual volunteer" describing and answering questions about images.[12] How might we as librarians leverage this for our purposes? If the focus is on accurate and clear image descriptions and the tool touts strength in the area of art images in particular, how might we make use of this to improve alternative text descriptions in the inaccessible images we own or use?

Imagine an accessibility issue being reported about a file in your collection. Options will exist for librarians to get the jump on complex remediation using more mature AI text and character recognition, image alt-text descriptions, and audio descriptions. While these options might reduce one learning curve in that we steer clear of manually creating descriptions from scratch, we may be swapping out for another learning curve—acquiring the responsibility of better understanding the technology we use and its potential biases.

186 ••• CHAPTER 10

❯ Automated AI Speech-Recognition Captioning

Another area where interest in AI has been high is captioning. Automated captioning is now integrated into tools like YouTube, Zoom, and Microsoft Teams. Since the COVID-19 pandemic, auto-generated captioning has become much more common. While AI technology is not (by any stretch) perfect, such captioning is a boon for users with and without disabilities. For a user in a full house with children screaming or roommates cheering, the captioning can help ensure you aren't missing details of the interactions on your favorite show. But for a person with a hearing impairment, having captions is crucial. Accessibility is the universal benefit. Every time we make our materials, content, and tools stronger for those with disabilities, we improve the product for everyone.

In YouTube, automated captioning is a simple toggle option that most creators forget to review. However, if the automated captioning in a tool like YouTube is not accurate for the video you upload, you can easily edit it. It is the responsibility of all content creators to ensure that their materials are usable and accessible. As a content creator, automating the captioning process gives you a stepping-stone to meet your captioning goals without having to start from scratch. For stretched-thin librarians, this kind of assistance can be the saving grace when creating tutorials, promotional videos, and other video content. Streamlining our accessibility processes allows us to focus on the mission of inclusion in other ways. The literature and media are full of discussions of AI in the education sector. Articles detailing the use of AI to create learner-centered feedback or personalized learning modules are published regularly. There are many intersections between education and library services. AI could prove particularly useful in creating or helping to create tutorials and modules on doing research, using databases, and even honing one's search language or overall research topic or thesis.

Automated speech recognition still has a way to go as it currently struggles to represent all speech accurately. Anyone with dictation software or those who use assistants like Siri or Google Assistant can tell you that queries are, more often than not, unable to produce desirable results. The terminology is often unique, and the assistants and users need to be trained. Users must learn the language, for example, of saying

"Hey Google." In turn, users might need to train the assistant to learn the user's language, specifically when it comes to discipline-specific terms like medical conditions. Non-anglicized speakers, names or terms, dialects, speakers with speech impediments, speakers with disabilities that impact their speech patterns, videos with background noise, and product names are much more likely to confound current captioning technology. A good example is taken from a video interview with Ta-Nehisi Coates. During an interview for the *Atlantic* where he is introduced as a writer and senior blogger, the captioning misinterprets Coates's name as "Donna Hussey Coats."[13] Clearly, users can expect that it will be some time before large language models are able to learn how to properly caption proper names, discipline-specific terminology, words in multiple languages, and other complex terms.

Automatic speech recognition is possible via machine learning algorithms, but it is not perfect, as demonstrated in the Coates's example. It is critical to use tools that allow for editing of the automatically generated captions, and to make this editing a regular step in your workflow.

Librarians must remain vigilant by checking the captioning for any content we create and be willing to spend the time needed to edit out mistakes. Whether it is mistaking homophones like "eight" for "ate" or mistaking words like "candor" for "cancer," inaccuracies abound. It is not yet clear when the language models used to train the AI component of captioning will begin learning more diverse terminology, accents, and speaking styles. Automated speech recognition is improving every day, though, and we are already seeing a combination of traditional machine learning algorithms with more nuanced artificial intelligence that takes grammar and sentence structure into account.

The next generation of these tools will improve in precision and with diminished cultural bias. But don't be fooled. The training of all AI models needs to be continuous if we are to ensure that ever-shifting cultural norms and terms can be taken into account. We need to teach the tools how to contextualize the use of language so that it can distinguish the probability that "ate" is not the time or the number. The AI tools can also learn speech patterns to increase accuracy in live captioning. Since the COVID-19 pandemic, we have experienced an improvement in automatic speech recognition in popular videoconferencing platforms like

Zoom and Microsoft Teams. As with any other digital product, librarians need to review and evaluate the fidelity of any tools we employ, including those used by third-party vendors. Additionally, librarians need to ensure that contract language allows for some recourse if reliability fails on a large scale and becomes an impediment for users.

Customizable Options and AI Enhancements

OCR has been used for years to transform inaccessible texts into ones compatible with text-to-speech technology in operating systems and apps. Over time, voices have improved and users have been able to customize options for reading. Read&Write by Texthelp is an example of such a proprietary third-party application; used on many college campuses, it allows users to specify the type of voice they want to hear. Users may also control the speed, pitch, and pauses between words, sentences, or paragraphs. With the integration of SimplifyAI, Texthelp is beta testing user-centered features that can simplify words and sentence structure. While this is just one instance of such technology, it is clear that as these tools mature, they will better serve the mission of ensuring that articles and content are more digestible for an audience that understands their own needs.

The personalization of interfaces and results displays benefits from the customization that some tools allow. Still, one of the issues for many users is the inability to save their customizations without creating a sign-in or user profile. Users hesitant to create such profiles are often concerned about privacy issues. Few users are willing to read the fine print of terms agreements, vet the specific wording regarding what information is held along with the personalization filters, understand where the servers exist that hold such information, and know the local laws and regulations regarding the safekeeping of such information. One way to help patrons is to ensure that a contact within the library is familiar with these issues and is able to guide patrons interested in customized profiles so they can return to a common task like researching articles.

A user might want to summarize a research article. Database companies like Proquest are currently rolling out beta versions of an AI research assistant to help enhance and enrich the research process. The assistant is meant to help users "review, analyze and interrogate documents more effectively," as well as expand research topic suggestions and help the user create more targeted searches.[14] The tool is pitched as a collaborative effort between Clarivate and academic researchers and librarians to empower users to take their research a step further by diversifying results, suggesting topics, and summarizing articles. Clarivate claims it has focused on testing and governance as a way to build consumer trust. By the time this book is published, Proquest will have rolled out an AI assistant in at least twelve of its database products. Despite promises by the vendor, librarians interested in ensuring digital accessibility should vet these products carefully to ensure that interacting with them, from the perspective of users with disabilities, is barrier-free and that they positively contribute to the research and learning process.

❯ Patron Tools and Customizations

Using AI to summarize content or change its readability level will become more popular as it improves, making information available to more users in ways they can understand. Several tools could be integrated to help patrons with disabilities directly or indirectly at your library. In popular databases, tools have existed for a few years allowing users to specify font size or contrast level. Many large database platforms, like EbscoHost, include a read-speaker or read-aloud option. Yet, only recently have database vendors explored technology that can change the reading level of a document. AI is front and center in this effort. We know it can take complex language and bring it down to a specified reading level. With the ability to "translate" complex literature into more understandable chunks, AI holds great promise for those with a variety of disabilities. While establishing base readability and usability of content will help all users, it can be especially useful for users with a variety of learning and cognitive disabilities.

Similarly, AI can help us create more readable content before we release it to users. As Jingjing Wu explores in her presentation "Using ChatGPT to Evaluate and Improve Library Websites," one way would be to upload your website draft into the AI tool and prompt it to

> revise the provided web page content using user-centric language and front-loading style that quickly reveals key information. Employ clear

190 ••• CHAPTER 10

headlines and scannable layout to enhance overall understanding and readability. The suggested Flesch-Kincaid Grade Level is 8.[15]

By instructing the AI tool to "revamp content structure and expression to improve user experience"[16] at a specific reading level, we can eschew past practices of publishing a page only to have to remediate it when problems emerge. Of course, we can edit as we see fit and should do so, but an AI tool can help librarians to streamline this process. As new tools are constantly being developed, more librarians are thinking about how to leverage them to help patrons with disabilities. Tailoring your text to a base reading level that makes sense for your audience is a step forward in that mission.

▶ AI-Generated Audio Description

There are a few projects which are using AI for audio description (AD). Most of them are being developed by third-party accessibility vendors who promise the ability to verbally describe the visual actions and details in a video, such as clothing, facial expressions, background scenery, and more. These tools aim to insert such verbal descriptions into appropriate pauses in dialogue or narration within the videos. Of course, such technology will have some difficulties. Most of these tools might simplify a top as a "shirt" when it might be more culturally appropriate to call it a "sari." While the accuracy and cultural applicability of descriptions still pose a serious question, the ability of AI to properly predict insertion time for AD narration will emerge as one of its greatest strengths. Currently, creating audio descriptions is extremely labor-intensive, since it requires AD experts to calculate the total time of pauses and tailor the verbal descriptions to fit within those few precious moments so that the description does not impede the flow of the content. According to a recent study by Microsoft, Chu, Wang, and Abrantes, the automation of AD of "suitable length tailored to speech gaps" that can "swiftly adapt to various video categories" is not only possible but is a practical gain, performing with more consistency across frames via automated character recognition.[17] The development of AI-generated audio descriptions means increased latitude in what we can advocate for with vendors, and perhaps what we can reasonably do to meet user needs if we must outsource the creation of these descriptions. Librarians need to keep a sharp eye on how well the technology describes the action and images in a video. As of this writing, the technology is still rife with bias when it comes to describing images of non-Western subjects, clothing, gender fluidity, and other important characteristics. While the rise of AI is rapid, we expect automated audio description will, at most, remain an enhancement to the process, not a replacement for it. Nothing yet beats audio descriptions written and spoken by a trained human expert.

By and large, professionally created audio description is an expensive proposition. Since human intervention is still the gold standard for audio description, libraries must do their due diligence, and insist that contracts ensure that AD assets are available when streaming. If not, the vendor or platform should outline the process for requesting and acquiring necessary audio descriptions in a timely manner. Ensuring language is in the vendor contract detailing the inclusion of AD assets, or at least a road map for acquiring those assets in a timely manner, is crucial, given the bottom line for most libraries.

▶ AI Enhanced Sign Language

Artificial intelligence is now being used to interpret sign language and translate it in real time. Gesture recognition technologies are being used to convert sign language to text, which can then be spoken. Programs are beginning to emerge that aim to translate written text into sign language that an avatar will sign. Other integrations include a sign language video overlay that displays the signs as an option for viewers who prefer sign language interpretation. The day is not far off when libraries will engage these technologies for real-time translation and communication with patrons, but there are still risks embedded in these AI models.

Bias is a real concern for librarians, especially in international contexts. Bias can be baked into the AI when these models are trained "by researchers and startups in the U.S., where ASL is the primary language of the Deaf community, and consequently contain ASL."[18] British Sign Language, Chinese Sign Language, Australian Sign Language, and even International Sign Language, among others, will be omitted from training.

192 ••• CHAPTER 10

Those using other sign languages, outside of ASL, will be at a disadvantage and unable to communicate fluently.

Libraries need to understand that most AI-enhanced technologies are still inconsistent, incomplete, perennially prone to hallucination, and exhibit bias rooted in a corpus composed of professional sign language interpreters instead of crowdsourcing real-life examples. A review of algorithms concludes that this application risks "misrepresenting sign language recognition as a gesture recognition problem, ignoring the complexity of sign languages as well as the broader social context within which such systems must function."[19] When only perfectly trained sign-language interpreters are used to train models, the more natural and colloquial use of gestures may be lost. To provide some service in this area, librarians must consider the current trade-offs before adopting the technology.

▶ Website Code

Several new AI tools can be useful in guiding website editors to ensure that code is more accessible. An early February 2023 blog on Intopia by Joe Watkins, a noted accessibility expert, provides a wonderful example of how AI can assist us with writing more accessible code. Using ChatGPT as both the tool and the example, Watkins prompted ChatGPT to evaluate its inaccessible code and present options to increase its accessibility. "In the end, the service was able to come up with an accessible solution to its own accessibility barriers" by working through questions such as why the tool relied on ARIA labels to achieve accessibility when it could have depended on straight HTML code. Watkins keenly understands code and how it can be misused. He reminded the AI tool to consider "the first rule of ARIA," and the engine came back reflecting that "it's often stated that the first rule of ARIA is to use native HTML elements whenever possible, and only use ARIA when there is no native HTML equivalent that meets the needs."[20] By the end of the discussion, ChatGPT had rewritten its code using HTML and CSS and without using ARIA, as Watkins had prompted. The blog post illustrates both how we can leverage AI and how AI can learn from these interactions as every exchange becomes part of the corpus.

Such interactions are becoming more commonplace, even among those inexperienced with coding, and we now see librarians using AI to fill known professional development gaps. For web designers looking to shift left in their thinking (moving accessibility into the approach and design earlier in the process), it provides an opportunity to jump-start this work and learn more about accessible web design along the way, assuming that prompts are carefully crafted.

As with any tool discussed thus far, the guidance from the tool should be checked and double-checked. We often see AI fail in ways we did not expect; and the surveillance of products, as well as attention to the main tenets of accessibility, are all that stand between us and embarrassing mistakes. According to Dekel Skoop, "the availability of an accessibility ecosystem that combines AI-powered solutions and manual remediation services is not just a temporary fix but a catalyst for a deeper change. It facilitates a shift towards proactive accessibility, where accessibility is integrated into the web development process rather than being an afterthought."[21] There is no escaping the need for ongoing training and development if librarians are to continue leading and creating inclusive information ecosystems.

Libraries Using AI

Interview with **Jingjing Wu**, *Web Librarian, Texas Tech University Libraries**

What are your top tips for libraries using AI to improve accessibility?
As a web librarian, I focus on using AI to enhance website accessibility. Here are my key recommendations:

1. **Test and evaluate AI tools.** Always validate AI suggestions before implementation. For instance, after using AI tools to assess web page performance, I cross-check the suggested code improvements against performance metrics, using tools like Google PageSpeed Insights to ensure their effectiveness.

2. *Continuous training of AI tools.* The web accessibility scanning tool we use allows us to approve or disregard AI suggestions to provide feedback. I hope our input will help customize the tool to meet our specific needs, enhancing its relevance and effectiveness.

3. *Final decision-making authority.* While AI tools provide suggestions for improving web accessibility, I ultimately decide which recommendations to implement. For example, when evaluating content flagged for high readability scores, I review AI's concise suggestions. Here's a comparison:

   Original: The University Library has entered into Transformative Agreements with publishers that allow Texas Tech researchers to publish open access with significant discounts on article processing charges (APCs), and in some instances, with full funding available for APCs.

   AI suggestion: The University Library has made new Transformative Agreements with publishers. These agreements help Texas Tech researchers publish open access. Researchers get big discounts on article fees. In some cases, the library covers the full fee.[i]

   My revision: The University Library has made new Transformative Agreements with publishers. These agreements help Texas Tech researchers publish open access. Researchers receive significant discounts on article processing charges (APCs). In some cases, the library covers the full APCs. (This revision maintains the term *APC* for clarity among researchers.)

What advice would you offer for writing prompts to improve website accessibility?

Be specific and provide context. When I first explored using ChatGPT to evaluate and improve web accessibility in early 2023, I assumed that accessibility-related vocabulary and standards were "common sense" for AI. If I were to conduct these evaluations again, I would ensure that my prompts include both web content/code and relevant accessibility standards. This clarity helps the AI understand my expectations better.

What tips do you have for using prompts beyond the website? What are your considerations in approaching AI for help with other matters?

1. *Understand AI's role.* In preparing the workshop on AI-powered tools for literature reviews, I was initially impressed by their capabilities. I compared them with traditional literature review processes and recognized how AI contributes in terms of semantic search engines, the summary of relevant papers, the extraction of information via research methods, and Q&A on specific papers. Understanding AI's role in the new procedure is crucial for evaluating the tools effectively.

2. *Leverage AI's strengths while acknowledging its limitations.* Take AI-powered semantic search engines as an example. They improve relevance, consider context, and handle complex queries. However, their effectiveness relies heavily on the quality and volume of training data, which can introduce biases, interpretation errors, and privacy concerns. Additionally, the scope of these semantic search engines can be unclear—users may not know where the articles come from or what databases are used. This can lead to missed important publications, especially in fields like the humanities, where closed-access publishing is prevalent. While these tools can enhance the efficiency of literature reviews, it's important to verify information independently before including it in research.

3. *Use AI recommendations within your understanding.* In R for Beginners workshops, I will introduce students to integrating RStudio with GitHub Copilot, an AI-powered coding assistant. Since most attendees are graduate students who will apply their R coding skills to research projects, incorporating an AI-powered coding assistant aligns perfectly with this objective. The first 7.5 hours will focus on basic R concepts and coding, with the final 30 minutes dedicated to demonstrating Copilot. I will highlight common mistakes that Copilot makes in its coding suggestions and explain how to refine prompts for better results. My goal is for students to view Copilot as a learning coach and research assistant, rather than relying solely on its code suggestions.

What good resources can you offer for writing prompts?

I recommend "ChatGPT Prompt Engineering for Developers" by Andrew Ng and Isa Fulford on Coursera.[ii] This was the first course I took on prompt engineering, and I still consider it the best one available. It covers core concepts in LLMs and provides hands-on experience with ChatGPT APIs.

* I acknowledge the use of ChatGPT in refining the wording for clarity.

Notes

i. Text generated by Silktide when identifying content with higher readability scores, Silktide, September 19, 2024, https://app.us.silktide.com/ttu/, edited for style and content.
ii. Andrew Ng and Isa Fulford, "ChatGPT Prompt Engineering for Developers," Coursera, www.coursera.org/projects/chatgpt-prompt-engineering-for-developers-project.

Notes

1. David Russell Schilling, "Knowledge Doubling Every 12 Months, Soon to Be Every 12 Hours," *Industry Tap* (blog), April 19, 2013, www.industrytap.com/knowledge-doubling-every-12-months-soon-to-be-every-12-hours/3950.
2. "Fact2 Guide to Optimizing AI in Higher Education," 5, www.fitnyc.edu/gateways/employees/faculty-academic-support/cet/aitaskgroup-fact2-document-101223.pdf.
3. Todd Miller, "Weighing the Merits of AI for Information Access," *Computers in Libraries* 44, no. 2 (March 2024): 16.
4. W. Cho, "Artists Score Major Win in Copyright Case Against AI Art Generators," *Hollywood Reporter*, August 13, 2024, www.hollywoodreporter.com/business/business-news/artists-score-major-win-copyright-case-against-ai-art-generators-1235973601/; G. Appel, J. Neelbauer, and D. A. Schweidel, "Generative AI Has an Intellectual Property Problem," *Harvard Business Review*, April 7, 2023, https://hbr.org/2023/04/generative-ai-has-an-intellectual-property-problem; K. Madigan, "Mid-Year Review: AI Lawsuit Developments in 2024," Copyright Alliance, July 25, 2024, https://copyrightalliance.org/ai-lawsuit-developments-2024/.
5. UN Environment Program, "AI Has an Environmental Problem. Here's What the World Can Do About That," September 21, 2024, www.unep.org/news-and-stories/story/ai-has-environmental-problem-heres-what-world-can-do-about.
6. S. Ren and A. Wierman, "The Uneven Distribution of AI's Environmental Impacts," *Harvard Business Review*, July 15, 2024, https://hbr.org/2024/07/the-uneven-distribution-of-ais-environmental-impacts.
7. J. Coleman, "AI's Climate Impact Goes beyond Its Emissions." *Scientific American*, December 7, 2023, www.scientificamerican.com/article/ais-climate-impact-goes-beyond-its-emissions/.

8. Martin Frické, *Artificial Intelligence and Librarianship: Notes for Teaching*, 3rd ed. (SoftOption, 2024), 259, https://softoption.us/AIandLibrarianship.
9. Ross Andersen, "Does Sam Altman Know What He's Creating?" *The Atlantic*, July 24, 2023, www.theatlantic.com/magazine/archive/2023/09/sam-altman-openai-chatgpt-gpt-4/674764/.
10. Frické, *Artificial Intelligence and Librarianship*, 325.
11. "Books for All: Protect the Freedom to Read in Your Community," New York Public Library, www.nypl.org/spotlight/books-for-all/nationwide.
12. "Introducing Be My AI (Formerly Virtual Volunteer) for People Who Are Blind or Have Low Vision, Powered by OpenAI's GPT-4," www.bemyeyes.com/blog/introducing-be-my-eyes-virtual-volunteer.
13. Jennie Rothenberg Gritz, "The Anger behind the Story," *The Atlantic* (blog), August 22, 2012, www.theatlantic.com/video/index/261133/the-anger-behind-the-story/.
14. "ProQuest, Launches AI-Powered Research Assistant," https://about.proquest.com/en/blog/2024/proquest-part-of-clarivate-launches-ai-powered-research-assistant/.
15. Jingjing Wu, "Using ChatGPT to Evaluate and Improve Library Websites," September 7, 2023, 13, https://repository.ifla.org/handle/123456789/2964.
16. Wu, "Using ChatGPT," 27.
17. Peng Chu, Jiang Wang, and Andre Abrantes, "LLM-AD: Large Language Model Based Audio Description System," ArXiv, May 2024, https://arxiv.org/abs/2405.00983.
18. Danielle Bragg et al., "Sign Language Recognition, Generation, and Translation: An Interdisciplinary Perspective," ArXiv, August 22, 2019, www.proquest.com/docview/2280230983?parentSessionId=ihe18bjZKA%2FEMudPEH3kvk8%2BacoqcdhQrFKzTTKzh50%3D&pq-origsite=primo&sourcetype=Working%20Papers.
19. Bragg et al., "Sign Language Recognition," 3.
20. Joe Watkins, "Using ChatGPT to Make ChatGPT's Experience More Accessible," Intopia, February 14, 2023, https://intopia.digital/articles/using-chatgpt-to-make-chatgpts-experience-more-accessible/.
21. Dekel Skoop, "How AI Is Revolutionizing Web Accessibility," https://learn.g2.com/ai-for-web-accessibility.

• • •

CHAPTER 11

Best Practices for Working with Vendors

A Deaf student majoring in film studies needs captioned versions of all of the films shown in her classes.

A blind law student needs to access newly published court opinions using a screen reader.

A patron with low vision stops by the reference desk at the local public library to ask about digital access to movies with audio descriptions.

In these cases, the materials being accessed are held in subscription databases. One of the challenges of ensuring complete digital accessibility at libraries is that many of the digital tools used in libraries are purchased or licensed from vendors who may have different priorities or areas of focus. This leaves library team members with limited control over the accessibility of these products. For this reason, effective partnerships with vendors around accessibility are a key step in improving digital inclusion. In many cases, vendors are very receptive to this feedback but adopting an organized and methodical approach can maximize impact across libraries.

Working with vendors can fall into different categories, especially depending on the type of vendor relevant to the project. For vendors that work primarily with libraries, particularly libraries in countries with accessibility laws that apply to them, it is often safe to assume that the vendor will have at least some knowledge of accessibility requirements and the workflows related to them. In the rare instances where this is not the case, these vendors are often open to receiving feedback and integrating accessibility into their workflows. This is because most of their customers are subject to the same legal rules and select vendors based on their ability to work within these requirements. However, even among these vendors, there will be varied approaches to accessibility and differing amounts of resources put into optimizing accessibility, as opposed to just meeting legal minimums. This means that it is still helpful to evaluate prospective vendors based on their approach to accessibility.

Vendors who primarily work with non-library customers, and particularly those who work extensively with commercial customers or customers in jurisdictions without significant accessibility requirements, may not have as robust an infrastructure for accessibility work. These vendors may not all have VPATs available for all of their products and may not be prepared to make rapid improvements to their products to help libraries meet their accessibility obligations and ensure that their services and collections are inclusive for all users. While this is an important factor to be aware of when deciding to work with a vendor, it can still be useful to work with such vendors to make it clear that this is a priority for library customers, and is therefore worth investing resources in. As will be discussed in more depth later in this chapter, these situations are where it can be particularly useful to work with other libraries using the same vendor to share the results of user testing and to demonstrate the importance of accessibility to both the libraries that work with the vendor and those libraries' patrons. Of course, each vendor will exist along a spectrum between these two extremes, and these generalizations may not describe every vendor working with libraries. Regardless of the type of vendor, following some best practices when working with them will ensure that accessibility remains an ongoing priority and is optimized across all the platforms used at the library.

❯ Integrate Accessibility into Your Workflow

As discussed in previous chapters, it is vital to include an evaluation of accessibility in the overall evaluation of any new software or hardware that is being considered for use in the library. This should start from the early stages of considering a purchase or subscription. If the purchase or subscription requires a request for proposals (RFP) process at your institution, accessibility considerations should be included from that point if at all possible. Asking specific questions in the RFP about accessibility features, and the future road map for additional features, can help to differentiate among vendors and ensure that the successful proposal is from a vendor who offers the necessary accessibility features and is flexible enough to incorporate changes to meet evolving requirements. Potential questions to consider integrating into the RFP include the following ones:

- What accessibility standards (such as WCAG) does the vendor use to evaluate its products?
- What process does the vendor use for testing and evaluating the accessibility of its products?
- What level of compliance with these standards does the vendor guarantee?
- How does the vendor test the accessibility of its products?
- What future accessibility plans and improvements does the vendor have on the horizon?
- What process does the vendor use for updating its products to meet changing accessibility standards (e.g., new versions of WCAG standards)?
- What types of support does the vendor offer for accessibility problems identified by customers or users?
- How can customers place requests for new accessibility features, and how are those requests treated?

This information can help in choosing a product and can also guide future interactions with the vendor around accessibility topics. Some of these questions might be answered by an up-to-date VPAT, which can also be requested at this point in the process. Especially in situations where multiple vendors are being compared for a purchase or project, integrating accessibility into the RFP process can be the only way to make it a factor in the ultimate decision. Failure to consider accessibility at this stage can leave the library locked into a relationship with a vendor who is unable to meet minimum accessibility standards, which can cost both time and money later on to find solutions for issues patrons encounter.

In addition to asking vendors for information about the accessibility of its products, it is also important to incorporate independent verification in the decision-making process. This can take the form of internal evaluations at your institution (as discussed in more detail in chapter 7, "Automated and Manual Testing," which also provides additional details on VPATs), or it can take the form of a more simplified process. When the vendor is able to provide a VPAT, basic automated testing can be effective in verifying the accuracy of the information shared in that VPAT, which is particularly important given research suggests many VPATs contain errors and inaccuracies.[1] While more recent research suggests there may be a trend toward greater accuracy in vendor-created VPATs,[2] it is still worthwhile to conduct independent testing, particularly at the beginning of a relationship with a vendor. This will ensure the decision to enter into an agreement is made with full information. Moreover, in situations where the decision is made to purchase or subscribe to a platform that is not fully accessible, this will also offer an opportunity to make plans for how to assist disabled patrons who encounter barriers in a platform with known accessibility issues.

▶ Vendor Limitations

Vendors, especially smaller or independent ones, will struggle with some of the accessibility principles discussed throughout this book. More often than not, they want to improve their products to meet consumer needs and "do the right thing," but they may lack the expertise or knowledge to do so. Other vendors will routinely seek out feedback to make continuous improvements because they do have that ability.

▶ Include Accessibility in Negotiations

Beyond simply discussing accessibility with a vendor while evaluating a product, it is also worthwhile to consider how accessibility can be included in contract negotiations. Including accessibility in the terms of the contract at the point of negotiation can be an effective way to create a shared set of expectations with a vendor and also ensure accountability around accessibility throughout the term of the contract. Where the institution has an EIT policy or other policy regarding the procurement of accessible resources, these can be particularly helpful in driving the negotiation process. Moreover, including accessibility in contract negotiations is becoming a more common practice across the profession. Evidence of this exists not only in the literature but also in libraries' collection development policies, which may mention how accessibility factors into their purchase or subscription processes.[3] As this practice grows, model contract provisions have also proliferated.[4] These model provisions are an excellent tool for working in this area because they offer support for those who may not be comfortable negotiating new language. They can also be a way to negotiate in connection with other similarly situated libraries, despite the absence of a formal consortial relationship with them. This second point can be helpful because vendors will see the same language being requested repeatedly, thus emphasizing the shared interest in accessibility across the library community. There has also been a growth in other support for library professionals who want to dive deeper into how accessibility can be effectively integrated into their existing negotiation workflows. For example, the Triangle Research Libraries Network published their freely available "TRLN Guide to Negotiating Accessibility in E-Resources Licenses" in 2022. This document seeks to help library professionals "understand the rationale behind the elements included in the model language, the implications of omitting or softening the components of their preferred language, and how they can advocate for their libraries' accessibility language needs with providers."[5]

While model provisions are very useful, they may not meet the needs of all libraries. In particular, for libraries in jurisdictions with specific local accessibility requirements, regulations, or laws, it may be difficult to find a model provision that fills these specific needs. However, it is possible to negotiate an individualized provision for accessibility rather than using one of the model provisions in existence. Ideally, such a provision would particularly focus on setting very specific expectations. Libraries could negotiate to include:

- Reference to specific local or national-level laws with which the product must comply

- Reference to specific institutional standards or policies to which the library is subject
- Reference to a specific WCAG version and compliance level
- Specific assistive technologies that are of particular interest, such as a specific tool that the library offers on computer equipment
- Features that are particularly relevant for a specific tool, such as captions, transcripts, and audio descriptions in the case of a streaming video platform
- Set procedures or deadlines for responding to accessibility issues that are reported to the vendor
- Requirements that a VPAT be provided and when it must be provided (for example, biannually, annually, or when specific types of changes are made to the platform)
- Ensuring that the library team has the right to modify or remediate any vendor-provided content that is not accessible
- Specific contacts at both the library and the vendor for communication regarding accessibility changes or issues
- Specific consequences with regard to ongoing accessibility issues, such as lowered prices or an ability to cancel the license during the term of the agreement

And as already mentioned, for those who don't feel comfortable negotiating new language around the topic of accessibility, a wide array of model provisions exist for both U.S. and international libraries.

In some cases, if a product does not currently meet the necessary accessibility standards, it may be possible to include improvements in the ultimate agreement that is negotiated. In these cases, it is essential to ensure a clear understanding between the library team and the vendor about the specific needs and expectations. As Barbara Kawecki writes about library and vendor relationships, "documentation allows both the library and the vendor to clarify roles and expectations within the scope of the project, with implementation timelines and benchmarks built into the process."[6] This applies equally to projects around accessibility improvements. If the decision to purchase software or subscribe to a database rests on specific accessibility improvements the vendor has promised will be forthcoming, it is worthwhile to clearly document these, potentially even in the contract. This can take the form of specific deadlines and details about the exact nature of the necessary features or the specific level of compliance with accessibility guidelines that is expected. Such documentation might also include specifications about how the evaluation of the final product will be undertaken, such as whether the library will have an opportunity to conduct its own tests or whether an independent third party will be testing the product. In addition, the provisions of the contract should include specific consequences for failing to meet the accessibility requirements by the agreed-upon deadline, potentially including an option to terminate the relationship with no penalty to the library.

Even if a product already meets the library's accessibility standards, it is worthwhile to consider including ongoing accessibility compliance as a requirement in the contract. Given the way digital platforms continually evolve, and the fact that new accessibility guidelines and requirements are periodically released, it is critical to make sure the vendor makes an ongoing commitment to accessibility. Hopefully, this commitment will be evident from their answers to questions on the topic and their existing accessibility documentation. Including this in the contract can add an additional layer of assurance and protect the library from future problems and complaints.

If a library currently subscribes to a product, it is still important to track accessibility information and use this in future negotiations. If there are frequent issues and they are not promptly addressed, this can be a point of discussion and negotiation going forward. As an example of this practice in action, the Grand Valley State University Libraries have memorialized this approach in their collection development policy, noting that "labor devoted to troubleshooting, improving metadata quality, in-house development to meet accessibility and usability standards, resolving errors, unsatisfactory customer support experiences, data analysis, accessibility, and other issues not explicitly covered by a service level agreement or license agreement are considered during negotiations, renewals, cancellations, and acquisition of new materials."[7] In a similar vein, the Stewart Library at Weber State University notes in the library's collection development policy that licensed resources that do not meet their accessibility requirements "should come with discounted pricing to address the cost of remediation and individual accommodations."[8] Being able to point to a history of accessibility issues can be important when seeking to bring this topic into the negotiation at the point of renewal because it will make a more concrete case for negotiating a lower price, a specific standard of service around accessibility issues, or even indemnification of the library if accessibility complaints about the product arise during the term of the contract.

Contract negotiations can also be a central component in educating vendors about the impact of accessibility issues, as vendors may not have direct experience with the work libraries must do to remediate content or otherwise work to mitigate accessibility barriers that exist in the platform. In his 2020 survey of existing model accessibility provisions and the key points for the negotiation of said provisions, Michael Rodriguez noted that "negotiating accessibility clauses is not a chance to browbeat vendors but rather to educate them and advocate for inclusive access—and ultimately for libraries to walk their talk."[9] This can help to demonstrate the connection between negotiating about accessibility and the other approaches to working with vendors as suggested in this chapter.

▌ Prioritize Regular Communications about Accessibility

While it can be easy to leave discussions of accessibility to the initial negotiations with a vendor, or the hopefully rare situations where users encounter major accessibility barriers, it is imperative to make sure that there is an ongoing discussion of accessibility throughout the term of a license agreement. Researchers who have studied the relationships between vendors and librarians have argued for the importance of regular meetings with vendors to "provide an opportunity for reflection and evaluation of these relationships."[10] It is vital to ensure that accessibility is a topic that is regularly discussed at these meetings. There are many ways accessibility can fit into the conversation. First, be sure to ask about any outstanding features the vendor has said will be coming, or more generally about the accessibility plan the vendor hopefully outlined at the beginning of the relationship. Checking in regularly offers opportunities to verify progress is being made and to find out about any changes in future plans in a timely fashion. Second, track any questions or issues that didn't rise to the level of immediate reporting to the vendor so they can be discussed in these meetings. In these cases, be prepared with specifics and be ready to send those specifics, with the necessary documentation, to the technical team if the primary vendor contact is not the correct person to address them. Third, these regular meetings offer an opportunity to discuss evolving standards and expectations with the vendor during the course of a contract. Examples of this would include learning how the vendor plans to approach any newly emerging standards, such as new versions of the WCAG standards, and any shifts in assistive technologies, such as changing preferences for specific assistive tools and changing functionality within those tools.

Finally, during these meetings, vendors will often mention new features, platforms, or products they have in development to gauge the interest of their customers. Think about accessibility from the very start of these discussions. For example, if a vendor mentions a plan to add a library of video content to their database, ask about the accessibility of the video player. Will these videos have transcripts, captions, and audio descriptions? Be sure to ask other relevant questions about what can be expected in terms of accessibility from day one of the new feature, platform, or product. This is crucial information to have when deciding whether to allocate funds to this new item, and it also demonstrates again to the vendor that accessibility is a priority and not an aspect that can be left for later stages in the development process. For the same reason, if the vendor is pitching a new platform or product, it is important to ask for a VPAT in the early stages of discussions so there is time for the vendor to create and share one before any decisions are finalized.

Another aspect of regular communications is to e-mail vendors as issues arise rather than waiting for the next regularly scheduled meeting. Raising accessibility problems promptly can not only help your library patrons but also make the vendor aware of an issue that may well be impacting users at other libraries as well. For two reasons, you shouldn't assume that other subscribers will raise these same issues. First, not all subscribers may have a clear process for receiving patron reports of issues, or for tracking these problems and notifying the vendor of them. Second, it can be helpful for multiple libraries to reach out about the same issue to demonstrate to the vendor it is a priority across their customer base and, therefore, an issue that should be addressed promptly.

❯ Share What You Learn

A part of effective communications with vendors is to share information you have learned from the use of their products at your library. This can be as simple as usage data or information about the number of accessibility requests the library receives about their product, but it can also be more in-depth information. It is important to have an effective and accessible way for patrons to report accessibility barriers they encounter when using the library's digital content, and it is equally valuable to track and share this information with vendors when it pertains to their platforms. This workflow should take into account the different ways complaints might be shared, such as via a formal feedback form, as a comment at a reference point, or from faculty who have encountered students who report problems. Regardless of how accessibility problems are reported, they should be systematically gathered and saved for use by the library team and for sharing with the vendor to help advocate for improvements.

As both formal and informal user experience testing has become more common in libraries, they can offer an avenue for collecting accessibility information to share with vendors. This is, of course, dependent on including users with disabilities and those who use assistive technologies in user testing, which should be standard protocol. Assuming that is the case, this testing can provide valuable information that can supplement any user testing being done by the vendor, which may not involve as many tasks related to accessibility or include users who use a variety of assistive devices. User testing data can be particularly useful when discussing issues with vendors because these are often the same types of testing approaches their internal teams use. This makes the information clearer and more relatable to the vendor representatives. In some cases, it might even be possible to partner with vendors on joint user testing to ensure accessibility is considered as early as possible in the design of new platforms or major redesigns of existing platforms.

No matter how the information is collected, the key is to share it with vendors. It is easy to assume vendors are doing their own testing or already have information about accessibility requirements and needs, but this is not always the case. Sharing this information can ensure accessibility issues are addressed promptly and remain a priority at all points in the design process.

▶ Build Partnerships

Partnerships are another key way to work effectively toward the widespread accessibility of vendor products and find quick solutions to any problems that present themselves. These partnerships allow library employees to exert influence on vendor products more effectively than individual action at the point of contract negotiations and can also ensure that accessibility is considered earlier in the design process than would otherwise be the case. Additionally, as with all partnerships, they can lead to a broader sharing of perspectives and information that can help to move innovation in accessibility work forward and give a voice to more perspectives. There are two major types of partnerships that can help in working with vendors, which will be considered in turn.

Partnerships with Vendors

When opportunities arise to partner directly with vendors, these are often the most effective way to contribute to the ongoing development of the vendor's products. These partnerships can take several forms, from serving on a long-standing advisory board that is consulted regularly about the vendor's proposed changes and new products, to participating in a short-term focus group or even pop-up user experience testing. Regardless of the format, these partnerships offer great opportunities to contribute to the future of the vendor's products and make sure accessibility is top-of-mind at all points in the process. Many vendors will approach customers, particularly those with whom they have long-term relationships, about testing and other opportunities, but at other times they may send out open calls for volunteers. Even if the vendors you work with have not mentioned such a partnership, it can be worth proposing one, particularly if they announce they are starting work on a new platform or product, as this is an opportunity to make sure accessibility is not overlooked until the end of the process.

For those who do not feel they have the expertise to regularly raise accessibility issues in these settings, consider whether you have colleagues or even patrons with this expertise who might be willing to have their name put forward to participate in focus groups and user experience testing opportunities. Vendors are often happy to include participants from a wide range of institutions in these tests, but they might not consider including individuals who use assistive devices or who are disabled without prompting and the suggestion of specific individuals. Connecting vendors with specific disabled users can be a great way to ensure they are included in this process and have an opportunity to provide direct feedback on the products while they're being developed. Since many vendors may not have disabled individuals on their development team or even as part of the user testing population, it is helpful to connect interested users with them to provide insights that might otherwise not occur to the development team.

Partnerships with Other Libraries

Partnerships with other libraries can also be helpful in working effectively with vendors. Anytime libraries can come together to speak to vendors with a single voice on important topics can help demonstrate the widespread interest in these topics. There are many ways libraries have worked together specifically to advocate for improved accessibility. One of the largest-scale examples of this work is the Library Accessibility Alliance. Originally formed as the Library E-Resource Accessibility Group of the Big Ten Academic Alliance in 2015, this group has brought together the member institutions of seven consortia to date to work collectively on major accessibility initiatives, including training, e-resource accessibility evaluation, model licensing language, and other resources.[11] While this is a particularly extensive example of this type of collective work, smaller-scale collaborations can also have a significant impact. Several library systems have worked together to create shared resources, including professional development resources,[12] VPAT repositories for e-resources licensed by member institutions,[13] and other documentation.[14] At an individual level, librarians can also come together to form communities of practice, committees that are part of professional groups, and other types of affinity groups involved in accessibility work, all of which can help to share a consistent and effective message with the vendors regarding accessibility and the meaningful inclusion of all disabled users.

Ultimately, all of these actions are aimed at the same goal, which is to emphasize to vendors that accessibility is a top priority for libraries, not only due to libraries' legal obligations in many jurisdictions, but also because of the impact that this work has on libraries' ability to offer inclusive collections and services. Negotiating with vendors will also educate them about the impact of inaccessibility, of which some vendors may not be aware, particularly newer or smaller companies. By prioritizing this work with vendors, libraries can have an impact on accessibility that will reach beyond the walls of the library to help all users of these platforms have more equitable access to the information and services offered through them.

TOP TIPS

Working with Vendors

Interview with **Sarah Brennan**, *Lead Product Manager, ProQuest/Clarivate*

What do you see as the key accessibility changes or improvements on the horizon for e-resources?

One recent change of note is that WCAG 2.2 includes nine new success criteria, some of which are aimed at making resources more accessible to those with learning or cognitive disabilities. One example is around authentication, providing alternative methods to remembering a password. Allowing a user to enter via an emailed link, rather than memorizing and typing a password, is one way a resource becomes more accessible to a user with a cognitive disability and removes what was previously a barrier to entry. I'm pleased to see WCAG expand to include these types of disabilities in their success criteria and hope it's a positive trend for the future.

Speaking more broadly, recent advances in generative AI and machine learning should translate to increased achievements and accuracy in accessibility tools, which could lead to more inclusive design and more personalized user experiences for those with disabilities. A concrete example might be increased usability of assistive technologies that use voice navigation, based on natural language processing improvements. It's encouraging to see AI being applied to accessible design and it's exciting to think of the potential improvements these technological advancements can bring.

What would you like librarians to understand about a vendor's perspective on meeting accessibility standards? What challenges do you face?

Sometimes, libraries view vendors as adversaries or obstacles, but we see ourselves as collaborators and partners, and we view accessibility as a shared goal. We're eager to work with libraries to solve problems creatively together.

Making accessibility improvements to a large-scale platform requires many cross-functional teams, including design, engineering, product, and QA. What may seem like a small change on the surface can actually take weeks or months to implement successfully.

We view accessibility as a journey. Making digital resources more accessible is a series of incremental steps over time. It's an iterative process that's never completed or finished and is always a work in progress that requires continual effort and prioritization.

What is the best way for librarians to communicate accessibility concerns to your team?

Our team is always available by phone, e-mail, webform submission or chat, or in-person meeting. Any communication method that's convenient for your library will be effective at reaching us. There's nothing more important to us than hearing from library customers, and no library should ever hesitate to get in touch with us to raise an accessibility concern or question.

How does your team identify accessibility issues and collect feedback around these topics?

ProQuest has an internal team of UX designers who are focused (and credentialed) on accessibility in digital resources. We place importance on being aware of current trends, thought leadership, and legislation around accessibility.

Product teams and sales executives also attend library conferences, regularly read library periodicals and literature, and stay informed on trending topics in our space. In addition to all of the above, regular discourse with our library customers fuels our awareness and ensures we are listening to our customers' evolving needs and priorities.

What are your top tips for communicating with vendors and ensuring accessibility issues rise in priority?

One of the very best things about librarianship is the collaborative network of peers. Information-sharing is the defining element of what we do! If your library has a question or concern about accessibility, chances are other librarians share that same question or concern. Reach out to your network of librarian groups (e.g., listservs, state library associations, local consortia, or regional networks, conferences you regularly attend, etc.). Working with others can help amplify your voice as well as create a proactive community of support and advocacy.

Notes

1. See, for example, S. K. Willis, and F. O'Reilly, "Filling the Gap in Database Usability," *Information Technology and Libraries* 39, no. 4 (2020), https://doi.org/10.6017/ital.v39i4.11977 ("Of the 227 databases, only 10 databases were found to fully match the claims the vendor made on the VPAT for the 11 criteria assessed from the ARG"); M. Zavala, and M. Reidsma, "Trust, but Verify: Auditing Vendor-Supplied Accessibility Claims," *Code4Lib Journal* 48 (2020) ("While not all vendors exhibited the same problems, every vendor we tested had accessibility issues that were not reflected in the VPAT"); and L. DeLancey, "Assessing the Accuracy of Vendor-Supplied Accessibility Documentation," *Library Hi Tech* 33, no. 1 (2015): 103–13 ("The Compliance Sheriff scans found numerous compliance issues not indicated on the VPATs. 9 of 17 vendors stated that they were fully compliant with checkpoint (a) (alt text for images), but Compliance Sheriff found problems in 14 of the 17 platforms scanned").

2. A. Sturgill and E. M. Gould, "Trends in VPATs Over Time," *Journal of Electronic Resources Librarianship* 35, no. 4 (2023): 249–59 (though the authors did note that "despite the positive trend the authors identified of VPATs being more correctly completed in recent years, there is still a high degree of variation in how VPATs are completed").

3. See, for example, M. Rodriguez, "Negotiating Accessibility for Electronic Resources," *Serials Review* 46, no. 2 (2020): 150–56; S. J. Adams, C. Halaychik, and J. Mezick, "Accessibility Compliance: One State, Two Approaches," *The Serials Librarian* 74, no. 1-4 (2018): 163–69; and K. Ostergaard, "Accessibility from Scratch: One Library's Journey to Prioritize the Accessibility of Electronic Information Resources," *The Serials Librarian* 69, no. 2 (2015): 155–68. For example, Michigan State University asks vendors "to accept/insert accessibility language into our e-resource licenses/contracts," specifically asking that vendors add the Big Ten Academic Alliance's Standardized Accessibility License Language. Michigan State University, "Collections Accessibility," MSU Libraries Accessibility, https://lib.msu.edu/accessibility/collections.

4. Rodriguez, "Negotiating Accessibility for Electronic Resources."

5. B. Ashmore et al., "TRLN Guide to Negotiating Accessibility in E-Resource Licenses," 2022, bit.ly/trln-a11y-eresource-license.

6. B. Kawecki, "Transforming Library Vendor Relations: Turning Relationships into Partnerships," *Against the Grain* 30, no. 2 (2018): 15.

7. Grand Valley State University Libraries, "Collection Development Policy," March 29, 2023, www.gvsu.edu/library/collection-development-policy-106.htm.

8. Stewart Library, "Collection Management Policy," Weber State University, August 18, 2022, https://library.weber.edu/sites/default/files/PDFs/about/Policies_and_Procedures/Collection%20Development%20Policy%20-%2008182022%20Draft.pdf.

9. Rodriguez, "Negotiating Accessibility for Electronic Resources,"153.

10. Kirsten Ostergaard and Doralyn Rossmann, "There's Work to Be Done: Exploring Library–Vendor Relations," *Technical Services Quarterly* 34, no. 1 (2017); 13–33, doi: 10.1080/07317131.2017.1238196.

11. Library Accessibility Alliance, "About Us," www.libraryaccessibility.org/about.

12. For example, Consortium of Academic and Research Libraries in Illinois, "PDA Event: Accessibility Series: Social Media Accessibility Basics," www.carli.illinois.edu/pda-event-accessibility-series-social-media-accessibility-basics.

13. For example, Consortium of Academic and Research Libraries in Illinois, "VPAT Repository," www.carli.illinois.edu/products-services/eres/vpat-repository; SUNY Office of Library and Information Services, "SUNY Library Vendor Accessibility Repository," January 3, 2024, https://sunyolis.libguides.com/vendor_accessibility; CUNY Library Services, CUNY VPAT Repository, "Accessibility Toolkit for Open Educational Resources (OER)," October 27, 2023, https://guides.cuny.edu/accessibility/vpats.

14. SUNY Office of Library and Information Services, "Accessibility and SLS," September 2023, https://sunyolis.libguides.com/sls-accessibility.

CHAPTER 12

Preparing the Profession

In order to make the necessary changes to our digital accessibility landscape, libraries must be prepared to devote staff time and expertise to this work. This can prove challenging in a period when both budgets and staff sizes are shrinking, and many librarians may feel ill-prepared to tackle significant digital accessibility barriers. This chapter will explore the existing landscape of digital accessibility skills in the library profession and consider the implications for library and information science curricula. This chapter considers where gaps exist and how we educate the next generation of library professionals, and instill a passion for equitable access at a scale unlike anything we have experienced before. These topics are vital to creating an ambitious, but necessary, plan for our profession to address accessibility head-on and ensure an inclusive future at our libraries.

▶ The Rise of Disability

Global rates of disability are increasing as the population ages. Worldwide there was a 41.5 percent increase in the number of adults 60 and over with hearing impairments between 1990 and 2010, and a 48.6 percent increase in the number of older adults with visual impairments.[1] Those rates do not account for other disabilities that also impact digital equity, such as mobility or cognitive impairments. Second only to millennials by some counts, our largest generation ever (Baby Boomers) is getting older and this will affect everything we do, especially with regard to disability and inclusion.

Essentially, this concurrence of an aging population, a global pandemic with a mass-disabling trajectory, and a younger population experiencing a higher incidence of disability has created a perfect storm, a tipping point for our profession and ultimately our culture.

Long COVID (a "range of new or persisting symptoms that can last weeks or months" after an initial COVID-19 infection) was classified in July 2021 as a disability under the ADA in a statement from the U.S. Department of Health and Human Services.[2] Long COVID is undoubtedly a factor in the changing disability landscape, among our patron base as well as in our own ranks. It is undeniably changing the nature of who we are, how we do our jobs, and for whom, especially regarding accessibility.

Where digital accessibility is not yet even explicitly integrated into jobs as fundamental to access and equity, librarians are starting to take action. According to Stephanie Rosen, an accessibility specialist at the University of Michigan Library:

> Across North America, academic librarians are quietly converting print materials into accessible files, testing databases for usability, and applying universal design principles to services, spaces, and instruction. Most of us do this work under unassuming job titles like director of access services or humanities librarian.[3]

Rosen insists our libraries are "part of a larger ecosystem" where we can have a grassroots impact on change that benefits everyone. She notes that "advocacy is key to promoting accessibility among partners whose work affects ours: vendors of electronic resources, publishers of content, creators of educational technology."[4]

While we do see some library positions devoted to accessibility as a focus, the vast majority of institutions will infuse that focus throughout all positions, mostly in an effort to comply with regulations and insulate themselves against accessibility complaints while slowly creating a new, more equitable information landscape. The latter may not be the explicit goal but is most certainly a side effect of the legal complaints and lawsuits.

❱ Occupational Outlook

The occupational outlook for librarians (updated in April 2024 by the Bureau of Labor Statistics or BLS) lists the largest employer of librarians as elementary and secondary schools at 35 percent; "local government, excluding education and hospitals," was next at 31 percent, followed by "colleges, universities and professional schools (state, local and private)" at 18 percent.[5] The overarching projection is a 3 percent increase in the number of librarians between 2022 and 2032. The BLS's assumption of this percent change is based on the current age of the workforce in libraries, suggesting that "many of those openings are expected to result from the need to replace workers who transfer to different occupations or exit the labor force, such as to retire."[6] However, there will be more pressure on government actors within these sectors to support digital accessibility in light of the new Department of Justice rule of 2024 that focuses on "digital accessibility" as integral to the spirit of the ADA.[7]

The rise in opportunities will also come with a rising expectation that job candidates will be able to fill some digital accessibility gaps in organizations. A 2021 *Wall Street Journal* article analyzed accessibility jobs and claimed a 78 percent increase in the number of job listings with "accessibility" in the title from the year before. This built on the 38 percent increase from the first months of the pandemic, when organizations scrambled to offer more reliable services to a wider consumer base.[8]

Hiring additional staff or creating new positions in libraries to adjust to changing needs, while aspirational, is simply not an option with shrinking budgets. Budget savvy and stalwart advocacy will be leadership competencies in high demand to ensure a strategic and sustainable approach to comprehensive universal design and an equitable information ecosystem. Without increased funding, librarians will be asked to do more with what they have, or with even less than they currently have. Digital accessibility done well in libraries will require a team approach and a deep understanding of accessibility barriers, information poverty, and their repercussions.

A point worth considering when analyzing your accessibility workflows is at what stage stakeholders have a direct influence over digital accessibility. The life cycle of a product or service can be positively affected by a diversity team approach that will most likely have a universal approach or perspective. The technology team, while holding a theoretical frame for their work, will most likely be trying to just keep up with stopgap measures, checklists, and random site audits if they are not truly shifting their design and thinking about accessibility to the beginning of the process before those technical expedients are necessary.

A 2018 study of European job ads related to digital accessibility analyzed a total of 89 vacancies for 48 different positions. The focus of most of these skills is technical, but some indicate more of a disposition and mindset. The Rajšp et al. study "identified 13 technology-independent high-level skills that a developer should master to be truly competent in Digital Accessibility:

- Understanding Web Accessibility,
- Managing the technical aspects of Web Accessibility,
- Enabling publishing of accessible web content,
- Understanding accessible visual web design (and CSS),
- Creating accessible images,
- Creating accessible multimedia materials,
- Accessible page structuring,
- Developing site navigation and orientation,
- Creating accessible tables,
- Creating accessible forms,
- Basics of accessible scripting and WAI-ARIA (Accessible Rich Internet Applications),
- Creating mobile accessible solutions,
- Accessibility conformance evaluation."[9]

Of these skills, several overlap with those needed by librarians working to provide equal access. Particularly critical are understanding web accessibility, understanding accessible visual web design, creating accessible images, creating accessible multimedia materials, creating accessible tables, creating accessible forms, and accessibility conformance evaluation. "Understanding" and "evaluation" done well are both iterative and reflective processes that integrate a wider picture of the importance of accessibility, as well as the reverberations of its presence or absence.

The focus of these skills is rooted in intentionality—pushing the emphasis to a "shift left" mindset that "means thinking about accessibility at the start of every step we take when we deploy new software or services," according to Microsoft's partner software engineering director, Patrice Pelland.[10] While file- and document-specific creation protocols are covered in depth in chapter 5, "Digital Media and File Accessibility," and are certainly critical to ensuring inclusion, it is important to hone in on the trend here of specifically seeking candidates who focus on maintaining the necessary mindset and approach to sustain digital accessibility as a practice.

In their study of job listings, Rajšp et al. looked at "all stages of ensuring Digital Accessibility," including "the design phase, development phase, evaluation phase, and conformance testing phase." They summarized the changing landscape in the European Union: "Not only are new professions being created, existing positions are constantly adapting to the new accessibility norms and technologies."[11] This trend is not specific to libraries, but it points to a sea change in how we embrace this work and forecasts some of the skills librarians can bring to lay the groundwork to fulfill their mission.

❱ Library and Information Science Curricula

The new millennium has not brought a dramatic shift in the status quo for library and information science curricula over the years. Several studies have looked at the historically ableist approach of library and information science (LIS) programs overall. Today, at least in the United States, we are at a turning point, with more legal regulations ensuring equal access and a rise in lawsuits and complaints where such access is inadequate. While there is ample discussion about the needs and satisfaction of library users with disabilities, there is much less on the library and information science curriculum concerning accessibility. Lauri Bonnici, Stephanie Maatta, and Muriel Wells conducted the first U.S. National Accessibility Survey of librarians serving the National Library Service (NLS) for the Blind and Physically Handicapped (BPH) in 2009, completing a deep dive into the existing literature at the time. The authors note that "only two studies have examined library education programs that attempt to prepare graduates to work with special needs populations," citing both Gibson 1977 and Walling 2004.[12] Bonnici et al. note in a follow-up study that "LIS education is severely lacking in courses preparing graduates to work with populations with physical access challenges."[13] Clear in their findings is a "keen awareness among library professionals providing NLS/BPH access that sufficient funding for libraries, increased advocacy campaigns and available leadership that understands the complex system of services to persons with disabilities are crucial to the migration to equitable digital access."[14]

Both the Gibson and Walling studies, while seminal works, are now dated. The former was written well before the establishment of the Americans with Disabilities Act in 1990, and the latter was written fourteen years after the passage of the ADA. One would think there would have been more progress on the front of inclusion since then, and certainly some progress has been made, especially around physical accessibility. But sadly, even as we look to update their conclusions, Bonnici et al.' s illustration of the issues at hand should not surprise anyone: funding limitations which result in poor staffing, support, and training, all complicate the growing demand for a "universal access philosophy practiced by information professionals [which] would assure that no individual is left without access to information."[15]

As JJ Pionke suggests in his 2020 study, "Often there is a disconnect between what is being taught, what is being learned, and what is needed."[16] Pionke's study reveals that only 2 percent of library graduate students surveyed felt "extremely well" prepared to assist patrons with disabilities. A whopping 39 percent felt "slightly well" and a full 20 percent felt "not well at all."[17] Together, almost 60 percent of graduates' educational expectations were not met. Pionke examines the perceived gaps and charts a history that confirms the information and practical application vacuum felt by graduates of LIS programs regarding disability, and he calls for LIS programs to include specific information on how exactly to be more inclusive. In examining the comments of his participants, Pionke further surmises that "libraries continue to subscribe to a retrofit model of accessibility rather than an inclusive Universal Design model that has accessibility incorporated into the beginning stages of planning/designing services, software, and the like, and not added as an afterthought."[18] The inextricable link to information technology skills is evident, as is graduates' desire to approach disability with a better understanding of proper etiquette, language, and understanding of the barriers they unwittingly create. By not having accessibility "baked into every relevant course" and treated "not as a second thought but as another track of thought," creating a practice for accessibility to be at the "center of our thoughts,"[19] LIS programs miss crucial opportunities to connect theory to practice and to our new realities.

At a time when we are clearly experiencing more disability as a society and need a more inclusive information ecosystem, data continues to show what Bonnici et al. concluded in 2015, specifically that "library education in the USA may not be preparing for the expected mass exit of professionals versed in serving special access needs."[20] We will need library professionals with "knowledge of the information access challenges, the ability to work with information and communication technologies to assure access to electronic sources of information, and the ability to secure funding to assure that equality of access will be crucial for the next generation of library professionals to be successful."[21]

For more than a decade before the printing of this work, studies on the limitations of LIS curricula in keeping up with technological changes have made clear that "libraries have traditionally played a key role in providing access to information and disseminating it across a community. That role has now extended to include facilitating access to innovative technologies."[22] A 2022 study by Yadav looks at LIS curricula in India and similarly posits that "the impact of the digital technologies on the library and information science profession necessitates that the LIS schools bring their curricula up to speed."[23] Here, the author speaks to the benefit of information professionals with computing skills and knowledge about programming, web designing, hardware, and software. However, these alone mean little if professionals can't apply these skills without "a deep understanding of ethics and ethical reasoning."[24] Internationally and within the United States, the marriage between the practical and the theoretical remains a need and expectation for the profession to fulfill its mission.

Bonnici et al. suggest that the "adoption of universal access philosophies while simultaneously aligning with strategic partners and initiatives at the national level" might shift the course we are on.[25] Over the years, the American Library Association (ALA) has attempted to advocate for more inclusion and codify the needs for both specific skills and the theoretical framework under which they operate. The most recent update to ALA's Core Competences of Librarianship clearly calls for a praxis that "incorporates the concepts of social justice, equity, diversity, and inclusion."[26] The ALA clarifies that "social justice in the library context includes the knowledge and skills necessary for library professionals to create and support library collections, services, personnel, facilities, and programs that foster equitable access to and participation of all people to use the library and its resources."[27] The question becomes how and when the curriculum will catch up.

▶ Skills

We have discussed the increasing levels of disability globally, the growing need for digital accessibility, its relationship to information technology, and the central role libraries play in ensuring equal access to information by following best practices. In this section, we look at the specific skills being sought for those in digital accessibility positions. Research in the field of digital accessibility, while not centered on librarianship, has given us a glimpse of the skills needed to implement digital accessibility across most organizations and information ecosystems.

Not surprisingly, Rajšp et al.'s content analysis of existing digital accessibility job ads counts "librarian" among the titles studied. Specifically, the job title "Emerging Technology Librarian"[28] stood out as directly relevant, as it included digital accessibility as a need and skill. While the study did not include any mentions of the more popular title of "Electronic Resources Librarian" (the data set likely lacked this title due to timing and the size of the set), similar skills would be required of most electronic resource librarians. The study did not comment on the "librarian" listing as an outlier among the other job titles, likely because the idea of a librarian is central to the mission of digital accessibility. They examine the skills identified as most relevant to digital accessibility jobs, including

- User testing
- User experience
- Usability testing

- User interface design, etc.
- Accessibility compliance evaluation
- Inclusive design
- Designing and developing WCAG-compliant websites
- Automating accessibility testing

Singh and Mehra (2013) point out that all of the studies focused on changing job descriptions showed "the introduction of new job titles—such as digital librarian, web services librarian, electronic resources librarian, metadata librarian, and emerging technology librarian—in the workplace, thus reflecting a new focus on information roles meshed with new technologies."[29] While there is a widespread realization that someone needs to be a "point person for digital accessibility,"[30] it is not clear that libraries, on the whole, have anyone aside from the ubiquitous electronic resources librarian to fulfill this role. This is the one standard library position which unequivocally includes a "shift left" mindset focused on digital accessibility. According to the North American Serials Interest Group's (NASIG's) Core Competencies, the electronic resources librarian is "committed to . . . the library's dual role as content access provider and content generator."[31] With an understanding of conformance and the library's role in advocacy, NASIG confirms that "both vendors and librarians must commit to understanding what makes a product accessible," and the electronic resources librarian is well suited to do just that. Ultimately, it is the electronic resources position's proximal relationship to the workflow of digital accessibility that solidifies its place as a central resource, advocate, and gatekeeper when it comes to equitable resources.

According to Bronstein, who looked at skills from an Israeli perspective, "personal competencies began to appear in job advertisements for reference librarians in the early 1990s, emphasizing oral and written communication skills because librarians need to be able to communicate effectively with patrons."[32] Aside from these, the personal competencies mentioned in job ads also traditionally include "leadership," "creativity," and "computer skills," and often mention teamwork and "strategic and relationship management." A 2013 survey by Robati and Singh looked at over 100 competency statements that were expected of special librarians. Of the 122 competency statements rated on a Likert scale by participants, the one area that, not surprisingly, came to the fore at any level of education was information technology skills, specifically the "ability to operate computers and familiarity with computer technology."[33] This study was just one in a series of calls in the literature to focus on being nimble when it comes to sharpening graduates' skills in dealing with information and computing technology.

Changing Our Hiring Practices

Spina and Cohen discuss changing interview practices at various ARL college and university libraries that were surveyed. They point out that there are some libraries that "take more proactive approaches," including "providing interview questions ahead of time, providing sign language interpreters, and asking about issues of transportation around campus and between buildings."[34] They further explain that

> other interesting suggestions include making sure interviews were always taking place in an accessible room, asking candidates about dietary restrictions prior to arrival on campus, and notifying the candidate ahead of time about what accommodations are available while they are on campus.[35]

The Digital Library Federation (DLF) has a wiki with a growing list of recommendations for creating a more unbiased interview process. Tips like ensuring both the speaker and audience have a microphone available, offering periodic breaks, and even having a plan to intervene if anyone asks or says something inappropriate, can make or break the interview process for either side involved.[36] Karen Miller of Bradbury Miller Associates suggests stakeholders take the time to "look for ableist language in job descriptions," and encourages clients to rewrite or remove such language. One example she gives is "requiring an individual to hold a driver's license as opposed to having reliable transportation available."[37] This is something many people don't consider and may take for granted. Unless there is a specific reason, how someone gets to work is likely not your concern, and this may be a legacy from older, boilerplate job descriptions. Reconsidering every element of the hiring process and viewing it from the perspectives of several known disabilities is useful. Understanding disability may be intersectional and an individual may face several barriers in your process is, frankly, necessary. The goal is to find the right match for your library, and the benefits of leaning into an increasingly diverse workforce often outweigh the perceived disadvantages.

The library profession has an opportunity to commit to accessibility at all levels, from the services we provide to our communities, to our hiring practices, to our curriculum. Making this commitment allows libraries to meet and exceed their legal obligation, creating inclusive and supportive communities and workplaces for disabled individuals. It is vital that we move toward a greater emphasis on accessibility and a deeper understanding of disability in LIS education and ongoing professional development for the members of our profession.

Advice from an Executive Search Expert

Interview with **Karen Miller**, *President/CEO, Bradbury Miller Associates*

Have you been in discussions on inclusion regarding digital accessibility?

Our firm runs approximately thirty searches per year, primarily for upper management/CEO-level positions in public libraries. The firm has been in existence since 1983. Digital accessibility hardly ever comes up except when we bring it up in planning a more accessible search. When we do, people are generally surprised and amazed.

What have you done to ensure a more inclusive candidate search?

We have started sending interview questions to candidates ahead of their scheduled interview. We also add the interview questions to the chat box during virtual interviews as the candidates are being asked—allowing the candidate to review them in real time and refer back if there are difficulties in hearing or understanding. From my perspective, the more we can reduce fear and anxiety in the candidate and allow for a more authentic conversation, the more likely we are to get to know the real person, which is who will show up day after day at the job site. I want the candidate to concentrate on sharing their experience and approach to work because that is what matters in the end—and if that person has a disability but is capable of doing the work, we want them to have the best chance of getting that job. It's all about bringing different voices to the table—someone shouldn't lose the opportunity to do the work because they couldn't hear the questions being asked or technology failed them in some way.

Where have you found some fruitful discussions about accessibility?
I volunteer for ILEAD Ohio,[i] which is a fantastic and unique mentorship program for current or future Ohio library leaders (sponsored by the State Library of Ohio and OhioNET) to do team-based problem-solving projects. One of the most recent cohorts for ILEAD focused on disability—the latest generations of library professionals are much more aware of and thoughtful about the topics of disability and accessibility and there is still so much to learn.

Note

i. ILEAD Ohio, https://library.ohio.gov/libraries/training-and-development/ilead-ohio.

Notes

1. Wan He, Daniel Goodkind, and Paul Kowal, "International Population Reports," n.d., 45.
2. U.S. Department of Health and Human Services, "Guidance on 'Long COVID' as a Disability under the ADA, Section 504, and Section 1557," July 2021, www.hhs.gov/civil-rights/for-providers/civil-rights-covid19/guidance-long-covid-disability/.
3. Stephanie Rosen, "What Does a Library Accessibility Specialist Do? How a New Role Advances Accessibility through Education and Advocacy," *College & Research Libraries News* 79, no. 1 (January 5, 2018): 23, https://doi.org/10.5860/crln.79.1.23.
4. Rosen, "What Does a Library Accessibility Specialist Do?," 24.
5. Bureau of Labor Statistics, "Librarians and Library Media Specialists," www.bls.gov/ooh/education-training-and-library/librarians.htm.

6. Bureau of Labor Statistics, "Librarians and Library Media Specialists."
7. Federal Register, "Nondiscrimination on the Basis of Disability; Accessibility of Web Information and Services of State and Local Government Entities," April 24, 2024, www.federalregister.gov/documents/2024/04/24/2024-07758/nondiscrimination-on-the-basis-of-disability-accessibility-of-web-information-and-services-of-state.
8. Ann-Marie Alcántara, "More Companies Are Looking to Hire Accessibility Specialists," *Wall Street Journal*, September 1, 2021, sec. C Suite, www.wsj.com/articles/more-companies-are-looking-to-hire-accessibility-specialists-11630501200.
9. Alen Rajšp et al., "Preliminary Review of Jobs, Skills and Competencies for Implementation of Digital Accessibility" (Faculty of Organization and Informatics Varazdin, 2019), 93–99, www.proquest.com/docview/2366654690/abstract/BD38A33C61814969PQ/1?sourcetype=Conference%20Papers%20&%20Proceedings.
10. Lukas Velush, "Shifting Left to Get Accessibility Right at Microsoft," *Inside Track Blog* (blog), May 13, 2024, www.microsoft.com/insidetrack/blog/shifting-left-to-get-accessibility-right-at-microsoft/.
11. Rajšp et al., "Preliminary Review," 95–96.
12. Bonnici et al., "Second National Accessibility Survey: Librarians, Patrons, and Disabilities," *New Library World* 116, no. 9/10 (2015): 515, https://doi.org/10.1108/NLW-03-2015-0021; Merrillyn C. Gibson, "Preparing Librarians to Serve Handicapped Individuals," *Association for Library and Information Science Education* 18, no. 2 (1977): 121–130, https://doi.org/10.2307/40322534; Linda L. Walling, "Educating Students to Serve Information Seekers with Disabilities," *Journal of Education for Library and Information Science* 45, no. 2 (2004): 137–148, https://doi.org/10.2307/40323900.
13. Bonnici et al., "Second National Accessibility Survey," 505.
14. Bonnici et al., "Second National Accessibility Survey," 8.
15. Bonnici et al., "Second National Accessibility Survey," 523.
16. JJ Pionke, "Disability- and Accessibility-Related Library Graduate-School Education from the Student Perspective," *Journal of Education for Library and Information Science* 61, no. 2 (April 2020): 254, https://doi.org/10.3138/jelis.2019-0036.
17. Pionke, "Disability- and Accessibility-Related Library Graduate-School Education," 259.
18. Pionke, "Disability- and Accessibility-Related Library Graduate-School Education," 262.
19. Pionke, "Disability- and Accessibility-Related Library Graduate-School Education," 262.
20. Bonnici et al., "Second National Accessibility Survey," 8.
21. Laurie J. Bonnici, Stephanie L. Maatta, and Muriel K. Wells, "US National Accessibility Survey: Librarians Serving Patrons with Disabilities," *New Library World* 110, no. 11/12 (2009): 52, https://doi.org/10.1108/03074800911007532.
22. Vandana Singh and Bharat Mehra, "Strengths and Weaknesses of the Information Technology Curriculum in Library and Information Science Graduate Programs," *Journal of Librarianship and Information Science* 45, no. 3 (September 1, 2013): 220, https://doi.org/10.1177/0961000612448206.

23. Akhilesh K. S. Yadav, "An Evaluation of Library and Information Science Curricula and Professional Perspectives in India," *International Information & Library Review* 54, no. 3 (July 3, 2022): 243, https://doi.org/10.1080/10572317.2021.1988393.

24. Yadav, "An Evaluation of Library and Information Science Curricula," 250.

25. Bonnici et al., "Second National Accessibility Survey," 513.

26. American Library Association, "2022 Update to ALA's Core Competences of Librarianship," January 18, 2023, www.ala.org/educationcareers/2022-update-alas -core-competences-librarianship.

27. American Library Association, "2022 Update to ALA's Core Competences."

28. Rajšp et al., "Preliminary Review," 95.

29. Singh and Mehra, "Strengths and Weaknesses of the Information Technology Curriculum," 221.

30. Faye O'Reilly, "Digital Accessibility as a Core Competency for E-Resources Librarians," *Serials Review* 46, no. 2 (April 2020): 115, https://doi.org/10.1080/ 00987913.2020.1782631.

31. "NASIG Core Competencies for E-Resources Librarians," www.nasig.org/ Competencies-Eresources.

32. Jenny Bronstein, "An Exploration of the Library and Information Science Professional Skills and Personal Competencies: An Israeli Perspective," *Library & Information Science Research* 37, no. 2 (April 1, 2015): 130–38, https://doi.org/ 10.1016/j.lisr.2015.02.003.

33. Alireza Peyvand Robati and Diljit Singh, "Competencies Required by Special Librarians: An Analysis by Educational Levels," *Journal of Librarianship and Information Science* 45, no. 2 (June 1, 2013): 125, https://doi.org/10.1177/ 0961000613476728.

34. Carli Spina and Margaret Cohen, "SPEC Kit 358: Accessibility and Universal Design," May 2, 2018, Association of Research Libraries, https://publications.arl .org/Accessibility-Universal-Design-SPEC-Kit-358/2.

35. Spina and Cohen, "SPEC Kit 358."

36. "Designing an Inclusive Interview Process," DLF Wiki, July 16, 2020, https://wiki .diglib.org/Designing_an_Inclusive_Interview_Process.

37. Karen Miller, interview with Karen Miller of Bradbury Miller Associates, August 26, 2024.

• • •

CHAPTER 13

Digital Accessibility On a Budget

A school librarian has identified that some students would benefit from access to a screen reader, but she isn't sure if there is room in the budget for a JAWS license.

The team at a rural public library would like to offer circulating assistive technologies and is searching for outside funding to make this new collection possible.

A new academic librarian realizes that there are gaps in his knowledge about digital accessibility and wants to learn more on the topic.

C reating an accessible and inclusive digital experience for library patrons can be an expensive undertaking that requires a significant amount of employee time and expertise. Digital accessibility also encompasses providing access to technologies and tools, both for patrons and for those responsible for checking and maintaining the accessibility of the library's digital presence. At a time when most libraries are short staffed and facing shrinking budgets, these aspects of digital accessibility can present significant challenges. But, there are ways to make effective accessibility improvements without investing a lot of time or money into the work. The key is to focus on efficient and high-impact activities, while also finding external sources of support for this work. This chapter will offer some tips for increasing accessibility opportunities and training without breaking the budget or over-taxing employees who are already stretched thin.

229

230 ••• CHAPTER 13

❯ Optimize Your Current Resources

The first step to take toward improved accessibility can be achieved for free. It is to optimize the library's current assets. This step may take some staff time but is otherwise not resource intensive. It can encompass a few different activities. First, as discussed in chapter 2, "The Wares: Spaces, Hardware, and Software," many operating systems already have assistive features, such as screen readers or screen magnifiers, built into them. Ensuring that these are enabled and providing documentation about how they work in an accessible format can improve accessibility without the need to purchase any new technology. In addition to offering documentation for those who will be using the tools, training staff on how to use these tools or helping patrons with them is a vital part of making them available in the library. Second, the digital content that the library provides access to should be evaluated for accessibility features and barriers. Once this information is collected, it can be shared proactively with all users in the library's catalog or discovery layer, on the library website, and integrated into research guides that feature these databases. It might even be helpful to create specialized outreach materials about platform accessibility features that are shared on the library's social media accounts and distributed to partners, such as disability services departments or relevant community organizations.

Finally, the placement of furniture, hardware, and equipment should be audited to ensure that they are arranged for accessibility and ease of use, which can be done using free tools, such as those provided by Project ENABLE.[1] While ideally an institution will provide workspaces with dedicated accessibility features and assistive hardware, an initial step toward improved access is to reconsider how technology spaces are organized. One common problem in libraries is that spaces are too crowded, which prevents those using wheelchairs, crutches, or walkers from navigating through the area. Spreading out computer stations can be a good way to improve access. Along the same lines, offering a greater variety of workstation options, such as setting up technology workstations in areas with different types of lighting, different types of chairs, different height tables, and different noise levels, can ensure that as many people as possible have access to a space that will meet their needs. This type of furniture audit can help in prioritizing future purchases of assistive technologies and accessible hardware by identifying where gaps exist in the library's current offerings.

❯ Identify Free Resources

It can be easy to assume that web accessibility testing tools will be expensive, but there are a range of free resources available for those institutions that have limited funds. Many of these tools are discussed in chapter 2, "The Wares: Spaces, Hardware, and Software." However, it is worth highlighting a few tools that can be particularly helpful when starting accessibility work with no available budget.

WebAIM's WAVE—The free web accessibility evaluation tool from WebAIM known as WAVE is useful because of its versatility. For library workers who cannot install tools on their computers, the web-based testing tool available at wave.webaim.org allows users to paste a URL into the provided box to evaluate the accessibility of the page. In addition, WAVE also offers a free browser extension for those who can install such tools, which is helpful for evaluating digital content that is behind a login page, such as databases. The browser-based tool is available for Chrome, Firefox, and Microsoft Edge and both the web-based and browser-based tools are fairly intuitive.

Accessibility Insights—This Microsoft tool is free and open source, which makes it a great option for those with limited budgets. It does require the installation of either a browser-based tool, currently available for Chrome or Microsoft Edge, or a Windows desktop app. It has different testing options, including a Fast Pass option, which is "a lightweight, two-step process that helps developers identify common, high impact accessibility issues in less than five minutes."[2]

AudioEye Color Contrast Checker—There are many free color contrast checkers available online, so there are definitely options to test out to find the one that works best for you. AudioEye's color contrast checker offers a nice balance of functionality and additional background information on how color contrast works and why it is important that can be useful for those who are new to this topic. It also offers an option to preview the selected colors in greyscale.[3]

CADET—This tool from the National Center for Accessible Media at WGBH is a fully featured caption and audio description creation tool.[4] It does require downloading and installation, and it is worth noting that your library likely already has caption authoring tools available in your video creation software, if you have one, but this is a good option when you are working on both captions and audio descriptions, and you are working with a limited budget.

YouTube—For captions alone, YouTube offers access to a web-based caption editing platform with a free account. If your institution has a YouTube account, uploading videos, waiting for them to be automatically captioned, and then editing those automatic captions can be a fairly efficient workflow for caption creation if you do not have the budget to pay for external caption creation.

NVDA—While NVDA is not the most popular screen reader in most surveys, it is free and open source, making it a good option for those who want a screen reader for testing and evaluation purposes. It is available for Windows computers.[5]

VoiceOver—If your library has any MacOS or iOS devices, whether desktop computers, laptops, or mobile devices, you already have access to VoiceOver, the screen reader that is built-in to Apple devices. Since this comes automatically installed on these devices, it is another great option for those working at institutions that limit the ability to install new content. VoiceOver also has helpful documentation online that helps with the learning curve to become a regular user of this tool.[6]

Your institution may also already have paid access to tools that the library team could make use of, such as subscription-based web accessibility testing tools or accessibility training resources, such as Deque University. It is worthwhile to check with relevant departments, such as IT or the disability services office, to see if any of these tools are available, particularly before opting to make a purchase or subscription.

▶ Evaluate New Purchases and Contracts

As mentioned several times throughout this book, the most budget-friendly way to approach accessibility is always to consider it at the beginning of the project. Too often, accessibility is overlooked in the early stages of selecting a new CMS, evaluating a database for potential subscription, choosing furniture for a space, or drawing up the plans for a renovation. If accessibility is forgotten and problems are only discovered after work has been done or money has been spent, it will virtually always take more time and money to fix the issue. For this reason, accessibility considerations should be integrated into every new purchase decision, contract negotiation, and RFP process. This is discussed in more depth in chapter 11, "Best Practices for Working with Vendors," but any discussion of being budget conscious around accessibility work necessitates this approach.

When selecting new furniture or designing new spaces, flexibility will almost always serve the library well. If the choice is made to prioritize usability and accessibility at the time of purchase, it might be possible to spend a small amount more, for example, to purchase an adjustable height workstation, which will save libraries from having to purchase additional workstations at various accessible heights in the future. When advocating for allocating the budget toward flexibility, it can be helpful to point out that spending a little more on an item that allows the individual user to easily adjust it to meet their needs will not only save money down the road because new purchases will not be needed but also will cut down on the amount of employee time that is spent assisting users who are trying to make use of inaccessible spaces or fixtures.

For databases, content management systems, and web content designed by third parties, as discussed elsewhere in this book, a good way to cut back on the cost of accessibility compliance is to ensure that this is contemplated in the initial contract. For example, if the library is contracting with an outside party to create a new library website, the RFP should include questions about the company's accessibility expertise and practices, and the contract should specify that if issues are found, they must be fixed, ideally at no additional cost. This will save time and money in the future and ensure that the new site will be accessible from day one. For database subscriptions, it may not be possible to insist that the vendor make specific changes for a single subscriber, but given that many libraries are now focused on digital accessibility and legal compliance, it is often possible to negotiate into the contract that a minimum level of WCAG compliance is maintained. Particularly when this is not possible, it is important to negotiate a clear process for reporting issues to the vendor. Taking these steps at the beginning of projects will set the library up for optimal accessibility in a budget-friendly way.

❱ Affordable Employee Training

Training library employees on digital accessibility is a vital part of ensuring that the library's web presence and services are accessible. At many libraries, digital content creation is distributed across employees in many departments, many of whom may not have extensive training in how to ensure the accessibility of the materials they create. Studies conducted by JJ Pionke demonstrate that significant percentages of both library school students and current library employees do not have a high level of comfort around troubleshooting assistive technologies, updating or creating accessible websites, and updating or creating accessible research guides.[7] This research points to the importance of making employee professional development a core component of all digital accessibility work. While this may sound expensive, there are ways to make it more affordable.

Community partners can be a useful resource in developing professional development opportunities. Recruiting a member of the community who works with assistive technologies or is an expert on digital accessibility to present to the library team can help to build buy-in for the importance of this work. It can also bring new skills into the library at low or no cost.

This is particularly true if the library is part of a larger organization that has trained IT or disability services professionals on hand to provide this type of training. An alternative for public libraries that do not have access to professionals with these skills would be to see if there are local community groups offering this type of training who would be interested in using the library as their meeting place. Additionally, some larger library systems, consortia, or educational institutions may have access to databases like LinkedIn Learning, which offers tutorials on accessibility-related topics and even provides certificates for completion so employees can use these for review and promotion. Whether partnering with community groups or other libraries, the benefits are clear: more engagement with concepts of accessibility and the prospect of networking with other like-minded professionals interested in honing skills and knowledge in this area.

Another approach to affordable library professional development around accessibility is to turn to vendors. When it comes to accessibility features of the platforms that libraries subscribe to, the vendor can often offer free training for employees. While this training may not always focus on accessibility features, it is definitely worth asking for specific training around accessibility best practices, particularly when this is a new subscription or a new platform that the library will be using to create and share content. Vendors should be able to also provide written documentation that can explain how to use accessibility features effectively. Outside of the vendors that the library already has a relationship with, many other digital accessibility vendors offer free webinars on accessibility best practices and updates on accessibility requirements. 3PlayMedia is one example of a vendor that offers how-to guides, webinars, podcasts, and more related to digital accessibility.[8] In addition to their paid services, Deque also offers a variety of free webinars as well as hosting a free conference on digital accessibility annually. Other organizations, such as WAI and WebAIM, also offer free professional development resources and tutorials. Many large educational institutions have created guides and tutorials that are freely available to anyone. Using the free resources available online, it would be possible to create a menu of options that would meet many of the needs of employees across library departments.

While free professional development resources are available, it can be very helpful to formalize this process by creating a team that works together through set accessibility training materials. This can not only keep everyone on track, but it also offers a built-in community for discussion and collaboration. There are many ways that this can be structured. If your library is part of a larger system, you might consider a cohort of employees interested in digital accessibility who could undertake both training and accessibility testing work together. This approach was used at the State University of New York to build skills around evaluating library databases for accessibility and proved to be a supportive and successful way of encouraging professional development on this topic.[9] For those institutions that aren't able to devote an extended period of time to this type of professional development, the ten-day accessibility challenge format implemented by SUNY Oswego is a perfect way to build accessibility skills through brief, daily activities. This challenge asked participants to participate in readings, optional discussions, and activities during the ten-day period with a goal of improving the accessibility of one of their documents with each day focused on a single skill that was designed to be approachable by those with varied levels of experience.[10] This type of activity could be modified to fit the needs and expertise level of any organization able to allocate time over the course of two weeks to accessibility training. While offering professional development on digital accessibility to your library's employees might initially seem daunting or potentially expensive, there are ways to start building skills at no cost and with only a limited amount of time to devote to the work. This type of professional development can ensure that all employees are prepared to contribute to the accessible and inclusive environment that the library offers.

▶ Find Partners

Accessibility work is most successful and efficient when it is a collaborative effort. Building a community of others who are committed to this work can extend impact and offer support for professional development by sharing skills. For those who work in libraries with multiple individuals interested in accessibility or those at institutions with multiple libraries with accessibility needs, forming a team or committee devoted to accessibility is a great first step. This approach can make the work feel less overwhelming, as it can be divided across those with differing interests and expertise. It can also allow members of the group to share expertise, building everyone's knowledge and comfort with accessibility work over time. A team approach to this work also helps to ensure that accessibility is integrated into decision-making and workflows across the library, which can be very difficult when all accessibility work falls to a single individual. At most libraries, it is not possible to have any one employee devote all their time to accessibility work, so adopting a team approach can help to spread the work out in a way that makes it possible to achieve the library's accessibility goals with the limited staff time available.

It can also be useful to collaborate beyond the library on accessibility efforts. As with internal groups, these broader partnerships can facilitate growth in skills and provide a support network for those just starting out with accessibility work. For academic libraries, this can mean building a working relationship with the disability services department, but at other types of libraries, there might be opportunities to partner with IT, HR, and other departments to share accessibility resources and knowledge as well as to advocate for making accessibility a priority across the institution. For libraries that are associated with governmental institutions, such as public libraries and other governmental libraries, building these relationships can also be useful in persuading these partners to help make changes that the library might not be able to unilaterally make, such as major website redesigns.

Building partnerships across the wider community can also be a key part of creating an accessible and inclusive online experience at the library. One great resource for those wanting to learn more about accessibility is local affinity groups, such as those for accessibility professionals and web developers. These groups are usually free and can offer opportunities to learn about new technologies, connect with others working in this field, and build skills. Accessibility meetups often host in-person events for networking focused on accessibility and also offer recordings or hybrid options for these events and sessions focused on developing new skills. For many accessibility professionals, our discussions can be enhanced by an understanding of how accessibility is valued even in adjacent professions. Getting outside of the library can be a way to find out about new innovations that may not yet be common practice in libraries, so it can be

238 ●●● CHAPTER 13

a particularly valuable approach to professional development. For those in areas where these groups are not available, there are online groups that can offer just as much support and training.

It can also be helpful to reach out to local organizations of people with disabilities, which can range from nonprofits to educational institutions to social groups. While some of these groups may be limited to only members with disabilities, other groups host educational programming and may be open to partnering with the library on programming or helping to recruit participants for user testing. Connecting with these groups is a great way of building a stronger understanding of your community's needs and interests. This is invaluable in setting priorities around accessibility initiatives at the library and finding resources that will be regularly and enthusiastically used. Over time, this can help to make sure that purchases are impactful. Additionally, building an authentic relationship with groups for people with disabilities can also help to demonstrate the library's commitment to inclusion in a way that will encourage more people to visit the library and use its services.

❱ Identify and Apply for Grants

Some accessibility projects cannot be done at a low cost. The unfortunate reality is that some of this work will be expensive, particularly if renovations or new websites are required. While the majority of web accessibility projects can be tackled with incremental improvements over time, at times it may be necessary to find money for a major project. In these cases, outside funding might be available to help limit the impact on the library's budget. Grants are often a good way to approach funding for these projects. These can include public grants, in the form of local, state, or federal grants available to support improved inclusion of people with disabilities. Your larger organization, such as a campus, system, or consortium may offer grant funding for this purpose as well. Some private organizations also provide grants, such as the ALA, which provides multiple grants that can be used to support accessibility projects. One such grant that can support a wide range of accessibility initiatives is the Libraries Transforming Communities: Accessible Small and Rural Communities grant.[11] This grant is geared towards small and rural libraries, as the name suggests. It requires that applicants include "community input-gathering sessions" to ensure that the final grant activity makes a significant impact. The grant has been offered for multiple rounds and can give libraries the funds needed to make real changes to improve inclusion within their community. In addition, there are grants that are focused on specific types of disabilities. For example, the Reference and User Services Association (RUSA), which is a division of ALA, offers the Stephen T. Riedner Grant for Life Enhancing Library Programs for People Living with Dementia to support new services or programming for people living with dementia.[12] While this grant does not require a technological component, nothing precludes organizations from applying for support for digital programs or services. RUSA also sponsors the annual ETS Best Emerging Technology Application Award, which does not provide funds up-front, but does provide a monetary award to recognize innovative technology developments and applications that can be applied to accessibility initiatives.[13]

Even if a grant is not specifically designed to support accessibility initiatives, it may be possible to make the case for an accessibility initiative. Any grant that aims to improve inclusion, such as services to elderly patrons or updated facilities, can easily fit with an accessibility project. In addition, for grants related to digitization or the creation and distribution of open educational resources or other open access resources, funding for the necessary accessibility work that will be part of the project can be incorporated into the funding request. When writing these types of grants, it is important to explain why the accessibility component is central to expanding the reach of the project and ensuring that the end result is inclusive and meets legal requirements. This can not only get funding for this work but also makes the overall grant application stronger in the eyes of many funding organizations.

Grants can also be used to support library professional develop ment. These grants may not be limited to accessibility-related professional development, but they can allow library employees to take classes, attend conferences, or pursue advanced certifications related to digital accessibility. One example of an accessibility-specific grant of this type is the Big Ten Academic Alliance's Library Accessibility Mini-Grant Program, which provides funding for library employees at member institutions to pursue professional development opportunities related to accessibility.[14] Other professional organizations offer a variety of professional development support and conference travel grants that can be used to develop accessibility skills or attend conferences with programming related to digital accessibility. As an example, the ALA Learning Roundtable offers the annual Pat Carterette Professional Development Grant[15] to support a range of types of professional development, and many other national and local organizations offer similar grants to support conference attendance or other professional development.

Grant writing can feel overwhelming, but it is important to remember that there are resources available to support this work at many institutions. For those at academic institutions, there may be an office that can assist with the preparation of grant applications. Even at organizations that do not have this formal support available, there may be experts who have written successful grants in the past who can help with the process. Looking beyond your institution to the larger community, such as consortia, systems, or professional organizations is also a good option. Even if you cannot identify this support, it is worth applying for grants to support this work. Accessibility initiatives fall squarely within the kind of work that many funding organizations hope to support, which makes it worth applying.

▶ Make the Case for Dedicated Funding

Another alternative for funding accessibility initiatives is to advocate for funding within the library's budget for this work either for one-off initiatives or for ongoing support of digital accessibility at the library. Given the budget limitations many libraries face, this may seem like an overwhelming option. However, there are ways to make the case for a budget increase. The first element of this sort of request is to conduct an evaluation of the library's current accessibility status. This should incorporate multiple types of information to make a strong case for spending more on digital accessibility.

First, it is important to understand the legal requirements that apply to the library. This can be both related to technology spaces within the facility and the library's online presence. Given the upcoming change in regulations that apply to many libraries under the ADA, it is particularly important to understand whether the library is going to be subject to increased requirements in the near future. This information can be used to advocate for a short-term budget increase to fix known problems or for hiring additional employees with expertise and experience in digital accessibility to be responsible for improving and maintaining the library's digital presence over time. Outlining the legal risks of not allocating more funds to this work is a persuasive way of making sure that more money is dedicated to this work.

The next step in the process is to collect both quantitative and qualitative data about accessibility. This can include information about the number of requests or complaints the library receives regarding accessibility, the number of issues found on the existing website, or the number of patrons who participate in specific services or programs aimed at patrons with disabilities. This is also where user research with disabled patrons can be very useful. Including actual anecdotes, quotes, and information gathered through usability testing, focus groups, and other user tests can make a big impact on those who may not have as much first-hand experience with the importance of accessibility at the library. Ideally, a variety of data should be collected and presented as part of making the case for the specific budget request that is being submitted. However, never underestimate the value of general information about the needs of the community that will be met with this budget increase. These needs should cover not only how the budget request will allow the library to meet the needs of patrons with disabilities but also any other communities that will also benefit. For example, will the budget improve services for non-English speakers? Will it improve services for elderly patrons? Will it improve services for young patrons? All of these are possibilities depending on the type of initiative you are pursuing funding for and can help to make a strong case for increasing the funds allocated to this work.

Even if your library has limited funds and employee time to allocate to accessibility work, there are ways to nevertheless make a real impact. It is important not to feel overwhelmed and to instead look for partners for learning, for support, for funding, and more to achieve your accessibility goals. This work is ongoing, iterative work that will not happen overnight.

CHAPTER 13

But, there is no reason to feel it is impossible. There is a lot of support available for improved accessibility in libraries and there are many free resources available to those interested in learning more about digital accessibility. The important first step is making a commitment to this work and to finding ways to support it within the available budget and time at your library.

Grant Funding for Accessibility

Interview with **Renee Grassi**, *author, trainer, librarian, administrator, teacher, and accessibility consultant*

Tell us a little bit about one of your successful accessibility grant projects.

In 2017, the Minnesota Department of Human Services launched the application process for their Disability Services Innovation Grant program. The goal of these grants was to promote innovative ideas to improve outcomes for people with disabilities in the state of Minnesota. Colleagues from Dakota County's Social Services Department shared this opportunity with me, offered help and support throughout the process, and encouraged that my library apply based on our already established commitment to serving the disability community. At the time, I was youth services manager at Dakota County (MN) Library, overseeing youth and family services across a collar county of the Twin Cities serving approximately 420,000 residents. With an already established partnership with Dakota County's Social Services and support from Dakota County Library's leadership, I wrote Dakota County Library's successful application, which resulted in a grant award of $100,000 to fund accessibility-related projects across our nine-branch library system. Dakota County Library was the first library ever to receive an Innovation Grant from the Minnesota Department of Human Services.[i]

This grant project had five major goals:

1. Design library spaces and environments to be more welcoming and inclusive for individuals with disabilities.
2. Provide inclusive programs, services, and experiences for individuals with disabilities to participate in community life.
3. Provide learning opportunities for Dakota County residents to increase their awareness on issues related to disability and inclusion.
4. Build staff capacity and knowledge in inclusive and welcoming customer service for individuals with disabilities.
5. Build stronger community connections with self advocates/people with disabilities, family members, service providers, and disability organizations.

To achieve these goals, the grant project identified eight major grant projects and activities:

1. Online Accessibility Consultant
2. Community Engagement Consultant
3. Library Programs
4. Staff Training
5. Accessible Library Technology and Equipment
6. Marketing and Promotion
7. Accessibility Kits and Collections
8. Calming Spaces at three library branches

Dakota County Library's Innovations Grant funded a comprehensive and strategic plan that was multifaceted in its approach, impacting a wide range of areas of the organization. A portion of the funds was used to hire a consultant that performed an online accessibility assessment of the library's digital presence, including social media platforms, online public access catalog, online events calendar, and website. Another portion of the funds was allocated to hiring a community engagement consultant to engage people with disabilities and their stakeholders across Dakota County. The consultant's work included one-on-one interviews with disabled patrons and their stakeholders, facilitated conversations with staff, and a wide-reaching online survey for the public. Funds were also used to fund programs designed specifically for people with disabilities, as well as honorariums for disabled program presenters on various topics of disability. Dakota County Library also used grant funding for staff training workshops on a variety of topics. The Innovation Grant allocated funds for targeted marketing and promotional materials about the library and its services as a way to help increase awareness and engagement of disabled community members and their stakeholders with the library. This funding also supported the development of new collections called Life Skills Kits[ii] designed to expand access for people with disabilities and help support the development of social and life skills. The Innovation Grant also allowed for the purchase of large type high-contrast keyboards for computer workstations, as well as wheelchairs and walkers for all nine branches to support those needing physical support for in-person visits to the library. It was also used to fund new accessibility equipment to use to support disabled employees with various aspects of their jobs.

A significant portion of the funding financed the construction and design of Calming Spaces at three branches of Dakota County Library. In collaboration with local stakeholders, these spaces were designed and outfitted for individuals who need a comforting space to regulate while at the library. The library's new Calming Spaces were designed with attention to those with autism spectrum disorder, sensory processing differences, or other disabilities, and they are available for use by people of any age. Each space has a Calming Space guide that explains how to use the items available in the calming space, as well as a Calming Space Social Narrative for users to access online.[iii] In addition, calming space social narratives are available online to help prepare individuals for locating and using the calming space. Each Calming Space offers a variety of design features and supports, including

- Comfortable seating
- Adjustable lighting
- Sound machine
- Noise-reducing headphones
- Weighted blanket
- Visual timer

- Fidgets
- Tactile objects

You can learn more about my work collaborating with Dakota County's Social Services Department on their Autism Grant, which built the relationship and foundation for the Library to learn about funding opportunities, as well as my work as Grant Manager for Dakota County Library's Minnesota Department of Human Services Innovations Grant, at targetingautism.com/resources.

What advice do you have for finding grants for library accessibility projects?

A successful grant application needs to effectively answer the question, "Why?" Your library's application needs to be compelling enough to persuade a committee that your project has the potential to have a positive impact and is worth funding. Libraries are perfectly positioned to be at the center for transformational community change. Philosophically and aspirationally, libraries exist for all people. They are free community spaces where everyone is welcome regardless of age, race, sexuality, gender expression, class, or disability. However, there is a clear difference between visionary statements like these and the lived experience that disabled people across this country have had in libraries. Libraries need to close that gap and continue working towards accessibility and inclusion in all areas because it's a virtual part of our mission and vision. There were three core reasons for Dakota County Library's request for funding through the Minnesota Department of Human Services Innovation Grant and offered examples of ways libraries were best positioned to support those goals:

1. Libraries are vital community supports for people with disabilities because they offer

   - Free programs and services for all ages
   - Access to technology, free Wi-Fi and online resources
   - Opportunities for participation and socialization
   - Visibility of disability in the community
   - Life skill practice and support
   - Trusted and safe spaces

246 ••• CHAPTER 13

- Sense of belonging and connection with others and the community

2. Increased access to libraries equals increased opportunities for people with disabilities because they offer

  - Computer and technology classes
  - English language learning resources
  - Health and wellness programs
  - Homework Help
  - Resources for homeschool families
  - Employment support with job applications, cover letters and resumes
  - Online tax form and tax help
  - Access to printing, scanning, and faxing services

3. Everyone is a lifelong learner at the library because it provides access to

  - Anime and manga clubs
  - Arts and crafts programs
  - Movie programs
  - Music and dance performances
  - Science and technology programs
  - Storytime and play groups
  - Gaming and coding programs
  - Materials in accessible formats, such as video, braille, audiobooks, e-books, high-interest/low-reading level materials; and other hands-on kits

What tips would you offer to first-time grant writers?

In all of the successful grant applications I've written, I developed projects that were measurable in both qualitative and quantitative ways. Examples of quantitative outputs can include program attendance, numbers of books purchased, number of outreach visits completed, number of training hours, and more. Qualitative outcomes related to the desired change and impact the grant project hopes to achieve, such as an increase in knowledge, skill, awareness, confidence, and more. Grant sponsors and funders want to report on the successes and impact of their grants, so they are looking for applications that can provide clear and concrete examples of measuring success.

As an example, Dakota County Library's Innovation Grant identified several types of qualitative outcomes and measured them via both paper and online surveys for those who attended in-person and virtual programs. For example, as a result of attending grant-funded programs, community members were asked to answer Yes or No to the following outcome statements:

- Did you learn something new?
- Will you use the Library and its resources more?
- Are you more informed on issues and topics of disability and inclusion?
- Do you feel more welcome at the Library?
- Do you feel more connected to others and the community?

As part of the Innovation Grant, Dakota County Library also identified desired outcomes for staff trainings and workshops, asking staff the following questions:

- Are you more informed on issues and topics of disability and community inclusion?
- Do you feel more confident communicating with individuals with disabilities in the Library?
- Do you feel more confident providing customer service to individuals with disabilities at the Library?
- Did you learn something new that will help develop more positive and welcoming experiences for people with disabilities at Dakota County Library?
- Did you learn something new that will help develop more inclusive library environments and spaces for people with disabilities?

After only year one of the grant, Dakota County Library reported the following statistics in its narrative and budget grant reports to the Minnesota Department of Human Services:

- 98 percent of community members who attended a library program reported learning something new.

- 96 percent of community members felt more welcome at the library as a result of attending a library program.
- 94 percent of program attendees rated Innovation Grant–funded programs either Good or Excellent.
- 85 percent of program attendees reported they will use Dakota County Library more as a result of attending the program.
- 84 percent of program attendees reported they were more informed of issues related to disability and inclusion.
- 81 percent of community members reported feeling more welcome at the library as a result of attending a library program.
- 81 percent of program attendees felt more connected to the community.
- 200 Dakota County Library staff completed over 250 hours of accessibility-related training.
- Farmington Libraries ASL (American Sign Language) Celebration series, co-created by an instructor from the Metro Deaf School, welcomed over 200 people, who learned about communication abilities and Deaf Culture.

If you are not sure where to begin, look for training and learning opportunities in outcome and evaluation. The Public Library Association (PLA) offers an initiative for libraries called Project Outcome,[iv] which is a free online toolkit designed to help libraries understand and share the impact of essential library services and programs by providing simple surveys and an easy-to-use process for measuring and analyzing outcomes.

Do you have any specific advice for those pursuing accessibility grants?

Remember the phrase "Nothing for us without us." This slogan originates from the disability rights movement and refers to the concept of co-creation and sharing power with those who are disabled. When you are writing your grant application, think beyond the concept of service where the library is doing things for disabled community members. Disabled patrons have the right to access their public library just as non-disabled patrons do and have the right to participate in, engage, and even lead in all aspects of library work. So, build those relationships and work with your community, specifically the disability community. This should be the first step to any grant application—do not assume the library knows what the community wants and needs to increase and improve access. Leverage staff experiences by those who are disabled or who have disabled family members. Build trust and rapport with existing disabled patrons who already visit the library. Share power. When it comes to writing your grant application, invite disabled community members and library users to write letters of support for the grant and talk about their lived experiences relating to the impacts of the library and the grant. Here are three ways to do that.

1. Interview members of the community and include quotes in your application about why this project needs to be funded. Consider anyone from any background and life experience with disabilities, from a local student enrolled in your district's special education to a Library Board Trustee who may experience disability of their own.
2. Leverage community enthusiasm and suggestions. If you received a recommendation from a community member about an accessibility-related project they want to see happen at your library, contact them and offer to meet with them to discuss more.
3. Get local stakeholders involved. If your grant project serves students ages 22 or younger, contact your local school district's superintendent and ask for their support of the project. The Special Education and Transition/Life Skills Departments could be allies to the work you're doing and offer to collaborate. If your grant project serves older adults with Alzheimer's and Dementia, contact local memory care clinics or special recreation departments to let them know about your plans.

Do you have any specific advice about finding and securing funding for technology or accessibility projects?

- Align your application and project with your library's mission, vision, and values. If there are local city or county issues related to access, inclusion, and accessibility, use your application to talk about how the library is a partner in improving the quality of life for its residents and how the proposed grant application supports important local issues of voters and residents as well.

- Demonstrate alignment with your ordinance or state's standards. For example, if your grant project includes a construction project, include in your application the specific codes for accessible building construction that this project would satisfy. If your grant project helps improve compliance and access for your library's digital presence, talk about the WCAG 2.2 and Section 508 for online and web compliance. My home state's library association, the Illinois Library Association, has adopted a document of best practices entitled Serving Our Public 4.0: Standards for Public Libraries.[v] If your proposed grant project helps your library meet or exceed standards for library service in your state, include that information as well.

- Leverage the talents of others. This can be especially helpful when your time is limited and you have a small library staff, or if you lack grant writing experience and don't know where to start. Strong and trusted partnerships with local stakeholders could result in learning about a grant opportunity that could benefit the library. If this is the case, work with your local stakeholders in the planning of the project and collaborate on the initiative. This will help demonstrate the library has a strong partner and alleviate the pressure and responsibility of running a grant-funded project on your own.

- Do the research. Successful grant applications often provide data and research to demonstrate the need for the project. Identify as much statistical data as you can and include it in your application. The most successful grant applications I have developed included both national trends and hyper-localized data. Gather disability-related statistics and information from census.gov about your city or county, from your local school districts, the CDC's Disability and Health System, or another reputable source. Don't forget to cite your sources!

What advice do you have for managing grant projects after the funding is secured?

Tell your story—it's okay for libraries to celebrate themselves receiving the funding with a press release and a social media post. Write an op-ed piece in the local paper or submit a blog post on Patch.com. Strategies like these will help increase engagement with the library, as well as awareness that your library is working on important community issues of access and inclusion. And don't forget to thank your grant sponsor, too. Acknowledging the organization who funded your application will help build a positive reputation for them and also demonstrate to the community your library's commitment to fiscal responsibility using grant funding to improve and enhance customer experience for all. Be sure to take and store photographs about your grant activities, and also gather feedback and quotes from residents that you can use in marketing and promotional materials. Not only will these communication and marketing efforts help engage the public about your grant project, but it will also boost your library's reputation about its commitment to accessibility and inclusion. This will help build bridges of trust with individuals who may have had a negative experience at your library and demonstrate to them that you are dedicated to improving customer experiences for all.

Notes

i. April Witteveen, "Serving Children with Diverse Abilities, a Minnesota Library Blazes a Trail," *School Library Journal*, May 29, 2019, www.slj.com/story/serving-children-with-diverse-abilities-minnesota-library-blazes-a-trail.

ii. Dakota Public Library, "Life Skills Kits," https://search.dakota.lib.mn.us/client/en_US/default/search/results?qu=Life+Skills+kits&te=&rt=false%7c%7c%7cSERIES_TITLE%7c%7c%7cSeries+Title.

iii. Dakota County Library, "Calming Space Social Narrative," www.co.dakota.mn.us/libraries/Programs/Everyone/Documents/CalmingSpaceSocialNarrativeHeritage.pdf.

iv. Public Library Association, "Project Outcome," www.ala.org/pla/data/performancemeasurement.

v. Illinois Library Association, "Serving Our Public 4.0: Standards for Illinois Public Libraries," 2020, https://www.ila.org/store/product/8/serving-our-public-40-standards-for-illinois-public-libraries-2020.

Notes

1. Project ENABLE, "Americans with Disabilities Act (ADA) Accessibility Checklist," 2014, https://projectenable.syr.edu/projectenable_resoruces/view/141.
2. Accessibility Insights, "FastPass in Accessibility Insights for Web," https://accessibilityinsights.io/docs/web/getstarted/fastpass/.
3. AudioEye, "Check Your Color Contrast," www.audioeye.com/color-contrast-checker/.
4. GBH, "CADET," www.wgbh.org/foundation/services/ncam/cadet.
5. NV Access, "About NVDA," www.nvaccess.org/about-nvda/.

252 ••• CHAPTER 13

6. Apple, "Vision," www.apple.com/accessibility/vision/.
7. JJ Pionke, "A Secondary Analysis of the Library Profession's Self-Reported Competence and Comfort in Working with Patrons with Disabilities," *Library Management* 42, no. 6/7 (2021): 411–14.
8. 3PlayMedia, "Learn," www.3playmedia.com/learn/.
9. Colleen Lougen et al., "A Cohort Model Approach to Addressing Library Accessibility in a Large, Devolved Library System," *Library Resources & Technical Services* 68, no. 4 (2024).
10. Michele L. Thornton et al, "10-Day Campus Accessibility Challenge," *Journal of Postsecondary Education and Disability* 36, no. 1 (2023): 23–39.
11. American Library Association, "Libraries Transforming Communities: Accessible Small and Rural Communities," www.ala.org/tools/librariestransform/libraries-transforming-communities/access.
12. Reference and User Services Association, "Stephen T. Riedner Grant for Life Enhancing Library Programs for People Living with Dementia," www.ala.org/rusa/stephen-t-riedner-grant-life-enhancing-library-programs-people-living-dementia.
13. Reference and User Services Association, "ETS Best Emerging Technology Application Award," www.ala.org/rusa/ets-best-emerging-technology-application-award.
14. Big Ten Academic Alliance, "Library Accessibility Group Mini-Grant Program," https://btaa.org/accessibility-collaboration/LAG/mini-grant.
15. ALA Learning Round Table, "Pat Carterette Professional Development Grant," www.ala.org/learnrt/patcarterette-professional-development-grant.

• • •

CHAPTER 14

A More Inclusive Tomorrow

L ibraries have the opportunity to democratize information. Never has this concept been more crucial for all library users and workers. Research and fact-finding are ever more necessary in the world of AI-generated videos, fake news, and ubiquitous conspiracy theories. Library resources and services must be made available to those with disabilities, from research resources to registrations, to events. Leaving those with disabilities (permanent or temporary) behind without equal access to information is not merely an unfortunate by-product of the fast pace at which technologies change or the perennial budget deficits that keep many libraries short-staffed. It is contrary to our core values as expressed in the ALA's Library Bill of Rights and the Code of Ethics, where the very first ethical priority is "the highest level of service to all library users," including "equitable service policies" and "equitable access."[1] Despite the inherent challenges we face in a changing landscape, librarians can learn new approaches and hone their existing skills to meet the needs across a variety of library types.

Digital accessibility is a broad topic. This, combined with the fact that many librarians lack training and experience on the topic, can make it feel overwhelming, which can in turn make it difficult to get started on the necessary work. This can be even more the case when there are concerns around legal compliance. The most important advice we can give is to just leap in. Begin. Even starting small will move your library toward greater inclusion. Just one change can make all the difference to the disabled patron who is now able to access the library's resources independently. It may not be possible to solve every problem immediately, but starting the work will move your library forward. Improving inclusion is an ongoing process that rewards those who are always seeking to refine our spaces, systems, and resources to better serve our communities.

Remember, there is no reason that this work has to be the sole responsibility of a single person. Working together with colleagues as a team to improve accessibility can help everyone's skills to grow, increase their technical competence, and give them the advantage of multiple perspectives, and is the first step toward creating a culture of inclusion at your institution and in our profession. Whether you find partners at your library, in the larger library community, or even in adjacent professions that are also focused on accessibility, learning about accessibility and user differences will help you to build confidence, create camaraderie, and learn from your peers as you continue to expand your skill set and explore emerging technologies.

Cultivating this culture of accessibility and inclusivity is interactive and iterative, and it covers all aspects of the library. It is rooted in our understanding of barriers and our ability to ask ourselves questions about where they exist and why. The groundwork starts with ensuring that our computer labs and workstations are accessible and that we provide access to the hardware and software that patrons need to succeed. It extends to the library's web presence. Everything that the library offers online must align with the principles of web accessibility, from the library's website to its social media presence. Even the handouts, videos, and images that the library creates require careful design to be usable for all. How we communicate with our patrons and our colleagues, in any format, is at the core of our work. When we focus on inclusion, when it is part of our consciousness, our experiences are richer for it. Our partnerships are stronger. And our users and colleagues thrive.

As new technologies emerge and existing ones evolve, we may find it particularly challenging to maintain a focus on accessibility. But, as we have observed through the examples of XR and AI technologies, the central principles of accessible design and our existing best practices can guide us in this process. Ensuring that your library has workflows and procedures to fall back on when new projects and technologies emerge will set you up for ongoing success with respect to accessibility. It will also position you and your library to be leaders and advocates in this arena. A strong commitment to digital equity consisting of strong partnerships and clear practices to promote it will allow you to work with vendors to champion the importance of accessibility, improving inclusion far beyond the walls of your institution.

Every step we take to understand the changing landscape of disability and its impacts on the populations we serve and with whom we work gets us that much closer to inclusion. Creating more accessible spaces and procuring vetted hardware and software set the foundations for increased equity. Engaging users with your spaces and resources requires thoughtful and accessible communications, starting with a library website that clearly lays out both what you are doing to move toward greater accessibility and where you know challenges exist. How you meet those challenges will depend on your knowledge of accessibility, assistive technologies, and best practices in communicating with vendors. Ongoing training and partnerships can help you clarify that understanding and contextualize emerging technologies. You have just taken the first step by exploring this guide. And it is our hope that this book will help to set a path in your journey toward greater understanding and inclusion.

Note

1. ALA, "ALA Code of Ethics," www.ala.org/tools/ethics.

APPENDIX

Recommended Resources

There is a wealth of resources available to support those who want to learn more about disability and digital accessibility in libraries and beyond. Among the authors who regularly publish research on digital accessibility and disability in libraries and whom we would recommend are Jasmine Clark, Clayton Copeland, Martin Frické, Adina Mulliken, Renee Grassi, and JJ Pionke.

The resources in this appendix are some that we have found particularly useful and would recommend to readers interested in taking the next step toward a greater understanding of these topics.

Books

- Copeland, Clayton A., ed. *Disabilities and the Library: Fostering Equity for Patrons and Staff with Differing Abilities*. Bloomsbury Libraries Unlimited, 2022.
- Firth, Ashley. *Practical Web Accessibility: A Comprehensive Guide to Digital Inclusion*. Apress, 2024.
- Kalbag, Laura. *Accessibility for Everyone*. A Book Apart, 2017.
- Ladau, Emily. *Demystifying Disability: What to Know, What to Say, and How to Be an Ally*. Ten Speed Press, 2021.
- Shew, Ashley. *Against Technoableism: Rethinking Who Needs Improvement*. W.W. Norton, 2023.

Training Materials and Web Resources

- ADA.gov. www.ada.gov.
- Deque University. https://dequeuniversity.com.
- Microsoft Inclusive Design. https://inclusive.microsoft.design/.
- PlainLanguage.gov. www.plainlanguage.gov.
- W3C Web Accessibility Initiative. www.w3.org/WAI/.
- WebAIM. https://webaim.org.

Glossary of Acronyms

AAC	Augmentative and alternative communications
ACR	Accessibility conformance report
AD	Audio descriptions
ADA	Americans with Disabilities Act
AI	Artificial intelligence
ALA RUSA	American Library Association, Reference and User Services Administration
APA	Accessible platform architecture
AR	Augmented reality
ARIA	Accessible Rich Internet Applications
ASERL	Association of Southeastern Research Libraries
ASL	American Sign Language
BLS	Bureau of Labor Statistics
BTAA	Big Ten Academic Alliance
CART	Communication Access Real-time Translation
CCTV	Closed-circuit television
CMS	Content management system
CSS	Cascading Style Sheets
CSV	Comma-separated values
DAC	Digital Accessibility Committee
DAISY	Digital Accessible Information System

DAWG	Digital Accessibility Working Group
DLF	Digital Library Federation
DOJ	Department of Justice
EIT	Electronic and information technology
epub	Electronic publication
FCC	Federal Communications Commission
FM	Frequency modulation
GIF	Graphics Interchange Format
HTML	Hypertext Markup Language
IDEA	Individuals with Disabilities Education Act
IEEE	Institute of Electrical and Electronics Engineers
ILL	Interlibrary loan
IT	Information technology
JAWS	Job Access with Speech
LAA	Library Accessibility Alliance
LIS	Library and information science
MIDI	Musical Instrument Digital Interface
ML	Machine learning
MR	Mixed reality
NVDA	Non-visual desktop access
OCLC	Online Computer Library Center
OCR	Optical character recognition
OPAC	Online public access catalog

GLOSSARY OF ACRONYMS 261

POUR	Perceivable, operable, understandable, and robust
RFP	Request for proposals
SEO	Search engine optimization
SLIS	School of Library and Information Studies
SUNY	State University of New York
SVG	Scalable Vector Graphics
TRLN	Triangle Research Libraries Network
TTS	Text to speech
VPAT	Voluntary Product Accessibility Template
VR	Virtual reality
WAI	Web Accessibility Initiative
WAVE	Web accessibility evaluation tools
WCAG	Web Content Accessibility Guidelines
WebAIM	Web Accessibility in Mind
WYSIWYG	What you see is what you get
W3C	World Wide Web Consortium
XHTML	Extensible Hypertext Markup Language
XML	Extensible Markup Language
XR	Extended reality

About the Authors and Contributors

Carli Spina is an associate professor and the head of research and instructional services at the Fashion Institute of Technology in New York City. She regularly publishes, presents, and teaches about universal design, accessibility, and user experience in libraries. She is the author of *Creating Inclusive Libraries by Applying Universal Design: A Guide* (2021).

Rebecca Albrecht Oling (MLS, CPACC) is the director of digital accessibility at Purchase College, SUNY. Promoted to librarian there in 2024, Oling has worked to shape approaches to digital accessibility on her campus and beyond. Aside from her research and writing, she consults on accessibility best practices and leads trainings that empower people to create a more universal experience.

Both Spina and Oling have worked within SUNY to co-lead a group of librarians to hone skills and thinking in the accessibility area, resulting in the Library Procurement Accessibility Toolkit, an ongoing project. They currently co-chair a group reviewing the SUNY libraries' implementation of the Electronic Information Accessibility Policy.

264 ••• ABOUT THE AUTHORS AND CONTRIBUTORS

❯ Contributors

Dhruti Bhagat-Conway, MLS, is a senior UX designer with MIT Libraries and has over ten years of experience in UX design. Before MIT, she worked for several government (federal and local) organizations and libraries. She specializes in web accessibility to help all users have equal access to information. She is a Certified Professional in Accessibility Core Competencies (CPACC) and a Section 508 Trusted Tester.

Sarah Brennan began her career as a librarian at the University of Wisconsin, working in resource sharing. She moved into product management more than a decade ago and has been working in educational video ever since. First with Insight Media, then with Alexander Street, and now with ProQuest/Clarivate, she's focused on the mission of providing high-quality streaming video to libraries and maximizing the reach of filmmakers to bring their life's work to today's students.

Jasmine Clark is the digital scholarship librarian at Temple University. Her primary areas of research are accessibility and metadata in emerging technology and emerging technology centers. Currently, she is leading The Virtual Blockson, a project to recreate and gamify the Charles L. Blockson Afro-American Collection in virtual reality to teach high school students primary literacy skills. She is also doing research in 3D metadata and accessibility guidelines for virtual reality experiences. She is also the chair of the Digital Library Federation's Digital Accessibility Working Group.

Clayton A. Copeland, PhD, is the director of the Laboratory for Leadership in Equity of Access and Diversity (LLEAD) at the University of South Carolina's School of Information Science. Much of her research focuses on equity of access to information for people with disabilities. Copeland also pursues research interests in universal design and universal design for learning, literacy, facilities planning, technology, and materials and programming for children and young adults. She manages the Linda Lucas Walling Collection for Disabled Children and recently coauthored and edited *Disabilities and the Library: Fostering Equity for Patrons and Staff with Differing Abilities.*

ABOUT THE AUTHORS AND CONTRIBUTORS · · ● 265

Brady Cross is the associate librarian for collections, resource sharing, and technical services at the Tri-County Technical College's Learning Commons, in South Carolina. He has been with the college since 2019, where he also manages access services and spaces in the TCTC Learning Commons. Brady has authored and coauthored peer-reviewed journal articles, contributions to book chapters, white papers, and conference presentations about universal design, accessibility, and library design. He is also a regular guest lecturer at the University of Missouri's School of Information Science & Learning Technologies regarding library technology and accessibility design.

Renee Grassi, author, trainer, librarian, administrator, teacher, and accessibility consultant, is an advocate for equity, diversity, inclusion, and accessibility in libraries, schools, and communities. As a neurodivergent librarian herself, Renee has worked in public libraries for over seventeen years and coordinated grant-funded library initiatives that welcome and support disabled patrons, their families, and their caregivers. Renee graduated from Marquette University with a major in English language and concentration in secondary education. She completed her master's degree in library and information science at Dominican University in River Forest, Illinois. Learn more at reneegrassi.com.

Laura Harris is the web services and distance learning librarian at SUNY Oswego. She also serves as the liaison to several departments within the School of Education. Her current professional interests include accessibility (of course); inclusive and evidence-based instructional practices; instructional design; mid-career librarianship; and grumbling about bad web design.

Eve Hill is one of the nation's leading civil rights lawyers, and she is known especially for her work with clients with disabilities and LGBTQ+ clients. In government, academia, nonprofit, and private practice, Eve has successfully represented people with disabilities in a variety of contexts, from education to health care to housing. Eve also leads Inclusivity, Brown, Goldstein & Levy's Strategic Consulting Group, which works with organizations to promote the education, engagement, and employment of people with disabilities.

266 ⦿⦿● ABOUT THE AUTHORS AND CONTRIBUTORS

Karen E. Miller is the president and owner of Bradbury Miller Associates, an executive search firm specializing in serving libraries. Prior to her eleven years in consultancy, she has over twenty years of experience in leadership positions in public libraries. Her experience includes strategic planning, staff management and development, project management, successful levy campaigns, event planning, fundraising, and public speaking. Karen is an active member of the Ohio library community and serves as an annual presenter for the state's New Library Directors Workshop. She has proudly served as a mentor for the ILEAD USA-Ohio leadership program for Ohio librarians for twelve years.

Noah Roth is the electronic resources librarian at SUNY Broome Community College, where he manages the library's digital collections and online research tools. He has a strong interest in providing accessible resources to support diverse learning needs and has worked to collaboratively implement procurement initiatives to help improve access to resources for all users.

Lydia Tang is a senior outreach and engagement coordinator for Lyrasis, where she provides leadership for the ArchivesSpace hosting program and advances accessibility across the organization. She received her MLIS and Doctor of Musical Arts degrees from the University of Illinois at Urbana-Champaign. She is the 2020 recipient of SAA's Mark A. Greene Emerging Leader Award and was recognized in three SAA Council resolutions as a cofounder of the Archival Workers Emergency Fund, for the Accessibility & Disability Section's "Archivists at Home" document, and for her work revising SAA's "Guidelines for Accessible Archives for People with Disabilities."

Stacie Taylor is the operations manager of the Educational Streaming Account Management team at Swank Motion Pictures, where she has worked for over nine years. Stacie holds a degree in secondary English education from Southern Illinois University at Edwardsville, and she's leveraged her knowledge of the educational field to drive positive change in Swank's academic streaming platform. Her current role allows her to pursue her passion for education while stepping outside the traditional classroom setting.

ABOUT THE AUTHORS AND CONTRIBUTORS ● ● ● **267**

Jessica P. Weber is a partner at Brown, Goldstein & Levy, where she works on a range of civil litigation matters nationwide, with a focus on civil rights, including disability and LGBTQ+ rights, workplace justice, and appellate litigation. She has successfully litigated or resolved cases involving voting rights, accessible technology and document formats, access to health care and educational opportunities, employment discrimination, and wage and hour violations. Weber served as a law clerk to Judge Catherine C. Blake of the U.S. District Court for the District of Maryland and obtained her JD degree from Yale Law School.

Jingjing Wu is the web librarian in the Texas Tech University Libraries. She earned her MLIS degree from Wayne State University and a BE in optical instrumentation with a minor in information science from Zhejiang University. Her research interests include web technologies, user experience in libraries, and data analysis.

Index

A

A11yVR group, 171
ABBYY FineReader, 41–42
Abrantes, Andre, 190
Access Board, 14
accessibility
  legal requirements for, 13–16
  meaning of, 11–13
accessibility audits, 230–231
Accessibility Conformance Report (ACR), 136
Accessibility Insights, 70, 231
accessibility road maps, 150
Accessible Platform Architectures Working Group, 164, 170
Accessible Rich Internet Applications (ARIA) technical specification, 48, 62–64
accommodations, 8–9, 12–13, 126
ACRL's Framework for Information Literacy, 166
adaptation, support for, 153
ADHD, 40
Adobe Acrobat, 42, 110
advisory boards, 209
affinity groups, local, 237–238
agendas and materials, sharing in advance, 127
AI. *See* artificial intelligence (AI)
Alexa, 180
alternative text (alt-text), 51–52, 67, 82–84, 106–107, 121, 185

American Federation for the Blind, 25, 32, 37, 43
American Library Association (ALA), 43, 221–222, 238, 239, 240, 253
American Sign Language (ASL), 98, 99, 191–192. *See also* sign language
American Speech-Language-Hearing-Association, 32
Americans with Disabilities Act (ADA)
  applicability of, 14–15, 18
  compliance with, 89
  definition of disability in, 2, 7–8
  digital accessibility and, 217
  legal requirements of, 13
  long COVID and, 216
  operating systems and, 25–26
  regulation changes and, 241
  WCAG and, 48, 135
ANDI, 70
Android, testing and, 141–142
Apple, 26, 31, 141–142, 169, 232
ArcGIS, 103
archives, digital collections and, 131–132
ARIA Authoring Practices Guide, 64, 123, 192
artificial intelligence (AI)
  alt-text and, 84, 185
  audio descriptions (AD) and, 190–191
  benefits of, 183–184
  captioning and, 39, 40, 186–189
  communities for, 155

269

270 • • • **INDEX**

artificial intelligence *(cont.)*
    description of, 180–181
    generative, 212
    introduction to, 179–180
    OCR projects and, 184–185
    patron tools and, 189–190
    risks of, 181–183
    sign language and, 191–192
    tips for using, 193–196
    website code and, 192–193
Artificial Intelligence and Librarianship
    (Fricke), 184
ASCII art, 119
assistive input devices, 31–32
assistive technology, 24–25
Association of Southeastern Research
    Libraries, 138
astigmatism, 89
audio assistance, 37–38
audio descriptions (AD), 52–53,
    190–191, 232
audio files, 96–97
audiobooks, 184
AudioEye color contrast checker,
    231–232
audio-only files, 52
augmentative and alternative
    communication (AAC) devices,
    32
Augmented Archives project, 167
augmented reality (AR), 161, 163–164,
    165–166, 173–174
Aurasma, 166
Australian Sign Language, 192
authentication, 211–212
autism community, 11
Autism Grant, 245
automated testing, 75, 76, 84, 90, 140,
    142–143, 202. *See also* user testing
Axe Accessibility Plugin, 70
Axe-Con, 70
Azenkot, Shiri, 170

B

Barnes, Colin, 5
Barron, Simon, 79
BeMyAI project, 185
BeMyEyes project, 185
Bhagat-Conway, Dhruti, 66–70
biases, AI and, 182, 191
Big Ten Academic Alliance, 138, 155, 175,
    210, 239–240
Bonnici, Lauri, 219–220, 221
born-library resources, 96, 97
Bradbury Miller Associates, 224
braille
    embossers for, 35–37
    music notation and, 103
    refreshable braille displays, 35–37
Braille, Louis, 35
Brennan, Sarah, 211–212
British Sign Language, 192
Bronstein, Jenny, 223
browser extensions, 70
Bruce, Janine S., vii–viii
budgets/funding
    dedicated funding, 240–242
    employee training, 234–236
    free resources, 231–233
    grants, 238–240, 242–251
    introduction to, 229
    new purchases and contracts,
    233–234
    optimization of resources, 230–231
    partnerships, 236–238
built-in features and checkers, 100, 101,
    106, 110
Bureau of Labor Statistics (BLS), 3, 217
buttons, 83

C

CADET, 232
Cal Poly Pomona, 166
Calming Spaces, 244–245
camel case, 117

INDEX ◦•• 271

capitalization, 116–117
captions, 28, 38–40, 52, 96–97, 99, 110, 131, 151, 186–189, 232
Carson City (NV) Library, 166
CART (communication access real-time translation), 39
Census Bureau, U.S., 2–3
Certified Professional in Accessibility Core Competencies (CPACC), 67, 132
change, prioritizing, 76–77
ChatGPT, 179–180, 189–190, 192, 194, 196
Check Accessibility tool, 142
Chinese Sign Language, 192
Chu, Peng, 190
Clarivate, 189
Clark, Jasmine, 172, 173–175, 257
"click here" links, 86
closed captioning, 38–40, 52, 151. *See also* captions
closed-circuit television (CCTV), 32–33
Coates, Ta-Nehisi, 187
co-creation, 248
Code of Ethics, 253
cognitive support, 28–29, 30
Cohen, Margaret, 224
collections
    contract negotiations and, 203, 205–206
    XR and, 167, 174
color contrast, 51, 67, 84–86, 101–102, 231–232
color use, 84–86, 105
color vision deficiency, 51, 85, 169
comma-separated values (CSV) files, 105
communications
    digital displays and signage, 128–129
    e-mail, 121–122
    forms, 123–125
    GIFs, 120–121
    introduction to, 115–116

online events, 125–128
    social media, 116–120
communities, building, 154–159
communities of practice, 211
computer labs, designing accessible, 43–44
conformance levels, 60–61, 75, 86
conformance review/testing
    introduction to, 133–134
    manual testing, 140–142
    process of, 137–140
    tools for, 142–144
    VPAT and, 135–137
Congressional Budget Office (CBO), 3
content resizing, 140
content testing, 140
contract negotiations, 202–206
contrast, 26
conversion of file formats, 100
Copeland, Clayton A., 17–19, 257
Copilot, 195
copyright, 16
Core Competences of Librarianship, 222
Cornell Tech, 170
countdowns, 54–55, 124–125
COVID pandemic, 3, 38, 216
Cross, Brady, 43–44
CSS, 104, 192
customization, 28, 29, 89, 153, 188, 189–190

D

DAISY (digital accessible information system), 104
Dakota County (MN) Library, 242–247
Dakota County's Social Services Department, 242
dark mode, 26, 89
data files, 105–106
data security risks, AI and, 183
data visualizations, 83, 85, 103, 109
database subscriptions, 234

272 ⊙●● INDEX

Deaf culture/community, 9, 11, 191–192
decorative images, 108
dedicated funding, 240–242
dementia, grant regarding, 239
Department of Justice, 15, 18, 19, 26, 217
Deque University, 70, 132, 233, 235, 258
diagnosis, requirements regarding, 5, 7, 9
dictation, 27
Digital Accessibility Working Group, 150, 155
digital collections, 131–132
digital displays, 128–129
Digital Library Federation (DLF), 150, 155, 224
Digital.gov, 12
disability
 defining, 2–3
 invisible, 8
 language of, 10–11
 models of, 4–7
 percentage of population with, 2
 rise of, 215–216
 types of, 7–9
 See also individual disabilities
disability rights movement, 248
Disability Services Innovation Grant program, 242–247
discrimination, legislation preventing, 13–15
documentation, emerging technology and, 148–150
dyslexia, 40, 51, 116

E
EbscoHost, 189
education
 library, 17
 public, 14
Educause, 175
EIT plans, 42
elderly population, 3

electronic information technology (EIT)
 accessibility policy, 134, 145, 203
electronic resource librarians, 222–223
e-mail, 121–122
Embodied Labs, 163
emerging technologies
 communities for, 154–156
 comparable standards and, 151
 documentation for, 148–150
 general principles and, 151–153
 introduction to, 147–148
 working with users and, 153–154
emojis, 117–118
emoticons, 119
empty alt-text tags, 108
EN 301 549, 135
English as a second language, 40
environmental risks, AI and, 183
ePub, 103–104
EquatIO, 102
essential technology, 30–31
ETS Best Emerging Technology Application Award, 239
European Disability Forum, 91
experiential design, 174
extended reality. *See* XR (extended reality)

F
Federal Communications Commission, 151
file accessibility
 alternatives for, 110–111
 audio files, 96–97
 built-in features and checkers, 110
 images, 106–110
 introduction to, 95–96
 text files, 99–106
 video files, 97–99
file names, 59, 96, 106
fine motor support, 27
Firth, Ashley, 257

flashing content, avoiding, 55, 120, 129
flexibility, 50–51, 79, 89, 129, 153, 233
FLipMouse, 24
Florida Southern College, 166,
    171–172
focus groups, 209
focus mode, 28, 29
font style and size, 51, 67, 101
foot mice, 31
forms, 123–125
frequency modulation (FM) systems,
    37–38
Frické, Martin, 183–184, 257
Fulford, Isa, 196
Fuller, Buckminster, 179
funding. *See* budgets/funding
furniture/furniture audits, 230–231,
    233

G

Game Accessibility Guidelines, 171,
    174
gesture recognition technologies,
    191–192
Gibson, Merrillyn C., 220
GIFs (Graphics Interchange Format),
    120–121
GitHub, 170–171, 195
Global Initiative on Ethics of Extended
    Reality, 168–169
Goldberg, Larry, 170
Goodfeel, 103
Google Assistant, 180, 186–187
Google Cardboard, 166
governmental departments, emerging
    technology and, 150
Grand Valley State University Libraries,
    205
grants, 238–240, 242–251
Grassi, Renee, 242–251, 257
"Guidelines for Accessible Archives for
    People with Disabilities," 131

H

hallucination risks, AI and, 182
haptic integration, 30
Harris, Laura, 156–159
hashtags, 116–117
Hawking, Stephen, 23–24
heading tags, 80
hearing loops, 37–38
hearing support, 28
Hill, Eve, 92–93
hiring risks, AI and, 182
HTML, 62, 63, 67, 80, 82, 86, 88, 100,
    103, 106, 192
human captioning, 39

I

IAAP Certified Professional in
    Accessibility Core Competencies
    (CPACC), 67
icons, 83
identity, 8–9
identity-first language, 10–11
IEEE (Institute of Electrical and
    Electronics Engineers), 168–169
IKEA, 163
ILEAD Ohio, 226
ILL (interlibrary loan), 42–43
Illinois Library Association, 250
images, 51–52, 82–84, 106–110,
    118–119. *See also* alternative text
    (alt-text)
immersive readers, 29
immersive technologies, 161. *See also* XR
    (extended reality)
inclusion
    advocacy for, 6
    aiming for, 16–17
inclusive design, 152
inclusive instruction, 159
Individuals with Disabilities Education
    Act IDEA, 3, 7, 13, 14
induction loops, 37–38

274 ••• **INDEX**

Information and Communication
　Technology Standards and
　Guidelines, 14
information scarcity, vii
Information Technology Industry
　Council, 135
Instagram, 120, 179
instructions, clear, 123
intellectual property risks, AI and, 183
International Association of Accessibility
　Professionals, 91, 132
International Sign Language, 192
intersectionality, vii, 224–225
interview practices, 225
Intopia (blog), 192
IT and Development Subgroup, 150

J

jargon, 67, 79, 81, 102, 131
JavaScript, 62, 90
Job Access with Speech (JAWS), 31, 37,
　103
job descriptions, 224
job preparedness, XR technology and,
　166
job risks, AI and, 181–182
job titles, 222–223
joysticks, 31

K

Kalbag, Laura, 257
Kawecki, Barbara, 204
keyboards/keyboard navigation, 31–32,
　53–54, 141
keystrokes, 27
Kurzweil 1000, 42
Kurzweil 3000, 40

L

Ladau, Emily, 257
language
　natural, 180, 212

plain/clear, 56, 67, 81, 107, 123
preferences regarding, 10–11
screen readers and, 57–58
sign, 53, 98–99, 191–192
understandability and, 55–56
large language models, 39, 182, 187, 196
Larose, Karine, 79
Laskin, Kodi, 10
LaTeX, 103
lawsuits, overlays and, 91
layout, text, 118–119
learning disabilities, 40
legal requirements for accessibility, 13–16
legal tips, 92–93
Level Access, 70
Libraries Transforming Communities:
　Accessible Small and Rural
　Communities grant, 238–239
Library Accessibility Alliance, 138, 150,
　155, 210
Library Accessibility Cohort, 138, 155
Library Accessibility Mini-Grant
　Program, 239–240
library and information science (LIS)
　programs/curricula, 219–222
Library Bill of Rights, 253
Library E-Resource Accessibility Group,
　210
library profession, digital accessibility
　skills and
　curricula and, 219–222
　hiring practices and, 224–226
　introduction to, 215
　occupational outlook for, 217–219
　rise of disability and, 215–216
　skills overview and, 218–219,
　222–224
licensed content, 134–135
Life Skills Kits, 244
Lime, 103
Lime Aloud, 103
Lime Lighter, 103

LinkedIn Learning, 235
links
    accessible, 86–88
    color used for, 67, 85
    complicated images and, 109
    lack of text for, 82
    shortened, 118
Linux, 26
Lischer-Katz, Zack, 172
lists, 67, 80
literacy software, 40–41
live captioning, 38, 39
long COVID, 216
longdesc attribute, 109–110
Loretta C. Duckworth Scholars Studio,
    172
"Lunch at the Library" (Bruce), vii–viii

M

Maatta, Stephanie, 219–220
machine learning (ML), 181, 187, 212
MAGic, 33
magnification, 26, 32–34, 103
manual testing, 140–142
Marrakesh Treaty, 16, 19
MathType, 102–103
medical applications for VR, 163
medical documentation, 8
medical model, 4–5
Mehra, Bharat, 223
memes, 118–119
mental health support, 30
metadata, 59, 104
Microsoft, 25, 84, 110, 142, 188, 190, 231
MIDI (Musical Instrument Digital
    Interface), 103
Miller, Karen, 224, 225, 226
Minnesota Department of Human
    Services, 242–247
mistakes/errors, minimizing, 57, 124
mixed reality (MR), 161, 164–165
mobile testing, 141–142

model contract provisions, 203–204
moderators, online events and, 127–128
Mones, Erica, 10
mono audio, 28
mood support, 30
moral model, 4
MP3, 104
Mulliken, Adina, 257
multimedia, 52–53
MusicSharpeye, 103
MusicXML, 103

N

naming conventions, 59, 96
Narrator, 26
National Center for Accessible Media,
    232
National Center for Education Statistics,
    3
National Federation of the Blind, 43
National Library of Korea, 167
National Library of Medicine (United
    States), 167
National Library of Sweden, 167
National Library Service for the Blind and
    Print Disabled, 104, 219–220
natural language processing, 180, 212
navigation
    headings and, 80–81
    keyboard testing, 141
    links and, 87
    multiple means of, 53–54
    structure for, 56
negotiations with vendors, 202–206
newsletters, 122
Ng, Andrew, 196
night light, 26
North American Serials Interest Group
    (NASIG), 223
North Las Vegas (NV) Library District,
    166
Noteflight, 103

276 ••• **INDEX**

notifications, 124
Nuance, 40
null alt-text, 108
NVDA, 31, 232

O
OCLC, 42–43
Office, Microsoft, 84, 110, 142
Office of Civil Rights, 156
OhioNET, 226
Oklin, Rhoda, 5
OmniPage, 42
online events
   accessible, 125–128, 129–132
   tips for, 129–132
online public access catalog (OPAC),
   134, 149
operability, 53–55
operating systems, 25–26
optical character recognition (OCR), 33,
   34, 41–42, 103, 184–185
optimization, evaluating, 152–153
Orca, 26
organization, clear/logical, 54, 56, 81
orientations, XR technology and,
   166–167, 172
Otter.ai, 38
outline structure, 100
overlays, 89–91
overreliance risks, AI and, 182–183

P
pandemic, 216
partnerships
   building, 209–211
   digital media vendors and, 111–113
   employee training and, 234–235
   funding and, 236–238
Pascal case, 117
Pat Carterette Professional Development
   Grant, 240
PDF files, 41–42, 100, 142

Pelland, Patrice, 219
perception, 50–53
Perkins School for the Blind, 33
person-first language, 10–11
photosensitive epilepsy, 55, 120, 129
physical space, 25
Pionke, JJ, 220, 234, 257
plain language, 56, 81
Plain Writing Act (2010), 56
platforms, selecting for online events,
   125–126
Pokémon GO, 163, 166, 169
portable scanners, 34
POUR acronym, 50–59
PowerPoint, 110
predictive text, 28–29
privacy risks, AI and, 183
professional development, 234–235,
   239–240
programming, XR and, 165–167
Project ENABLE, 230
Project Gutenberg, 184
Project Outcome, 248
ProQuest, 188–189, 213
Prototype for the People program, 170
Public Library Association (PLA), 248

Q
QR codes, 128
qualitative outcomes, 246–248
quantitative outputs, 246–248
Quiver, 166

R
R for Beginners workshops, 195
Rajšp, Alen, 218, 219, 222
Read&Write, 40–41, 188
readability, 80, 81–82, 101–102, 189–190
reading level, 102
reading order, 100–101
Reference and User Services Association
   (RUSA), 43, 239

INDEX ••• 277

refreshable braille displays, 37
Rehabilitation Act (1973), 13–14
remediation skills, 18
requests for proposals (RFPs),
201
research
AI and, 188–189
XR and, 167–168
resources
free, 231–233
optimization of, 230–231
recommended, 257–258
Robati, Alireza Peyvand, 223
robustness, 58–59
Rodriguez, Michael, 206
Rosen, Stephanie, 216
Roth, Noah, 134–135, 145
Roux Library, 171–172
RStudio, 195
Rush, Kai, 167
Rutgers University–Camden, 166

S

SAS Graphics Accelerator, 103
scanners, portable, 34
scanning best practices, 35
Screen Reader User Surveys, 59
screen readers
alt-text and, 106, 108
built-in, 26
capitalization and, 116
data files and, 105
description of, 30–31
file structure and, 100
free, 232
hashtags and, 117
headings and, 80–81
links and, 86–87
memes and, 118–119
online events and, 127
PDF files and, 41
reading order and, 100–101

tables and, 88–89
testing with, 76
understandability and, 57–58
XR and, 169
search engine optimization (SEO), 59,
107
Section 508, 13–14, 66–67, 135
seizures, triggering of, 55
semantic search engines, 195
Serving Our Public 4.0: Standards for
Public Libraries, 250
Shew, Ashley, 257
Sibelius, 103
Siebers, Tobin, 5
sign language, 53, 98–99, 191–192
signage, 25, 128–129
Silktide Accessibility Checker, 69,
143–144
Silvers, Anita, 5–6
SimplifyAI, 188
simulators, 69
Singh, Vandana, 223
"sip and puff" switches, 23–24
Siri, 180, 186–187
SiteImprove, 144
Skokie (IL) Public Library, 166
Skoop, Dekel, 193
slow keys, 27
Smart, Julie, 4
social media, 116–120, 149
social model, 5–7
Society of American Archivists, 131
Soundbeam, 103
speech recognition, 27, 29–30, 38, 39, 40,
186–189
speech synthesizer boards, 32
Spina, Carli, 224
State Library of Ohio, 226
State University of New York (SUNY),
138, 155, 156–158, 236
Statista, 179
steno captioning, 39

Stephen T. Riedner Grant for Life
 Enhancing Library Programs for
 People Living with Dementia, 239
Stewart Library, Weber State University,
 205–206
sticky keys, 27
stigma, 4
streaming media, 112–113
stress-reduction tools, 30
structural elements, 80–81
structure, clear, 99–100
style headings, 80
success criteria
 color and, 86
 ePub and, 104
 understanding, 59–62
 updates to, 211–212
SUNY Broome Community College, 134
SVGs (Scalable Vector Graphics), 103
Swank Digital Campus Advisory
 Committee, 111–113
switch controls, 23–24, 27, 31

T

tab navigation, 54
tables, 88–89
Talking Book Library, 184
Tang, Lydia, 129–132
Taylor, Stacie, 111–113
team approach, 218, 236–237
Teams, 38, 40, 186, 188
Temple University, 172
terminology, 10–11
Tesseract, 43
text files, 99–106
text font style and size, 51, 67
Texthelp, 40, 188
text-to-speech (TTS) technology, 41–42
Therapeutic Games and Applications
 Laboratory (The GApp Lab),
 167–168
third-party experts, hiring, 139–140, 172

3PlayMedia, 235
timed elements, 54–55, 124–125
Title II, 18, 26
Trace Research & Development Center,
 48
trackpads, 31
training, employee, 230, 234–236
transcription services, 38–40
transcripts, 52, 96–97
translation support, 29
Triangle Research Libraries Network, 203
"TRLN Guide to Negotiating
 Accessibility in E-Resources
 Licenses," 203

U

UN Convention on the Rights of Persons
 with Disabilities, 2, 15–16
UN Environment Programme, 183
understandability, 55–58
Unified Web Site Accessibility Guidelines,
 48
United Nations, 12, 15–16
Unity Engine, 169
universal access philosophies, 221
universal design, 29, 44, 152, 153, 220
universal design for learning, 159
University of Michigan Library, 216
University of Oklahoma Libraries, 172
University of Utah, 91, 168
University of Wisconsin at Madison, 48
URLs, 86–87, 118, 128
U.S. National Accessibility Survey,
 219–220
UsableNet, 91
user data, 76
user experience design, 66–70, 213
user feedback, 76, 77, 111–112, 113
user testing
 emerging technologies and, 153–154
 importance of, 59, 75–76
 inclusive, 77–79

introduction to, 133–134
overlays and, 91–92
tips for, 68–69
vendor communications and, 208,
    209, 210
UX testing, 174

V

vendors
    building partnerships with, 209–210
    communications with, 206–208, 212,
        213
    employee training and, 235
    integrating accessibility and, 200–202
    introduction to, 199–200
    limitations and, 202
    negotiations with, 202–206
    questions to ask, 201–202
    sharing knowledge with, 208–209
    working with, 211–212
Verizon Media, 170
video files/content, 52–53, 97–99, 120
virtual assistants, 180–181, 186–187
virtual reality (VR), 161, 162–163
visibility, 8
vision, 51, 84–85, 116
vision support, 26
visual alerts, 28
visual content, describing, 127
VoiceOver, 26, 31, 169, 232
VPAT (Voluntary Product Accessibility
    Template), 75, 131, 135–138, 149,
    200, 201, 202, 207

W

WAI-ARIA 1.2 W3C Recommendation,
    63
Wall Street Journal, 217
Walling, Linda, 220
Wang, Jiang, 190
Washington, Erin, 163
Washington College, 167

Watkins, Joe, 192
WAVE, 70, 143, 231
Web Accessibility in Mind (WebAIM),
    30, 31, 59, 91, 143, 231, 235, 258
Web Accessibility Initiative (WAI), 15,
    47–49, 61–62, 64, 89, 155, 235
Web Content Accessibility Guidelines
    (WCAG)
    accessibility principles and, 50–62,
        151
    captions and, 39
    color contrast and, 101–102
    community and, 155
    conformance review and, 137
    description of, 48–50
    ePub and, 104
    legal considerations regarding, 15
    links and, 88
    magnification and, 33
    Section 508 and, 14
    sign language and, 98
    testing and, 75, 86
    Title II of ADA and, 18, 26
    updates to, 64–66, 211–212
    VPATs and, 135
    XR and, 169–170, 174
Weber, Jessica P., 92–93
Weber State University, 205–206
websites
    accessibility overlays and, 89–92
    AI and code for, 192–193
    assistive technology and, viii
    getting started with accessibility for,
        74–79
    introduction to, 73–74
    quick accessibility improvements for,
        79–89
Weisman, Sarah, 156
Wells, Muriel, 219–220
White Plains (NY) Public Library, 166
widgets (overlays), 89–91
Windows, 25, 26

workstations, designing accessible, 43–44
World Health Organization, 2
World Intellectual Property Organization, 16
World Wide Web Consortium (W3C), 15, 47, 64, 89, 104, 155, 164, 170, 175
Wu, Jingjing, 189–190, 193–196
WYSIWYG form–creation tools, 123

X
Xbox Accessibility Guidelines, 174
XHTML, 104
XML, 103, 104
XR (extended reality)
  accessibility practices for, 168–171
  background on, 162–165
  captions and, 151
  communities for, 155
  introduction to, 161–162
  in libraries, 165–168, 171–175
  XR Access, 170–171, 175
  XR Accessibility Project, 170–171
  XR Accessibility User Requirements, 170, 174
  XR Association, 170

Y
Yadav, Akhilesh K. S., 221
YouTube, 97, 186, 232

Z
Zoom, 38, 186, 188
ZoomText, 33
zoom/zoom apps, 26